PALGRAVE MODERN DRAMATISTS

ARTHUR MILLER

SECOND EDITION

Neil Carson

palgrave
macmillan

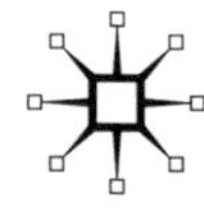

First published 1982
Second edition published 2008 by
PALGRAVE MACMILLAN
Houndmills, Basingstoke, Hampshire RG21 6XS and
175 Fifth Avenue, New York, N. Y. 10010
Companies and representatives throughout the world

PALGRAVE MACMILLAN is the global academic imprint of the Palgrave Macmillan division of St. Martin's Press, LLC and of Palgrave Macmillan Ltd. Macmillan® is a registered trademark in the United States, United Kingdom and other countries. Palgrave is a registered trademark in the European Union and other countries.

ISBN-13: 978–0230–50717–3 hardback
ISBN-10: 0–230–50717–4 hardback
ISBN-13: 978–0–230–50718–0 paperback
ISBN-10: 0–230–50718–2 paperback

This book is printed on paper suitable for recycling and made from fully managed and sustained forest sources. Logging, pulping and manufacturing processes are expected to conform to the environmental regulations of the country of origin.

A catalogue record for this book is available from the British Library.

A catalogue record for this book is available from the Library of Congress.

10 9 8 7 6 5 4 3 2 1
17 16 15 14 13 12 11 10 09 08

Printed and bound in China

FOR EDWINA, LYNNE AND CHRISTIE

Contents

Acknowledgements ix

Editors' Preface x

1 Beginnings (1915–39) 1

2 *The Golden Years* (1939) and *The Man Who Had All the Luck* (1944) 8

3 *All My Sons* (1947) 14

4 *Death of a Salesman* (1949) 20

5 Betrayals (1949–56) 29

6 *The Crucible* (1953) 37

7 *A Memory of Two Mondays* (1955) and *A View from the Bridge* (1955) 47

8 Celebrity (1956–61) 55

9 *The Misfits* (1956–61) 60

10 Refuge (1961–68) 65

11 *After the Fall* (1964) 73

12 *The Price* (1968) 81

13 Alienation (1968–2000) 91

14	*The Creation of the World and Other Business* (1972)	95
15	*The Archbishop's Ceiling* (1977)	100
16	*The American Clock* (1980–86)	105
17	*Incident at Vichy* (1964) and *Playing for Time* (1979–85)	110
18	Four One-Act Plays (1980–87)	116
19	*The Ride Down Mount Morgan* (1991–2000)	121
20	*The Last Yankee* (1991–93)	126
21	*Broken Glass* (1994)	130
22	*Mr Peters' Connections* (1998)	134
23	*Resurrection Blues* (2002)	139
24	Non-Theatrical Writing	143
25	*Finishing the Picture* (2004)	157
26	Conclusion	162
Notes		167
Bibliography		174
Index		178

Acknowledgements

The author and publishers wish to thank the following for permission to reproduce material:

The Wylie Agency on behalf of the author for excerpts from Arthur Miller, *A View from the Bridge*. Copyright © 2000 by Arthur Miller.

Every effort has been made to trace the copyright holders but if any have been inadvertently overlooked the publishers will be pleased to make the necessary arrangement at the first opportunity.

Editors' Preface

The *Palgrave Modern Dramatists* is an international series of introductions to major and significant nineteenth- and twentieth-century dramatists, movements and new forms of drama in Europe, Great Britain, America and new nations such as Nigeria and Trinidad. Besides new studies of great and influential dramatists of the past, the series includes volumes on contemporary authors, recent trends in the theatre and on many dramatists, such as writers of farce, who have created theatre 'classics' while being neglected by literary criticism. The volumes in the series devoted to individual dramatists include a biography, a survey of the plays, and detailed analysis of the most significant plays, along with discussion, where relevant, of the political, social, historical and theatrical context. The authors of the volumes, who are involved with theatre as playwrights, directors, actors, teachers and critics, are concerned with the plays as theatre and discuss such matters as performance, character interpretation and staging, along with themes and context.

BRUCE KING
ADELE KING

1
Beginnings (1915–39)

Arthur Miller has been called the greatest dramatist of the twentieth century. While that claim may be open to challenge, the writer's death in 2005 brought to a close a sixty-year career of astonishing variety and distinction. As playwright, novelist, essayist and indefatigable spokesman for artistic and human rights, Miller achieved an international celebrity quite exceptional in its scope. Although his sensibility and values were quintessentially American, having been formed during the years of Roosevelt's New Deal and the post-war McCarthy era, his plays speak to a world-wide audience. *Death of a Salesman*, the definitive exploration of the inherent contradictions of the American Dream, has been applauded internationally, including in Communist China; *The Crucible*, an indictment of Anglo-American puritanism, is instantly recognizable wherever tyranny reigns. As a result, Miller is widely respected as a courageous champion of humane liberalism.

If the playwright has occasionally been revered as something of a prophet abroad, however, he has not always been so honoured in his own country. In America his social criticism is sometimes resented by those who fail to recognize its roots in a profound patriotism. Another obstacle to a fully balanced assessment of Miller's achievement is the fact that his reputation is almost entirely based on the plays of his middle years. Of the dramas, novels, short stories, essays and travel books published since his last major Broadway triumph in 1968 there is widespread ignorance and misunderstanding. Consequently, in spite of his international celebrity, Miller remains something of an enigma.

There are several reasons for this. One is the changing nature of American theatre. Whereas Broadway had once been the nursery of serious American drama, rising costs and changing demographics had gradually deprived it of that function, forcing dramatists like Miller to rely on the off-Broadway and regional theatres which attract smaller and more specialized audiences. Another reason is that Miller found himself increasingly at odds with the theatrical innovations and revolutionary enthusiasms fashionable during the second half of the twentieth century, preferring to follow his own path of dramatic experimentation and social criticism. Embittered by the disappointment of his own millennial hopes, he seemed unable to share the certainties of the anti-Vietnam and civil rights protesters, and was gradually isolated artistically and philosophically. Broadway audiences, accustomed to popular musicals, were baffled by the startling departures from simple realism in his later plays, while newspaper reviewers found it difficult or impossible to follow the convoluted intellectual arguments presented in them. As a result, the later work never received the public exposure and critical attention it deserves. Only now, perhaps, after the playwright's death, do we have the necessary perspective and objectivity to form a balanced judgement of his total oeuvre.

***

Arthur Asher Miller was born into a wealthy New York Jewish family on 17 October 1915 and grew up in a period of unprecedented economic growth and swelling American confidence following the First World War.[1] His boyhood home was a luxurious eleven-room apartment on 110th Street overlooking Central Park where his mother enjoyed the help of a Polish maid and from which his father travelled to work in a chauffeured limousine. In the summers the family escaped the city heat to a rented waterfront house on Long Island. As the middle child between an elder brother, Kermit (born 1912), and a much younger sister, Joan (born 1922), 'Arty' often felt the odd one out. He was overshadowed by his brother who was not only a better student and athlete, but (sharing his father's light colouring) regarded quite literally as the blue-eyed boy of the family. Arthur, on the other hand, was tall and gangling, with ears that stuck out and the dark eyes and complexion of his mother. Temperamentally, too, he seemed closer to his imaginative and sometimes dramatic mother, and after the birth of his sister he began to feel displaced. Thereafter he looked more and more to his friends for an understanding of the world.

Those friends were almost entirely Jewish. Religion was not a subject of much discussion in the Miller home. Indeed, conversations on any subject were rarely probing, family members being fairly reticent. Nevertheless, Jewish culture permeated their lives. The food, the rituals, the jokes were Jewish as were the traditional values they unquestioningly adhered to. While Mr Miller's business brought him into contact with people from many different backgrounds, there was no thought that the children would be raised outside the faith and, when the time came, the boys went to Hebrew school to prepare for their *bar mitzvahs*.

Arthur was not a student. The only place he seemed able to make his mark was on the athletic field. It was after school that he came alive – playing baseball, skating on the pond in Central Park, riding his bicycle around the neighbourhood and up towards Harlem. He came to love the city. Its energy and diversity enthralled him; its sounds fascinated him. He delighted in the variety of the accents of its multi-racial population. The city seemed the embodiment of the American experiment, tangible evidence of the new life possible for those fleeing the tyranny and poverty of Europe.

Certainly for Arthur's father, New York had proved to be the promised golden door. Arriving alone from Eastern Europe in 1891, Isidore Miller, age six, had been met by his parents and six siblings who had emigrated to the city a few years earlier. The family was then living in a two-room tenement in the Lower East Side from which they ran the S. Miller and Sons garment business. Young Isidore attended school briefly, but left before he learned to read and remained illiterate for the rest of his life. It was a liability that didn't hold him back. Starting off at a sewing machine in the family business, he soon graduated to salesman and by the age of 26 was rich enough to marry. His bride, Augusta ('Gussie') Barnett was the eighteen year-old daughter of an uptown Jewish family who had just graduated as a qualified teacher. By the time their first son, Kermit, was born in 1912, Isidore owned his own business, the Miltex Coat and Suit Company, employing about 800 people. In 1929, however, all that changed.

Like most of his associates, Isidore Miller had for some years been putting all of his savings and much of his capital into common shares which he hoped would give him a better return on his money than his regular business. When the stock market collapsed in 1929, therefore, he was left virtually bankrupt with a viable company but impoverished customers. After a few months, when it became apparent they could no longer afford the rent of the apartment, the family was forced to move. At Gussie's suggestion, Isidore bought a house in the Midwood section of Brooklyn to be close to her two sisters who had moved there after the First World War. At the time, it was an area of unpaved streets with empty spaces behind the houses and the intimacy of a village. With no grocery store within four miles, the family kept a vegetable garden as well as rabbits and chickens. There the family settled into a house so small and cramped that fourteen-year-old Arthur had to share his bedroom with his irascible maternal grandfather.

The 'crash' of 1929 and the Depression following it were the major influences on the playwright's slowly developing view of life. The failure of the economic system called into question everything he had accepted as normal up to that time. His previous life had been a dream. The 'reality' was no longer the chauffeured limousines of New York, but the breadlines and the man fainting from hunger on a back porch in Brooklyn. Not only did the crisis affect the Millers' economic status, it also brought out inexplicable differences in the personalities of its victims. His father, whose success in business had been so astonishing, seemed overwhelmed by the catastrophe. The severely straitened circumstances of the family also affected his mother who became increasingly bitter and critical of what she considered to be her husband's foolhardiness in investing so heavily in the market. His brother, Kermit, characteristically generous, dropped out of university to help his father revive the family business. Arthur, on the other hand, resolved not to go down with the general collapse, although what he could do to escape was still not apparent.

When he graduated from high school in the spring of 1933, he realized that his marks were not high enough to get him into university and that, in any case, there was no money to send him. Over the summer he worked with Kermit striving to rescue the business, but in the fall he found a full-time job as a shipping clerk in an automobile-parts warehouse in Manhattan. During the two hours it took him to commute to and from work each day he began to read with a new seriousness. When a friend recommended that he apply to the University of Michigan, a State University where tuition fees were fairly reasonable, he did so but was turned down. Filled with a new resolve to escape into a wider world, however, he wrote again requesting special consideration of his case. To his delight he received an offer of probationary admission providing that he could show a bank balance of $500. Although earning a mere $15 a week of which he needed $2 for subsistence, he nevertheless managed to save the requisite amount and in September 1934 said goodbye to Brooklyn and headed West.

The University of Michigan was a whole new world. Whereas his previous environment had been predominantly Jewish, his new friends were the sons of die-makers, farmers, ranchers, bankers, lawyers, doctors or clothing workers from every part of the country. Unsure of his direction and lacking the memory for medicine or law, he registered in journalism and began to write for the student newspaper. University expanded his social and political horizons. He was attracted to the Marxist vision of a society in which people would no longer live off others' labour. Events in Europe such as the rise of fascism and the bombing of Guernica affected him deeply. By the end of his first year he began to feel that what he thought and did could have an effect upon events.

After a summer in Brooklyn where he witnessed again the gradual disintegration of his family, he returned to Michigan with a keener awareness of how his life had been changed by the apparent collapse of the capitalist system. He was also conscious of his own financial straits. His savings had long ago run out, and he was having to survive on the $15 a month he earned washing dishes and tending laboratory mice. When he met an attractive First Year psychology major who shared his political ideas and moral earnestness, he had to let her pay for their first date. Soon, however, he and Mary Slattery were sharing more than ideas and she encouraged him in his ambition to try for one of the Avery and Julie Hopwood Awards in Creative Writing.

Avery Hopwood had been a successful Broadway playwright, author of such American classics as *Getting Gertie's Garter*, and *Up in Mabel's Room*, who had bequeathed some $300,000 to the University of Michigan to establish annual awards for drama, fiction, poetry and the essay. Although Miller had never written a play (and indeed was even unsure of the length of an act), he sat down and, drawing from his own experience, wrote about a family very like his own in which he portrayed the conflict between a university student and his father and brother during a strike in the family garment business. As the title, *No Villain*, implies, the fault was neither with the workers nor the small businessman, but with a system that oppressed both. Although calling for the creation of a better society, the play was not so much a revolutionary cry as a study in generational and family dynamics. Finishing the work in less than six weeks, Miller just met the March 31 deadline and in May he received an award of $250. His playwriting career had begun.

Considerably encouraged by this success, Miller transferred out of journalism into English and enrolled in the playwriting course offered by Professor Kenneth Rowe. In Rowe's classes Miller was introduced to the dramatic literature of the past, especially the Greeks and the realistic works of the Norwegian playwright Henrik Ibsen. Through close analysis of plays such as *A Doll's House*, Rowe showed how each development in the well-constructed plot is an organic growth from character and situation. Rowe particularly admired Ibsen's emphasis on social problems and the way in which the playwright focused on questions of moral values, integrity and will underlying those problems. In Rowe's class, Miller revised *No Villain* which, under the title *They Too Arise*, won a $1250 Theatre Guild Bureau of New Plays Award and was produced in Ann Arbor and Detroit. He also wrote another semi-autobiographical play, *Honors at Dawn*, which in June won him his second Hopwood Award. During this year, however, he had learned that his method of playwriting was all wrong. The impulse to write about one's family, Professor Rowe had told his class, was a sign of weakness or of slackening of dramatic imagination. Autobiography should be avoided because characters based on the author are liable to be colourless. The foundation of drama is plot. Out of a story, told sincerely and in truth to life as the playwright sees it, a theme will emerge.[2]

Thereafter, Miller began to look outside his own experience for material for his plays. Through a friend who had become a psychologist at the Jackson State Penitentiary he researched prison conditions for a play he called *The Great Disobedience.* To his distress, this work was dismissed by the Hopwood judges as 'muddled and turgid'. The rejection was disappointing, but it did nothing to weaken Miller's resolve to become a playwright. Nevertheless, he had to face the possibility that success on Broadway might prove to be more elusive than it had been in the friendly atmosphere of the University of Michigan. So, in the spring of 1938, when he left Ann Arbor, waving goodbye to Mary whom he feared he would never have the money or self-confidence to marry, he headed back to New York in a state of exhilaration mixed with dread.

Laying siege to the Great White Way, while a cherished dream, was a long-term project and Miller's immediate concern was to support himself while he continued to write. Lacking any income of his own, he was forced to return home and live off the charity of his brother, Kermit, his father's business having finally collapsed altogether. Meanwhile, Mary Slattery had decided to drop out of university and moved to New York where she found a secretarial job with the publishing firm of Harcourt Brace. Miller helped her find a small apartment in Brooklyn Heights not far from the Brooklyn Bridge, but some distance from his family's home where, in accordance with their shared sense of morality, he felt obliged to stay. There, writing in the basement, he revised his family drama for a third time, re-titled it *The Grass Still Grows*, and tried to get it produced on Broadway. His first approach was to the Group Theatre, a permanent acting company with a strong social mission where the actors felt that their work could have an effect on the destiny of nations. The company had already staged several Jewish family dramas by Clifford Odets but, as a result of a number of anti-Semitic incidents reflecting the growing tensions in Europe, the atmosphere in the city had changed and Miller was told that his play was 'too Jewish'.

This disappointment was balanced, however, by news that his application to write for the Federal Theatre had been accepted. The Federal Theatre and Writers Project was set up in 1935 as part of President Roosevelt's Works Progress Administration to combat the massive unemployment in the theatre profession. It was originally intended simply as a relief project for theatre workers of all kinds, from circus performers to writers and actors, but under its dynamic and imaginative director, Hallie Flanagan, it became a radical challenge to traditional theatre. A left-leaning and experimental director from Vassar College, Flanagan sought to create a genuine people's theatre which would appeal to a working-class audience and reflect broad social concerns in productions spread across the country instead of restricted to New York City.

In November, 1938, therefore, as a newly employed staff member of the Federal Theatre, Miller began to draw his first regular salary since graduation. With it he rented himself a tiny studio apartment on 74th St in Manhattan and started to pursue a number of projects, including a play about the conquest of Mexico by the Spanish conquistador, Cortes. Unfortunately the work of the Theatre Project had begun to attract the ire of the popular right-wing press and the attention of the recently-convened House of Representatives Committee on Un-American Activities. HUAC, as it became known, was established to investigate the Nazi Bund and other right-wing and anti-Semitic organizations, but by early 1939 it had turned its attention to the dangers from the Left. Convinced that the Federal Theatre was a channel for Communist propaganda, members of the Committee voted to bar the use of WPA funds for any theatrical purpose, thereby silencing the playwrights. Out of work once again, Miller had to give up his apartment and return to his parents' home in Brooklyn where he continued to work on his Montezuma play, now called *Children of the Sun*. In August he sent the script to the Theatre Guild from whose reader he received complimentary comments but no offer of production. The world was beginning to seem hostile.

2
The Golden Years (1939) and *The Man Who Had All the Luck* (1944)

Children of the Sun (or *The Golden Years* as it finally became) was Miller's response to the growing threat of fascism in Europe and New York. In March of 1938 Germany had annexed Austria; in September, at the Munich Conference, England and France agreed to Hitler's demands for partitioning Czechoslovakia; and in November, on what became known as *Kristallnacht*, Jewish shops, synagogues and individuals were viciously attacked in many parts of German-speaking Europe. How could there be any doubt about the danger of Nazism? And yet everywhere people (and not only admitted Nazi sympathizers) seemed to be shutting their eyes to the reality. What could explain it? Thinking there might be some parallels with the astonishing conquest of Mexico by Cortes and the Spanish conquistadores in the sixteenth century, Miller consulted Prescott's *The Conquest of Mexico* and other historical sources. It became evident to him that Montezuma had not been defeated by force alone since his army outnumbered the Spaniards several times over. The deciding factor must, therefore, have been psychological.

The play begins with Montezuma and his nobles reacting to the news of the advance of the Spaniards towards their city. Since they are reported to be white and are coming from the east, Montezuma thinks that Cortes may be the God of Peace, Quetzalcoatl, who reigned in a legendary golden age and had promised to return sometime in the future. Several sacred rituals designed to interpret the significance of this extraordinary event fail to resolve the question, but when the helmet of Cortes recovered from the battlefield matches that of the statue of the god, Montezuma becomes convinced that he is indeed witnessing the promised second coming. Labouring under this delusion, and dreaming that his own empire which he acquired by violence may be maintained in peace, he is unable to recognize the savagery of the Spaniards for what it is, or to heed the warnings of his nobles. Instead he grasps at the similarity of the Spaniards' promise of 'peace on earth' to his own hopes, and fails to see how the Christian message is being corrupted by its practitioners. When the Spanish invaders take advantage of his trust and naiveté to seize him and force him to command his followers to lay down their arms, the Aztecs turn against him and he is wounded by an arrow shot by one of his own people. The play ends with Montezuma recognizing his folly and betrayal, but with a reminder of the nobility of his original conception. The dying king asks that the prophecy of Quetzalcoatl be read to him and the scribe, Talua, speaks the last words of the play:

> From out of the place where the sun comes up, warming the ocean sea, there shall come again the departed one, and with him, shining brightly from his hand, a year has come. The first of a sheaf of The Golden Years. *As he reads ... Cannon.*[1]

The Golden Years is journeyman work. Perhaps following Rowe's advice, Miller has chosen a story as remote from his own experience as can be imagined. Consequently, the characters and situations lack the particularity of observed life. The attempt to use poetry to elevate the tone of the piece is unconvincing (it being impossible to use Aztec speech rhythms as a basis for the rhetoric). The whole seems unduly indebted to Shakespeare or Hollywood epics, and frequently lacking in genuine feeling. On the other hand, it is an ambitious attempt on the young author's part to explore the tragic mode. Interestingly Miller follows the Shakespearean rather than the Greek model. The plot is epic (no lengthy exposition of past events) and the hero is flawed and culpable rather than a helpless victim of fate. The king's inability to act comes, not from any lack of will (he won his empire by conquest), but, like Hamlet's, from the peculiar ambiguity of the message from the other world. Wanting to believe, but doubting his senses, the hero seeks for certainty until it is too late. We pity the waste of a potentially great man and recognize his weakness in ourselves, but do not (as in Shakespearean tragedy), receive the assurance that the hero's death will be followed by the restoration of a providential order. The final effect is ironic – a juxtaposition of a dreamed-of peaceable kingdom and the actual reality of war. In *The Golden Years* Miller had found a dramatic situation he would use repeatedly in the years to come – a protagonist confronted by a reality he cannot see or accept because of the blinding power of his own passionately held hopes or fears.

Discouraged by his failure to get *The Golden Years* produced, Miller sat down to assess his position. He estimated that, in the two years since graduation, his total income, apart from the six months 'on the dole' with the Federal Theatre, was just $200 earned from a couple of radio plays and short stories. His projected Broadway triumph seemed as far away as ever. Instead of despairing, however, he decided to get married.

Without informing his parents, he and Mary drove to Lakewood, Ohio, where Miller was introduced to his in-laws. He felt ill-at-ease in the rather dour Catholic atmosphere of the Slattery home, but he made the necessary agreements concerning the education of any children and the couple were married on 5 August 1940. They returned to Brooklyn almost immediately where they moved into a small apartment at 62 Montague Street in Brooklyn Heights. Miller's family was not much happier than the Slatterys about the interfaith marriage (grandfather Barnett threw a clock at his daughter when told the news), but they could do nothing about it. Two weeks after the wedding, Arthur set sail on a freighter to research a play he was developing and Mary went to work as secretary to the head of medical books at Harpers Brothers. Whether or not it had been the original plan, at least in the short run it would be Mary who would have to support the family.

Back from his nautical researches, Miller completed his play, *The Half-Bridge*, but once again failed to gain the interest of any Broadway producer. With three failed scripts in his filing cabinet, he began to wonder if drama was indeed his métier and started to look about for a new literary project. In Ohio, Mary's aunt had told him about her husband, a happily married and successful businessman who had suddenly become obsessed with the idea that his employees were stealing from him. Persuaded by his friends to seek medical attention, he seemed at first to improve, but then, for no apparent reason, he committed suicide. Intrigued by the senselessness of the act, Miller decided to explore the subject in a novel. He worked steadily on the new enterprise but, after several months, found that he was unable to finish it.

Meanwhile the war in Europe had begun in earnest and in December 1941 any doubts about American involvement were swept away by the Japanese attack on Pearl Harbour. Suddenly the country was under arms, putting new pressures on the Miller families. Although recently married, Arthur's brother, Kermit, enlisted and became an infantry platoon commander. Arthur was rejected by the army, but took a job at the Brooklyn Navy Yard as a fitter's assistant on the night shift. Then in March 1943 came what he hoped would be his big break – a

Hollywood contract to write a film. To be based on the reports of the popular war correspondent, Ernie Pyle, and called *The Story of GI Joe*, the film would involve consultations in Hollywood, visits to several training camps in the Eastern United States, and pay a princely $750 a week. Filled with enthusiasm and new hope, Miller laboured on the project over the winter, resolving (like Pyle) to uncover the true face of war. In the spring of 1944, however, he was suddenly replaced and the film was finished without him. Bitterly disappointed, he reworked the material he had gathered into a book of reportage called *Situation Normal*, which he dedicated to Kermit, then fighting in Europe. But he was still almost penniless when Mary gave birth to their first child, Jane Ellen, on 7 September 1944. Then, at last, Miller's luck began to change. The abortive novel about the Ohio businessman (turned into a play called *The Man Who Had All the Luck* while Miller was working nights at the Navy Yard), appeared in an anthology of new American writing and was optioned by a Broadway producer.

The dramatized version of the novel eliminates the suicide and turns the story into a romantic comedy. David Frieber (naive, unsure of himself, reluctant to take chances) is supported and encouraged by his girl friend and then wife, Hester Falk. David's life seems almost supernaturally blessed. The implacable opposition of Hester's father to the wedding is overcome when the old man is killed in a traffic accident. Having built up a model business, David lands a big contract to repair tractors by taking false credit for work done by another mechanic and accepting the help of a friend willing to supply the money needed to buy machinery. As his business prospers, however, he becomes increasingly aware that most of his friends have been frustrated. One lost his legs in the war; another never had the children he wanted. But the most signal case of disappointment is that of his friend, Amos Beeves, who has trained with his father as a pitcher and dreamed of playing baseball in the big leagues only to be told that he has been ruined by his father's bad coaching.

These misfortunes seem to confirm David's apprehension that he too faces an impending disaster. Rejecting the idea that a man is simply a helpless victim of circumstances, he asserts that there is a law in the sky, and that people get what they deserve. The misfortune of others, he maintains, must be a consequence of their mistakes (Amos' father's bad coaching for example), and he feels that he has made no such errors. At the same time, he is convinced (somewhat inconsistently) that his good luck must somehow be paid for, but that once it is, he will be in the clear. He comes to believe that the predestined calamity will be the death of the baby Hester is carrying. On the strength of that belief he invests all his money in a mink ranch, certain that his bereavement will guarantee the success of this risky, but potentially profitable, enterprise. When the baby is born healthy, the guarantee expires, and David dreads that some kind of catastrophe will wipe out his mink farm and his fortune. Hester, meanwhile, suspects that her husband is losing his mind, and when she learns that the latest shipment of feed has been contaminated, she decides to cure him by making him face his fears. She persuades him to let the mink die, thereby wresting agency from the stars. 'There was nothing in the sky that gave you things, nothing that could take them away! It was always you.'[2] When David realizes that he has lost everything, he suddenly discovers a new peace of mind, convinced at last he doesn't really need the material goods he has been so furiously accumulating and that his destiny lies in his own hands.

But Miller was dissatisfied with the published version of the work and, in anticipation of the Broadway production, decided to improve it. He was uncertain about the ending which shifts the focus from luck to acquisitiveness. He also felt the piece lacked coherence, with each scene seeming like the beginning of a new play. Then one day it occurred to him that David and Amos should be brothers and suddenly he found that in writing about the relationship between a father and his son there was a fullness of feeling he had never known before.[3] He tightened the plot, eliminated a character and removed some of the improbabilities. But the most significant change he made was to the ending. In the second version it is Gus, the Austrian mechanic, rather than Hester who explains things. Gus fears that if the mink die, David (now called Beeves) will lose hope and with it the sense that he, not the stars, is in control of his life. As an immigrant, Gus can contrast the attitudes of Americans with those of the millions of Europeans who have given up the belief that they are 'the boss'.[4] He deplores the pessimism and superstition that make Americans feel they don't deserve their good fortune. When David enters, Hester tries to persuade him to let the mink die and threatens to leave him if he continues to be so obsessed with making money. After a brief (and uncharacteristic) scene of sexual jealousy, David learns he has, in fact, saved the mink inadvertently by his careful habit of checking the feed and meticulously removing the poisonous silkworms. Once again he seems to have demonstrated that 'luck' is simply the reward for one's own efforts. Gus agrees that David is both good (deserving) *and* lucky, but if luck is still a mystery, what is important is not the fact of being knocked down, but whether the individual lies there or gets up.

The somewhat confused conclusion of the play is evidence of the difficulty Miller had in choosing between fate and character as the determining force in the plot. This difficulty is a reflection of the fact that the overt story is only tangential to the secret story he was quite unconsciously trying to write.[5] Once he could relate the tale of the Ohio businessman to his own life, his imagination was released. He could explore the implications of the tale in terms of his own experience and deal with some of his own 'interior dragons' such as the dread felt by the successful survivor of a fraternal competition, a young man's perception of his father's hollowness, and the question of how far one's own success is deserved.[6]

The Man Who Had All the Luck is perhaps best understood as a failed attempt to confront the ultimate metaphysical questions directly rather than through a dramatic metaphor. The result is something like a moral allegory in which abstractions such as Law, Justice, and Luck are given a dramatic function, and the human characters become spokespersons for particular ideas or attitudes. Miller's imagination has been caught by a tale of waste which inspires in him a sense of what he often calls 'wonder', but which we might better understand as a kind of tragic awe. In an attempt to plumb the mysteries of fate, Miller the rationalist seeks to avoid the theological terminology normally used in a discussion of the meaning of life and death. He resorts instead to a rather less well-defined concept of luck. In the play the word is variously defined. Shory compares it to a blind force against which Man is as helpless as a jellyfish swept up by the tide. David, on the other hand, desperately needs validation of his life and feels that there must be a law in the sky which determines that individuals get what they deserve. Misfortune is an indication that that law has been infringed and some 'mistake' is being punished. At the same time, however, David comes to believe in a very different kind of luck, a sort of celestial bookkeeping whereby good fortune must ultimately be paid for by bad luck regardless of individual merit. It is a vision not unlike the medieval notion of the Wheel of Fortune which, in its endless revolutions, carries people indiscriminately upwards only to fling them down when they reach the summit. Miller's problems with the story reflect his own difficulty in reconciling his rationalistic beliefs with an atavistic hunger for a more consoling truth.

Miller's hopes for his first Broadway production were high but doomed to bitter disappointment. When *The Man Who Had All the Luck* closed after just two previews and four performances he was shocked and humiliated. In his hurt pride he vowed never to write another play. Fortunately, it was a resolution he was unable to keep.

3
All My Sons (1947)

In his disillusionment with Broadway, Miller decided to try his hand once again at fiction. This time the writing proceeded more easily and it took him a mere six weeks to complete a novel about anti-Semitism in New York which he called *Focus*. Although the book eventually sold some 90,000 copies earning Miller a substantial income in royalties and film rights, by the end of 1945 he felt that he had pitifully little to show for his seven-year struggle to carve out a literary career. Compared to his brother's Purple Heart, earned for bravery in the war, his novel and the few radio plays he had managed to sell seemed hardly worth counting. Indeed, his ambitions as a playwright had been cruelly mocked by rejection and failure. To make matters worse, Tennessee Williams' *The Glass Menagerie* had recently opened on Broadway to rapturous reviews. Whatever private doubts or resentments Miller may have harboured, however, Miller refused to surrender to them. So, in spite of resolutions to the contrary, early in 1946 he began work on yet another play. If this one did not succeed, however, he swore he would get into another line of work.

Since Broadway was essentially the home of realistic theatre, Miller resolved to master the mode. To avoid the misunderstandings that plagued *The Man Who Had All the Luck*, he determined to express no idea unless it were literally forced out of a character's mouth. As for a subject, he had been struck by a story Mary's mother had told him about a family from the Middle West that had been destroyed when the daughter reported her father to the authorities for selling faulty machinery to the army. Changing the daughter into a son, Miller expanded the conflict to involve two families, the Kellers and the Deevers, close neighbours, whose lives and fortunes become fatally intertwined.

Joe Keller has employed Steve Deever, his neighbour, in his machine shop, first as a worker, but later, as the business prospers, in positions of increasing responsibility. As war breaks out, the company obtains a valuable contract to supply airplane parts to the army, and both men begin to look forward to a prosperous future. Meanwhile, the children, George and Ann Deever and Larry and Chris Keller, have also become friends. By 1940, Larry and Ann are engaged and George idolizes Chris. At the outbreak of war, the young people leave home - the boys to join the armed forces, and Ann to move to New York. Then one day calamity strikes at the factory when the manufacturing process fails and a series of faulty cylinder heads come off the assembly line. Steve Deever phones Keller for instructions, and is told that Joe is too sick to come to the plant, but that Steve should disguise the cracks, ship the damaged cylinders out, and Joe would take responsibility. When the faulty cylinders cause the P40s in which they are installed to crash, Steve and Joe are arrested. At the initial trial both men are convicted but on appeal, Keller convinces the jury that Deever had acted on his own. As a consequence, Steve is imprisoned while Joe returns to his business. After the war, the children respond to the calamity in different ways. Ann and George turn against their father and do not even visit him in prison. Larry has been declared missing and is presumed dead by everybody but his mother who insists obsessively that he is still alive and has planted an apple tree in his memory. Chris returns to join the Keller firm and after some time begins writing to Ann in New York.

The play begins late in the story with Ann arriving on Chris' invitation to spend some time in her old neighbourhood. During her first night in the Keller's house, Larry's tree is toppled by the wind and the next day is removed. An atmosphere of domestic normality is established as bits of information about the past emerge in the course of the minimal forward action. Tension begins when Chris announces that he intends to ask Ann to marry him, and Kate insists that this is impossible since she is still engaged to Larry. Further trouble is foreshadowed when George phones to say he is coming to speak to Ann after having finally visited his father in prison. In the second act, Joe's guilt is gradually revealed to the audience, first by the suspicions of the neighbours, then by George's accusations, and finally by Kate's inadvertent remark that her husband has never been sick a day in his life. George's direct challenge to Joe is interrupted by the arrival of a neighbour with Larry's horoscope and George is persuaded to leave. When he is gone, Chris tries to reason with his mother about her objection to his marriage, but Kate is adamant saying, 'Your brother's alive, darling, because if he's dead, your father killed him... God does not let a son be killed by his father.' When Joe tries to tell Chris that he acted to save the business for his sons, Chris is overcome with revulsion and strikes him.

The third act brings the final revelation. Ann produces a letter she had received from Larry just before he went missing. In it Larry reports that he has read of his father's conviction and that he can't bear to live any longer. He tells her he intends to commit suicide and that if he had his father there he could kill him. At a stroke, the letter ends Kate's self-deluding hope and Joe's attempts to avoid responsibility for his actions. When Joe realizes that not only was he directly responsible for Larry's death, but that the other dead pilots were also his 'sons', he volunteers to turn himself in to the police. As he goes into the house to change his clothes, however, Kate tries to get Chris to dissuade him. Chris unrelentingly replies that being sorry is not enough, that one has to be better, to 'know there's a universe of people out there and you're responsible to it'. An offstage shot indicates that Joe has committed suicide rather than face the consequences of his deeds. Kate tries to comfort the overcome Chris by urging him to 'Forget now. Live.'

In general shape, therefore, *All My Sons* is a play of ripe circumstance with roots in nineteenth-century melodrama. Like its predecessors, it gets its effects by a skilful mixture of slowly revealed information about the past and sudden, unexpected incidents in the present. The form has been used to generate suspense and surprise in countless detective and courtroom dramas. In the wrong hands, it may seem merely mechanical - the plot unduly contrived, the final revelation unconvincing or arbitrary. But Henrik Ibsen had shown how, in the hands of a skilled playwright, the techniques could be refined to appear more psychologically convincing and to deal with deeper issues through symbolism and discussion.

To some critics, Miller's employment of these venerable techniques is too mechanical. The pace of the action, especially the first act, is slow, the symbolism of the tree awkward, and the reliance on coincidence and contrivance altogether too arbitrary. Some early critics also complained of the work's insistent didacticism, even going so far as to dismiss it as pure Communist propaganda. While it is possible today to smile at the tendency in the forties to find subversion everywhere, it must be admitted that not all of these criticisms are baseless. The action, what little there is of it, *does* plod; the tree symbolizing Kate's obsession ('You notice there's more light when that thing's gone') is not organically linked to the rest of the play; the strident condemnation of the evils of capitalism seems somewhat too sudden. Furthermore, some of the characters' actions (George and Ann's failure to visit their father in prison) seem determined more by the plot than by credible motivation. On the whole, however, critics who dismiss the play as old-fashioned or derivative tend to overlook the ways in which Miller has significantly altered his model.

To begin with, the 'villain' figure of the piece is very unusual. Joe Keller is evasive, manipulative, a perjurer and accessory to murder, but he is not 'evil' in the sense that Claudius in *Hamlet*, for example, is evil. Within the small circle of his family he is loving and generous, offering to find work for George and Steve in his factory (although the gesture is also self-protective). He is flawed rather than malevolent in that he has convinced himself that his motives excuse him. As Miller says, Keller looks on himself, not as a partner in society, but as an incorporated member who cannot be sued.[1] For him the ultimate value which finesses all others is family solidarity, and (especially) love between father and son. In this conviction he is supported by his wife who is, in effect, his accomplice. Kate too blinds herself to what she knows, convincing herself that only the death of their son, Larry, would incur true guilt. Her obsession with astrology is an attempt to probe the mystery of Fate and to support her faith that God would not allow a son to be killed by his father. (How she makes this connection, however, is uncertain since Larry did not fly the planes supplied with faulty cylinder heads.)

The avenging figures in this domestic revenge play, George and Chris, are also untypical. Of the two, George is the more conventional. It is Chris who is the puzzle. Outwardly supportive, he too suspects his father's guilt, but is able to suppress it during some two years' association with him in the family firm. There seems little in the work to attract him. After the scenes of death and self-sacrifice he has witnessed in the war, he is appalled by the selfishness and greed he sees around him in civilian life. The war has shown him the possibility of a better world of love and mutual responsibility and he feels that his participation in a system based on greed is a betrayal of men who died in the war. But he makes no personal effort to bring about that world. Indeed, he seems strangely passive and naive. His relationship with Ann seems more brotherly than impassioned and his disillusion, when it comes, almost adolescent in its intensity. Left to his own he would never have uncovered his father's crime.

Miller's attempts to bring these various elements together into a meaningful catastrophe are not entirely successful. The play is brought to a close in two climaxes. The first occurs in act two when Chris finally learns of his father's guilt. Appalled by the discovery, he is even more shocked by Joe's defence of his actions. Outraged that his father should put business interests above human life, he strikes out at him in rage and grief, but is unable to penetrate his incomprehension. The second climax is precipitated in the third act when Ann produces Larry's letter in which he announces his determination to commit suicide. This destroys Kate's obsessive denial and appears to drive Keller to take his own life. The usual assumption is that Joe kills himself out of a newly awakened recognition of the fact that he is as responsible for the deaths of the pilots of the damaged planes as he was indirectly for that of his own son. The meaning of the ending seems unusually explicit - that America is the land of dog-eat-dog capitalism instead of a community of love and responsibility of the kind to be found among soldiers in combat and implicitly in a socialist society.

But there are a number of ambiguities left unresolved at the end of the play. One concerns the nature of the catharsis produced by the catastrophe. Joe's death is tragic to the extent that he gains some insight into the cause of his downfall. On the other hand, it does not result in a restored order or revolution. Quite the contrary. Chris, urged by his mother to not 'take it on' himself and to 'forget', will probably take over the family business. (There is no hint that he plans to go into social work even if Ann would let him.) Society will not improve. Another ambiguity involves the meaning of Larry's letter. The precise relationship between Larry's death and those of the other pilots is obscure. Joe is unconcerned since he knows that Larry does not fly the affected P40s. Kate, on the other hand, seems convinced that if Larry is dead then Joe is somehow responsible. The letter reveals that Larry was so distressed by the discovery of his father's actions that he felt he could kill him. Since that was impossible, he planned to kill himself. Keller has stubbornly remained convinced that he has done nothing he needs to ask forgiveness for. When he reads Larry's letter, however, he at last feels that he cannot blame the world, and must take responsibility for his actions. The only thing he learns from Larry's letter that Chris had not explained to him is that Larry would have actually killed him whereas Chris has decided not to turn him in. Why then does Joe decide to put a bullet in his head? Is it because he has found that there is something bigger than the family (a universe of people outside to whom he is responsible)? Or is it that, like Larry, he cannot live without his illusions? All of the major characters in the play (except Ann) resort to self-deception to protect themselves from unpalatable truths. When their comforting illusion is destroyed, some (Kate and Chris) learn to survive and live in what Jim Bayliss calls 'darkness'. Others (Larry and Joe) find life without their dream intolerable. Joe Keller probably dies less out of a sense of guilt for what he has done than out of despair at the loss of his idea of family cohesion. Like later Miller protagonists, he sacrifices his life to the wrong dreams.

Miller's new agent submitted the finished script, now called *All My Sons*, to the Theatre Guild. When that organization delayed making a decision, however, Miller suggested that he approach a new producing partnership made up of his heroes from the Group Theatre, Harold

Clurman and Elia Kazan. They immediately accepted the play and it opened at the Coronet Theatre on 29 January 1947. Thanks in part to Kazan's brilliant direction, it ran for 328 performances, won the Drama Critics' Circle Award and transformed Miller's life. The playwright's ten percent share of the gross receipts amounted to $2000 a week for almost a year. In addition, the New York triumph led to productions in several foreign countries as well as to a movie contract worth $100,000 plus a percentage of the profits. The success which had for so long eluded him was his at last.

4
Death of a Salesman (1949)

With his new-found wealth Miller began to consolidate his life. He bought a converted stable house at 31 Grace Court in Brooklyn Heights with two rental apartments, a top floor where he could write, and space for the new baby which Mary was expecting. (A son, Robert Arthur, arrived on 31 May 1947.) In a further fit of extravagance, he purchased a farm in Roxbury, Connecticut, as a summer retreat. Then he returned to the endless search for material for his pen. At first he started working on a love story about working people in an industrial city to be called *Plenty Good Times.* In what was to become a recurring pattern, however, he found he could not finish the work and put it aside. Searching for other ideas, he was temporarily intrigued by the story he heard of a man who turned in two illegal immigrants in the neighbouring Red Hook district in violation of the code of honour of the local Italian community. But it was an incident from his own experience that eventually proved most fruitful. Some twelve months earlier, at the Boston tryout of *All My Sons*, he had encountered his uncle, Manny Newman, who instead of commenting on the play had blurted out, 'Buddy's doing really well.' The reference was to his son, Miller's cousin, whom his uncle had always thought of as being in competition with the Miller boys. This preoccupation with success and rivalry struck a chord with Miller, and he decided to investigate the family further. He interviewed his cousin in Manhattan, and the idea of a play began to form in his mind. In May he drove up to Roxbury where he spent six weeks building a cabin on the property to serve as his studio. When he finally did sit down to write, he finished two-thirds of a play in a single night. In another three months he had completed the manuscript which he titled '*The Inside of His Head*' and sent off to a producer. Walter Fried (who had co-produced *All My Sons*) and Kermit Bloomgarden agreed to accept it immediately and succeeded in getting Kazan as director and Jo Mielziner as designer. Rehearsals began in December and the play, renamed *Death of a Salesman*, opened in Philadelphia in January 1949, moving to New York the following month.

Death of a Salesman stands apart from almost all of Arthur Miller's other work. Nothing in *The Man Who Had All the Luck* or *All My Sons* prepared New York audiences for the quite extraordinary achievement of *Salesman*, and many critics have never forgiven the playwright for failing to repeat the triumph. *Salesman* is both the epitome of everything Miller had aimed for in the theatre and a separate and unique creation. When Willy Loman first appeared on the American stage, he was recognized as a kind of American Everyman - a universal symbol made real by hundreds of minutely observed details of speech, manner and psychology. The most novel feature of the play, however, was its form - a form for which Miller had been searching since the beginning of his writing career[1] and which made possible the rich interpenetration of past and present. The achievement was an enlargement of the scope of realistic drama, allowing for the inclusion of subjective experience normally excluded from the stage. It is this very richness of *Death of a Salesman* that is at once its greatest strength and its principal problem. The form permits an intricate interweaving of thematic material in which incidents are thrust into the play with a minimum of exposition and developed only so long as they are thematically relevant.[2] But this very mixture of present and past, actual and remembered, defies simple analysis and conveys to many readers and spectators an impression of narrative confusion. This is largely due to the fact that the story proceeds in two dimensions - real time and remembered time. The 'external plot' deals with the last twenty-four hours of Willy's life from his return home late Sunday night to his death Monday evening; the 'internal plot' treats the past from Willy's earliest memories of his own father to the fateful summer of Biff's failure in high school. The play's novelty is that the exposition is dramatized instead of being reported.

One way to approach the play is as a drama of social criticism not unlike *All My Sons* in which one might look for the central conflict in the opposed value-systems of the two main characters. According to such a view, *Salesman* is an indictment of the American capitalist system which values machines more highly than men. The central scene takes place in Howard's office where Willy's pleading for his job and invoking his human connection with Howard is cruelly juxtaposed with Howard's indifferent insistence that 'business is business' and with the mechanical imitation of human voices on the wire recorder. The difficulty with this interpretation is that it simplifies the play, ignoring the humane capitalist, Charley, and forgetting altogether that Willy is a very active collaborator in his own downfall.

Another related approach to the play is to see it as a domestic social drama in which the central character is Biff. This interpretation would identify the conflict as being between Willy's determination to make Biff into a success in capitalistic terms, and his son's search for a more authentic experience. Here the playwright's earlier examinations of father–son conflicts in *Luck* and *Sons* seem to anticipate the opposition between Willy's phoney doctrine of materialistic success and Biff's perception of a preferable ideal based on the freedom and companionship of the American West. But once again such an interpretation seems a distortion of the play. While it is true that Biff represents the possibility of individual integrity, it is not clear what kind of society he would fit into; nor is it at all apparent that we are to prefer Biff's rather unimaginative bumbling to his father's irrepressible hopefulness. Finally, the experience of the play makes it impossible for spectators or readers to respond to Biff as the central character because of the overwhelming presence of Willy.

It is the presentation of Willy's internal life that is the most striking feature of the play. Willy's memories do not materialize at random. They are triggered by certain incidents in the present, and Willy is changed by remembering them. Willy's first return to the past is the result of his recollection of the time when Biff seemed so full of promise. It is brought on by Biff's return home and the inevitable tension between the two men which is a consequence of Biff's apparent inability to settle down. It begins with Willy remembering his son waxing the car and proceeds to recollections of other details such as the way in which Biff 'borrowed' a football from the school locker-room. The guilt Willy felt even then about exaggerating his own accomplishments and encouraging his sons to disregard the law is suggested by the appearance of Linda in the memory.

Since Willy could never deceive his wife with quite the same facility that he could impress his sons, Linda serves as a kind of conscience, making him confess his true earnings and his real sense of inadequacy – 'The trouble is, Linda, people don't seem to take to me.' The temporary feeling of intimacy with his wife reminds Willy that he has not even been honest with Linda, and he attempts to justify his infidelity to himself – 'I get so lonely – specially when business is bad ... I get the feeling that I'll never sell anything again, that I won't make a living for you, or ... a business for the boys.' But even this rationalization is undercut by the intrusion of the image of the woman in the Boston hotel room and the reminder that, in some ways, he had been more generous to his mistress than to his wife. As he approaches the final unspeakable fear – the possibility that he has betrayed Biff too by the double folly of lying and being found out – the voices become more and more accusing. Nevertheless Willy represses the memories and cries out his denial – 'I never in my life told him anything but decent things.' When he returns to the present he is like a man who has glimpsed the ultimate horror and his immediate impulse is to protect his innocence. At first he tries to blame his failure on tactics or an error in strategy – 'Why didn't I go to Alaska with my brother Ben ... What a mistake!' But the memories pushing up into his consciousness will not let him accept that lie. The first recollection of Ben shows Willy's subconscious fear that the things he has been telling his sons are not always as decent as he has claimed – 'I've been waiting for you so long! What's the answer?'

This subtle exploration of Willy's subjective life has led many critics to approach the play as a psychological drama with strong Freudian colouring. According to this interpretation, the work concentrates on family relationships and especially on the conflicts between fathers and sons. This is a more fruitful path into the complexities of the work than the two previously discussed, for father–son conflicts are all-pervasive. Indeed one of the most striking characteristics of Willy is that he is both father and son. The quintessential boy–man, Willy is the eternal adolescent arrested at an early stage of development, unable to help his own son to a healthy maturity. In a very real sense Willy and Biff are more like brothers than father and son, and it is Biff who grows up first.

Willy's problems as a father are shown to be a direct result of his own deprivation as a son, and it is part of the richness of *Death of a Salesman* that its perspective encompasses three generations. Willy's memories touch on the critical moments of his life and the earliest of these concern his hazy recollections of his own father – 'All I remember is a man with a big beard, and I was in Mama's lap, sitting around a fire, and some kind of high music.' The music, of course, is the flute heard periodically through the play telling, Miller informs us in the stage directions, of 'grass, trees and the horizon'. The pastoral associations of the music are related to the wanderings of the Loman family 'through Ohio, and Indiana, Michigan, Illinois, and all the western states' where the elder Loman made and sold his flutes. But the father-image evoked by the music is much more complex than is sometimes suggested. For, according to Ben at least, their father was also a 'great inventor' who 'with one gadget' could make more in a week than Willy would make in a lifetime. The patriarch of the Loman family is therefore a shadowy ideal who embodies a variety of qualities. Musician, craftsman, salesman, inventor (as well as wife-deserter), he is a combination Wandering Jew and Yankee pedlar who has left a mingled heritage to his sons.

Since their father left when Willy was a child, he remains a dim figure in his son's imagination. Willy's determination to give strong guidance to his sons is a result of his sense of the lack of such guidance in his own life. 'Dad left when I was such a baby ... I never had a chance to talk to him and I still feel - kind of temporary about myself.' Willy has chosen to imitate the salesman side of his father, not through any urging on his father's part but rather as a result of circumstances. The most influential of these was his meeting with David Singleman, an old New England salesman who came to represent for Willy the father he never knew. It is Singleman's life, and more especially his death, that came to symbolize what Willy thinks he wants for himself. As he explains to Howard,

> Old Dave, he'd go up to his room, y'understand, put on his green velvet slippers - I'll never forget - and pick up his phone and call the buyers, and without even leaving his room, at the age of eighty-four, he made his living. And when I saw that, I realised that selling was the greatest career a man could want.[3]

Miller almost certainly intended the irony implied by Willy's interest in a job that required no more effort than lifting a phone, but the more dreadful irony relates to the interpretation of business which Willy derives from Singleman's example. What Singleman's achievement represents to Willy is a demonstration of the co-operative and benevolent nature of capitalism. Singleman's ability to sell by phone at age eighty-four was proof to Willy that he was 'remembered and loved and helped by so many different people'. This conclusion is confirmed by Singleman's funeral attended by hundreds of salesmen and buyers. Singleman represents free enterprise with a human face, and it is part of Willy's tragedy that he never realizes such a system does not exist.

Willy's inability to see the nature of the system in which he functions is the more extraordinary in that part of him worships the very ruthlessness that helps to destroy him. The other side of his father - the entrepreneurial and irresponsible side - is epitomized in the play by Ben who, as Willy's older brother, constitutes another substitute father-figure. The character of Ben differs from all the other figures in the play in several respects. There is a quality of unreality about Ben which suggests the generalized characters of Expressionist drama. He refuses to answer questions about himself and communicates cryptically – 'when I walked into the jungle, I was seventeen. When I walked out I was twenty-one. And, by God, I was rich!' There is no attempt on Miller's part to reveal Ben's psychological make-up, and indeed the character seems almost a two-dimensional projection of Willy's imagination, more like a ghost or *alter ego*. Psychologically he represents Willy's depression over his brother's recent death and the breaking of the last connection with his father. Symbolically he is the dark side of the American Dream – the ruthless pursuit of material 'happiness' at the expense of equality. He functions as a dramatic embodiment of those qualities of assurance, daring and lack of scruples which Willy secretly admires, but does not possess. The 'jungle' where no one fights fair is where Willy knows the wealth is to be found, but his own nature yearns for the security of home, garden and an adoring family.

One aspect of the play, therefore, deals with Willy Loman as a son trying to please a father he never knew. His own nature is ill-suited for the competitive world of business and he tries to adjust in two ways. He convinces himself and his sons that success is a product of being well-liked, but at the same time he encourages competitive and even unlawful behaviour. He fails because he never understands the inconsistency in his beliefs and that his desire for the emotional security of popularity is at odds with his dreams of material success.

Willy's failure to come to terms with his own father cripples him in his ability to be a father in his turn. Deprived of affection as a child, he smothers his own sons with love and oppresses them with the nakedness of his hopes for them. Here it is important to comprehend the paradoxical nature of the 'conflict' between Willy and his children. For what Hap, and especially Biff, have to fight is not indifference or hostility, but a surfeit of love. The terrible irony of the play is that Willy's struggles, sacrifice and final suicide are not for his own material advancement, but for his sons. Even when Biff is thirty-four years old Willy cannot rid himself of the compulsion to help him. When Charley gives him the advice of the practical realist – 'He won't starve...Forget about him' – Willy cannot take it, asking viscerally, 'Then what have I got to remember?' It is this overwhelming need to have his sons succeed that is the underlying drive of his life and the cause of his tragic agony.

When his sons understand this love, Willy is a 'prince'. But Biff has had an opportunity to get to know Willy better than Willy ever knew his father and he has come to realize that Willy is also a 'phoney'. It is the ambivalence of Biff's attitude to his father and the defensiveness it arouses in Willy that together cause the conflict between them. The form of the play, however, precludes a full examination of that conflict. Since only Willy's memories are dramatized, the opposition is seen almost entirely from Willy's point of view. It is his shock and guilt we feel when Biff discovers him in the Boston hotel room, not Biff's. And although we understand that Biff then loses faith in his father's ability to influence his teacher, and that he suddenly sees the discrepancy between what Willy pretends to be and what he really is, we never learn exactly how that shock affects his subsequent life.

True, we are told about the externals – that he burned his University of Virginia sneakers, refused to go to summer school to upgrade his math mark and then embarked on a seventeen-year programme of failure – but we never grasp the precise connection between Biff's disillusionment with his father and his own inability to know himself. For when the play begins, Biff is still torn between resentment of his father and emotional dependence on him. He feels 'like a boy', unable to compromise with the world, but uncomfortable at home. His rejection of his father as a 'fake' at fifteen has in no way altered his need to please him. It is only in the course of his last visit home that he comes to understand the emotional block that has been crippling him. After stealing the pen from Bill Oliver's desk he is finally prompted to ask the all-important question: 'Why am I trying to become what I don't want to be?' At that moment he realizes that 'all I want is out there, waiting for me the minute I say I know who I am!'

There is, on the face of it, no obvious reason why Biff did not make this discovery years ago (or conversely, what it was that triggered it at this particular moment). Miller himself came to see that Biff's achievement of self-understanding is not fully enough documented and is overshadowed by Willy's delusion and defeat. It is hard to agree with this criticism altogether because it seems evident that the play Miller has written is not, after all, fundamentally about father–son relationships; nor is the documenting of Biff's disillusionment central to Miller's concerns. Those are ultimately more philosophical than psychological.

The most fruitful approach to the play, therefore, is to see it, like *Luck* and *Sons*, as a drama about self-delusion. Miller's central preoccupation is not social, not psychological, but existential. Throughout his career the playwright has been preoccupied with the role the individual plays in his own fate. Why do people behave so differently in moments of crisis? Why, for example, were some men crushed by the Depression while others survived unscathed? Since the external factors were more or less the same for everyone in the 1930s, clearly the differences were within. Those who believed in the system felt guilty for their failure and gave up the struggle. The secret of survival seemed to lie in the discovery of the hidden laws governing the system. In the pursuit of this discovery the greatest obstacle was not the absence of facts, but the wilful blindness that rendered many people incapable of seeing those facts. At its core, *Death of a Salesman* is a play about the destructive nature of dreams.

The distinction between psychological and philosophical in this context is a fine one and perhaps involves no more than a difference of emphasis. For clearly the question of belief is both intellectual and emotional. It is Miller's insistence on this fact that underlies the peculiar blend of sex and politics in his plays. The mixture has confused some critics and annoyed others who do not see the connection between the subjects. In *Salesman*, for example, the scene in the Boston hotel room has seemed to some an unnecessary embellishment unrelated to the main theme of the play. Such critics would argue that Biff's discovery of his father's infidelity is not closely connected with his rejection of Willy's doctrine of being well-liked. Miller's point, however, is that the shock of Biff's discovery prevented him from seeing the truth about himself. His anger with his father serves as an excuse to avoid looking for the real causes of his failure which are in himself.

Looked at as a play about knowing, *Salesman* focuses on the conflict between facts as they are, and the attempts of various characters to ignore or disguise those facts. The conflict is not embodied in any particular moment of crisis (except perhaps in the last scene between Willy and Biff), but it is all-pervasive. The Lomans engage in constant deception to conceal the truth from themselves. In different ways Charley, Barnard, Howard and Ben each present Willy with facts that he will not recognize as such. Biff's gradual understanding of what has gone on in the house, and his determination to tell Willy the truth appear to the others as a betrayal. In the final confrontation between the two men, Biff cannot make his father face the truth. Willy has too much emotional capital tied up in his dreams of Biff's magnificence, and he prefers to sacrifice his life rather than his illusion. The ending is ironic in that Miller intends the audience to see that Willy is deluded and that a way out exists. As Willy says of Biff, the door of his life is wide open if he has the courage to go through it. The 'tragedy' of Willy Loman's suffering and death is that they are unnecessary.

Miller has often said that he was surprised by the reaction to *Salesman* because he had thought the play much more hopeful than audiences found it to be. Such remarks are a trifle ingenuous. For the epilogue Miller has written for the play (called a requiem in the text) is something of a dramatic *non sequitur* – an almost shameless exploitation of pathos. The scene of Linda at the graveside, her powerfully moving final speech with its achingly ironic concluding cry 'We're free ... we're free' and particularly the background flute music, are devices aimed unerringly at the tear ducts. The impression that Willy is a pathetic victim is reinforced by Charley who (somewhat inconsistently) provides in the epilogue the play's most eloquent justification for Willy's romantic hopefulness.

> A salesman ... don't put a bolt to a nut, he don't tell you the law or give you medicine. He's a man way out there in the blue, riding on a smile and a shoeshine. And when they start not smiling back – that's an earthquake... Nobody dast blame this man. A salesman is got to dream, boy. It comes with the territory.[4]

It seems clear from the rest of the play, however, that we are intended to blame Willy (as Biff certainly does) for having all the wrong dreams and for holding on to those dreams long after they cease to correspond with any possible reality.

The Broadway production was an astonishing triumph. It ran for 742 performances, won the Pulitzer Prize, the Antoinette Perry Award and the Drama Critics' Award. It earned its author royalties amounting to about $160,000 a year from the New York production, and an equal amount from two or three touring companies. Furthermore, it elevated Miller to a position of prominence where he became exposed to both adulation and criticism of a kind he had never experienced. After more than ten years of struggling to establish himself, the sudden success was heady and treacherously seductive. It began to change Miller in ways that some of his friends remarked on. Elia Kazan thought that Miller developed 'a hint of something swashbuckling'; Garson Kanin observed that Art Miller was gradually transformed into *Arthur Miller*.

5
Betrayals (1949–56)

The success of *Salesman* and the celebrity it brought fell like a thunderbolt on the Miller household. During the 1940s Arthur and Mary had lived in relative obscurity and it had been a simple matter to separate their private and professional lives. Of necessity they had existed quietly and the demands of their two young children occupied much of their energy and attention. The religious and temperamental differences between Mary and her mother-in-law and the fact that the children were being raised without a sense of their Jewish background imposed slight but perceptible strains on family relationships. But these problems seemed minor and the Roxbury farm enabled the young couple to secure some privacy and independence. Suddenly all that changed. As one of the New York stage's most exciting new talents, Miller found himself drawn more and more into the public spotlight. Dinner invitations kept him away from home several nights a week; his opinion was suddenly sought on a variety of topics, and he began what turned out to be a life-long practice of public pontification by writing in the *New York Times* about the nature of tragedy and its relationship to the common man. Most importantly, perhaps, he started to mix in the higher reaches of New York society and to make friends in the theatrical community. Mary never tried to become a significant part of the new orbit in which her husband had begun to move.[1]

Foremost among Miller's new theatrical friends was the flamboyant Elia Kazan to whom, in gratitude for his brilliant direction of the play, he dedicated the published version of *Death of a Salesman*. The two men had much in common. Both sons of failed immigrant fathers, they shared a strong socialist commitment and a belief that theatre could be a medium of social change. Beginning as an actor with the Group Theatre, Kazan had turned to directing and, after a series of Broadway hits culminating with *Streetcar Named Desire* and *Death of a Salesman*, was as celebrated as Miller himself. But there the similarities ended. Whereas Miller was emotionally restrained (some would say cold)[2] and morally straitlaced, Kazan embodied the passionate abandon of his

Greek forebears, and apparently refused to let marriage interfere with his amatory inclinations (amply encouraged in the Hollywood circles in which he moved). In these new circumstances, Miller slowly began to change. He became more reckless and curious about experiences outside the bounds of his behaviour up until that time.[3] Miller had never given the impression that he had been unhappy in his marriage to Mary, but gradually (as he remarked ruefully years later) 'The aphrodisiac of success came and sat between [them] in the car.'[4]

Sometime in the spring of 1949 Miller seems to have confessed his wayward (but as yet unsatisfied) impulses whereupon Mary became so jealous and suspicious that he felt he could no longer keep up the active social life he had been enjoying. Confined to barracks and more or less incommunicado at the Roxbury farm, he abandoned the film script about Mafia corruption on the Brooklyn waterfront he had been working on and instead spent the summer adapting Ibsen's *Enemy of the People.* The play tells the story of a town doctor whose discovery of dangerous pollution in the local spa is suppressed by the citizens fearful that the news will damage the tourist trade on which the town depends. Miller was attracted to the piece as another example of truth speaking to power. When it finally appeared on Broadway a year later, the play was generously received by the critics and served to confirm Miller's growing reputation as a champion of the Left.

The post-war years in the United States had seen a growing split between the liberal and conservative factions in all walks of life. Nowhere was this more pronounced than in attitudes to the Soviet Union. Whatever goodwill Americans had felt towards Russia as a wartime ally was rapidly dissipated during the late 40s as the Communists' intentions in Eastern Europe became ever more apparent. Many of those on the Left, who like Miller had been inspired by socialist ideas in the 30s, were slow to condemn a country which had helped to defeat Nazism and seemed to embody a hope for a society free of class privilege and race prejudice. The Right, on the other hand, saw Communism, not as the foreign policy of a single country, but as a secret international conspiracy to impose an anti-democratic ideology on the whole world. Had not the House Committee on Un-American Activities (HUAC) demonstrated the pervasive influence of Communist ideas in many aspects of American life?

Originally created in 1938 as a special (that is, not permanent) committee to investigate Nazism in America, the HUAC had been disbanded during the war. In 1945, however, it was revived as a standing committee, and its purpose redefined as an anti-Communist agency. Then, in 1948, its authority was considerably strengthened as a result of its role in the Alger Hiss case. Hiss was a high-ranking official in the State Department accused of being a Communist agent. Hiss vigorously denied the charges, but subsequent investigation established that he had perjured himself and that in all probability he had at some time been acting as a Soviet spy. The exposure of an international network of espionage reaching into the very heart of the State Department shocked and horrified Americans, most of whom were ready to back the efforts of HUAC to unearth more information about such a threat to the national security.

Years later Miller was to claim that both the Right and the Left were acting dishonestly during this period. Each had a hidden agenda: the Right's to dismantle the social legislation of the New Deal while pretending to defend liberty against Communism; the Left's to defeat capitalism while claiming to espouse constitutional protection against self-incrimination.[5] The result was a pseudo-judicial process that provided none of the protection of a proper court of law. Since witnesses before the Committee hearings were not technically accused of any crime, they were provided with none of the safeguards designed to protect witnesses in a criminal court. They could consult with lawyers, but their counsel could not speak on their behalf. There was no provision for cross-examination, so hearsay, prejudice, and allegation became part of the official record. Furthermore, far from protecting the identity of witnesses, HUAC did all it could to publicize its hearings so that 'unfriendly' witnesses could be exposed to an increasingly hysterical public opinion. Refusals to answer questions by pleading the First or Fifth Amendments of the Constitution were generally considered to be admissions of guilt, and the unlucky witnesses might face ostracism by their friends, dismissal from their jobs or even physical violence. Innumerable careers were damaged or destroyed by Committee investigations and more than a dozen suicides have been linked to appearances, or subpoenas to appear, before the HUAC.

Following the production of *Enemy of the People*, Miller returned to his film project. The work, to be called *The Hook*, was an outgrowth of his investigation of corruption on the Brooklyn waterfront in 1947 and the original plan was to produce the work jointly with Kermit Bloomgarten and Elia Kazan. By May of 1950, however, Kazan had decided that they needed the backing of a major studio and he proposed that the film be peddled in Hollywood. Accordingly, Miller travelled to Los Angeles to join Kazan who was finishing up the film version of *A Streetcar Named Desire*. Kazan took his less experienced friend under his wing and introduced him to a young actress then playing a small role in *As*

Young As You Feel. Her name was Marilyn Monroe and she was to turn Miller's life upside down. In the next few days Miller found himself so attracted to Marilyn that he knew he would have to leave Hollywood if he were not to endanger his marriage. During negotiations with Columbia Pictures, when Miller was pressured to alter his script to make the Communists rather than the Mafia the disruptive force on the waterfront, he seized the opportunity to flee back to New York; from there he telephoned Kazan to say that he was withdrawing from the project.

On his return, New York seemed even more tense than when he had left. On the domestic front, Mary remained cold and suspicious, a bitter contrast to the warmth and openness with which he had been greeted in Hollywood. He had been seeing a psychoanalyst in an effort to work through the problems in his marriage and his notebooks had begun to analyse dramatic situations in Freudian rather than Marxist terms. In working out the motivation of a particular character torn between a secure marriage and passionate adultery, he described the former as a neurosis which contained love, warmth and the memory of his mother, but also the renunciation of ecstasy. If adultery is 'wrong', he notes, a point must come when this seems not so horrible to the character, when he no longer needs his wife's acceptance to feel good about himself. 'Having found with another woman the heat of passion,' Miller asks, can the character 'give that up and find the old happiness with a wife? Or any physical happiness?'[6]

The political scene was, if anything, even more upsetting than the domestic. Anti-Communist hysteria was at a new height, fueled in part by the sensational treason trial of Julius and Ethel Rosenberg. Accused of passing atomic secrets to the Russians, the Rosenbergs steadfastly denied their guilt, and there was a sense among many on the Left that the prosecution masked a growing anti-Semitism. Equally disturbing were the stepped up rhetoric and aggressive tactics of HUAC. In the spring of 1951 the Committee launched a second investigation of Hollywood, attempting to get witnesses to implicate others who were members of the Communist Party. The net was drawing nearer. It threatened to entrap Kazan, a former Party member during his days with the Group Theatre. Miller could not be certain that he himself would not be targeted. Increasingly he considered the activities of HUAC and the attendant hysteria as a kind of witch hunt and to think about a dramatic response to the political turmoil.

In January 1952 Kazan was questioned in a secret executive session of HUAC and refused to identify his Communist associates. Although the hearing was supposed to be confidential, news of his testimony was leaked to the press. Under pressure from the President of Twentieth Century Fox film studios, who told him he would not direct another film in Hollywood unless he co-operated with the Committee, Kazan began to waver. He convinced himself that the kind of secrecy employed by the Communists had no place in a democracy, and called several of his friends, including Miller, to ask their opinion. On his way to Massachusetts to do research on the Salem witch trials, Miller stopped in at Kazan's summer home to be told that Kazan had decided to 'name names'.[7] Miller was so shocked that he broke off a friendship that had become one of the closest of his life.

Miller had been fascinated by the story of the seventeenth-century witches of Salem ever since he first read about them at university. He was struck by the 'terrible marvel' of people who 'could have such a belief in themselves and in the rightness of their consciences [that they would] give up their lives rather than say what they thought was false';[8] and if the courage of the 'witches' could provide an inspiration for the present age, the conduct of the judges might also be instructive. Miller 'wanted to tell people what had happened before, and where to find the early underlying forces of such a phenomenon'.[9] He called his Salem play *The Crucible.*

The work opened at the Martin Beck Theatre in New York on 22 January 1953, ran for 197 performances, and won the Antoinette Perry and Donaldson Awards as the most distinguished American drama of the year. But the opening night audience was cool, and many critics saw in the play a thinly disguised attack on the investigations of HUAC and, by implication, a plea of innocence for all of its victims. Miller began to feel a chill in the critical climate and to experience the darker side of celebrity. Framed in the spotlight of public indignation, he found it more and more difficult to protect his private life. It was a problem that would almost overwhelm him in the next few years.

An early indication of the hostile attention he was beginning to attract came when his application for a passport to attend the 9 March 1954 premiere of *The Crucible* in Brussels was turned down by the State Department on the grounds that his presence abroad would not be in the national interest. When pressed for clarification by *The New York Times*, a State Department spokesman explained that Miller's application had been rejected under regulations denying passports to people believed to be supporting the Communist movement, whether or not they were members of the Communist Party.

More disturbing evidence of official displeasure came the following year when Miller was invited to write a film to record the work of the Youth Board of New York City, an agency attempting to reach and rehabilitate members of the violent Manhattan street gangs. During the summer of 1955 he spent evenings with workers from the Youth Board visiting juvenile gangs and preparing a scenario for a film to be called *Bridge to a Savage World*. When news of Miller's involvement with the project spread, however, questions were raised in the press about the propriety of spending public funds to hire a writer with known socialist sympathies. *The New York World-Telegram* launched a personal attack on the playwright and in the next few months that paper was joined in its campaign by editorial writers, the American Legion, and other patriotic organizations. It seems that members of HUAC also suggested to the Youth Board that it should sever its relationship with the playwright. In spite of Miller's express denial that he was a Communist, the Youth Board finally voted in December to drop the project which by then had brought them too much unwelcome publicity.

Meanwhile the writing was going badly. Facing both private and public disapprobation, Miller struggled to finish *Plenty Good Times*, the working class love story he had been working on intermittently since 1947. He told *The New York Times* he hoped to complete the work by August 1954, but by the end of the year he felt he was writing 'under a certain curse'.[10] About this time, however, Miller's attention was caught by a new project. An actor and aspiring director appearing in the Broadway production of Clifford Odet's *The Flowering Peach* approached him to contribute a one-act play to a proposed evening of readings for an invited audience. Miller resurrected a memoir of his time working in an auto-parts warehouse in Manhattan which he worked up into a drama he called *A Memory of Two Mondays*. When the opportunity of a full Broadway production arose, he completed a second one-act play about the Brooklyn waterfront to serve as a curtain raiser. The two plays were presented under the overall title of *A View from the Bridge* on 29 September 1955.

During the rather hectic four-month period prior to this opening the various tensions in Miller's life suddenly came together in an explosive way. Hoping to save his marriage, he had broken off correspondence with Monroe but had been unable to forget her. In the years since he had been smitten by the young, unknown starlet in Los Angeles, Monroe has been transformed into one of the most glamorous figures in the film world. Then in February 1954, he learned that she had married the baseball player, Joe Dimaggio. So, as well as being the reigning

Hollywood sex goddess and an internationally acclaimed beauty, Monroe was now also the wife of the most famous sports figure in the country. The 'affair' seemed definitely finished. What Miller didn't know, however, was that Monroe, dissatisfied with her treatment by the Hollywood studios, had set up her own production company and moved east to be with her business partner, Milton Greene, in Connecticut. In May, at a party thrown by Lee Strasberg, Monroe's acting teacher at the Actor's Studio, the two met again. Miller left without learning where Monroe was staying, but the next day obtained her telephone number from Paula Strasberg. Thus began a clandestine romance, carried out furtively in the houses of friends, and soon in the apartment in the Waldorf Towers into which Monroe had moved from Connecticut. As the couple became more and more indiscreet, news of their association and then of their romance got into the newspapers. By mid-October, Mary Miller had had enough and asked Arthur to leave, whereupon he moved into the Chelsea Hotel, maintaining to the press that his separation from his wife had nothing to do with Marilyn Monroe.

By February 1956, the Millers agreed to a divorce, and in April Arthur travelled to Nevada to put in the requisite six weeks residency in a rented shack at Pyramid Lake fifty miles northeast of Reno. While Marilyn was in Hollywood making *Bus Stop*, Miller worked at expanding *A View from the Bridge* into a three-act drama. He also applied for a passport to go to England for a honeymoon and to be present at the making of *The Prince and the Showgirl* with Lawrence Olivier – the first project of the Milton Greene-Marilyn Monroe partnership. Once again his passport application was refused, but this time the refusal was followed by a subpoena to appear before the HUAC. On 11 June, Miller was granted an uncontested divorce on the basis of extreme cruelty 'entirely mental in nature'. Miller got his freedom; Mary got the house in Brooklyn, custody of the children, and a percentage of Miller's earnings until she remarried (which she never did).

Later that month Miller travelled to Washington to attend the 21 June Committee hearings and soon learned something of the astonishing publicity value of his new romantic partner. The Chairman of the HUAC session, Francis E Walter of Pennsylvania, offered to find a 'painless solution' to the hearing if arrangements could be made for him to be photographed with Marilyn. Miller refused and the hearing went ahead. Ostensibly called to investigate the unauthorized use of United States passports, the enquiry rapidly broadened its scope to encompass questions about Miller's political activities and sympathies. When asked to name fellow participants at a meeting chaired by a Communist writer in 1947, Miller repeated his denials of having ever belonged to the Communist Party and refused to give the names of individuals (already known to the Committee). As the session ended, Miller was asked if he felt something of a dupe for flirting with Communism in the 1940s. He replied wistfully, 'I was looking for the world that would be perfect. I think it was necessary that I do that if I were to develop myself as a writer.' Implying that he had failed to find that world in the Marxism that had attracted him in University and during the war, he concluded, 'What I sought to find from without I subsequently learned must be created within.'[11] Six days later Miller received an ultimatum to supply the names or face a citation for contempt of Congress.

Miller's defiance of the Committee was seen by many journalists as an act of heroism (as indeed it was). Even more newsworthy in the eyes of the popular press, however, was the announcement (finally made in Washington) that he and Monroe were to be married. There is no doubt that much of the fascination concerning this high profile romance was a result of the apparent incongruities of the union. At forty, Miller was widely considered to be America's leading playwright, generally regarded as a serious (even solemn) intellectual. Monroe, some eleven years his junior, the current Hollywood sex symbol, was a woman of extraordinary and luminous beauty, but of as yet unproven intellectual endowments. To many the relationship was a charming fairy tale; to others an astonishing misalliance. In either case it was a story of enormous newsworthiness.

6
The Crucible (1953)

As the title suggests, the central action of *The Crucible* is comparable to the purification of a substance by heat. John Proctor undergoes a metaphorical calcination in the course of which he is reduced to his essential, purified self. The movement of the play is reductive, stripping the central character of layers of protective covering until in the end he stands naked - totally exposed. It is a dramatic pattern very different from the conventional design of Greek or Christian tragedy. In these latter, the hero's suffering is seen to bear a direct relationship to some 'flaw' or error of judgement for which he must accept some responsibility. Usually, too, this suffering leads to some kind of insight into the inevitable relationship between character and fate, and to an acceptance on the part of the protagonist and the audience of the ultimate justice of his punishment. Miller's play, while it subjects the central character to suffering as great as any tragedy, does so to different effect. Proctor's story is not one of defeat and acceptance, but of triumph and vindication. Whereas the conventional tragic hero is a deluded or obsessed individual in an ordered universe, Proctor is a rational man in a universe gone mad.

Although Miller had long been fascinated with the Salem story, there can be little doubt that the immediate inspiration for the play was the fear inspired by the investigation of the Communist 'conspiracy' in America in the late 1940s and 50s. What came to interest Miller about the phenomenon of public terror, however, was not the workings of fear itself, but the much more bizarre and intricate mechanism of guilt. He became convinced that the root cause, both of the ferocity of the persecution and of the willing, almost eager, surrender of conscience on the part of the accused, was a deeply implanted sense of blame which in the case of the accused could only find release through confession. This handing over of conscience by individuals to the state seemed to Miller the central and informing fact of the 1950s. But the difficulty of exploring such subjects as guilt, confession, atonement and conscience in the modern context is that modern man's understanding of these phenomena is limited. Miller saw in the New England Puritans a group with the kind of moral self-awareness which would enable him to deal with the subject in a manner that would remain, in its essentials at least, realistic.

The Salem witch-trials represent one of the blackest pages of American history, a horrible aberration of that Puritan spirit of independence which has contributed much to the finest parts of the American national character. In a wave of hysteria that swept the town of Salem in 1692, nineteen adults and two dogs were hanged for witchcraft, and one man was pressed to death for refusing to plead. The evidence of supernatural influence brought against the accused consisted originally of the testimony of a number of girls and young women ranging in age from nine to twenty. This testimony was supported by a number of physical symptoms such as fainting or hysterical fits. Since those accused of witchcraft could save their lives by confessing and identifying other witches, it is not surprising that suspicion spread rapidly. The witch-hunt ended when a group of church leaders in Boston declared that the unsupported evidence of witnesses was insufficient to justify the death penalty. Before the court had been discredited, however, more than 150 persons had been accused and confined to prison to await trial.

The Salem witch-hunt shares similarities with many other persecutions in history, but in certain respects it is a peculiar product of its time. The Puritan theocracy of New England imposed numerous restraints on its citizens which contributed to an atmosphere of anxiety, repression, and psychological pressures compounded by the very real danger from Indian raids. Furthermore, the colonists were ill-prepared to understand aberrant behaviour or to deal with the hysteria that followed the discovery of witchcraft. In their exclusive reliance on religion as the foundation of science and law as well as ethics, the Puritan ministers were confounded by the fact that although the Bible stated explicitly that witches should not be allowed to live, nowhere did it define witchcraft or explain how its practitioners should be identified. The belief then current in Europe as well as America was that witchcraft was a contract or 'covenant' between an individual and the Devil to work for the overthrow of the Christian community. Witches were believed to communicate with the Devil in the shape of small animals or birds known as familiars, to be able to cause mischief to those they disliked by sending out their 'spirit', and to attempt to recruit others to their evil work by appearing to them in dreams or visions. The Salem judges, therefore, relied on three kinds of evidence: unusual marks on the witch's body that might be evidence of a 'witch's teat'; mischief following quarrels between neighbours; and, most especially, accounts of the activities of the witch's 'spectral shape'. Since this latter so-called spectral evidence was by its nature invisible to all but the victim or those gifted with 'second sight', the bulk of the testimony in the Salem trials is of a kind that is completely unverifiable.

There were several aspects of the Salem witch-craze that might well have baffled the most conscientious investigator. To begin with, the chief witnesses were perceived to be in genuine torment. Few of those who reported their actions could doubt that the symptoms of fainting, convulsions, bloody wounds and so on, were accompanied by real pain. Since it was inconceivable to them that apparently innocent children, some of them barely into their teens, would voluntarily inflict such pain on themselves, the inevitable deduction was that they were being afflicted. A second circumstance that seemed to most observers to corroborate the stories of the children was the fact that approximately one-quarter of those accused of witchcraft confessed to the crime and gave substantiating details. Finally, once the presence of agents of the 'invisible world' had been established, nothing could any longer be taken at face value. Since Satan himself had appeared glorious before he fell, no evidence of virtuous life was a guarantee that an individual had not been seduced by the Devil and was serving him while pretending outward piety. In such an atmosphere of twisted logic, hardly anyone once named could escape conviction.

Nevertheless, when every allowance is made for the complexity of the situation, it is a fact that the witch-hunt did not affect the whole of New England, but was confined to Salem and a few neighbouring villages. There were particular forces at work in Salem which set it apart and released passions that were elsewhere kept under control. It is this aspect of the case, perhaps, which contributes most to the peculiar fascination which the event has exercised over historians ever since. What was it that made the villagers of Salem so particularly susceptible to a madness, which, although by no means confined to Puritan New England, is nevertheless not a universal characteristic of human society? Marion Starkey in *The Devil in Massachusetts* attributes the hysteria to several causes: the unsettled political situation, the neuroticism of the adolescent girls, the presence in the village of the exotic slave, Tituba, and the particularly bitter rivalries and animosities between families and factions. In her account she focuses on the psychology of the children in whose adolescent emotionalism she sees the main cause of the tragedy.[1]

Miller's interest in the story was very different. He saw the accusations of the girls as little more than a catalyst for the reaction whose true causes were in the community. For Miller, Salem represented a microcosm of human society as a whole. His interest was less in the accusers than in the defendants, and especially those who confessed to their 'sins'. What conceivable feelings could lead an individual to admit to a crime he did not commit? The answer, he concluded, was 'terror and guilt'. The nature of that guilt, which suddenly made the dramatic structure of the play clear to Miller, was suggested by the discovery that Mary Warren tried to exclude John Proctor from accusations of witchcraft while she was denouncing his wife. This hint of a sexual interest in the girls gave Miller a form of motivation that would be more understandable to a modern audience and theatrically more effective than amorphous adolescent hysteria. Unfortunately, Mary Warren's role among the accusers was much smaller than that of Abigail Williams whose youth (she was twelve at the time) made unlikely the kind of sexual involvement that twenty year-old Mary Warren might have had with Proctor. Accordingly, the dramatist altered Abigail's age to seventeen and transformed her into a kind of pagan bacchante. By focusing primarily on the relationship of Abigail, Proctor and Elizabeth, Miller was able to explore two subjects of interest to him - the nature and effect of guilt and the right of society to judge the actions of its members.

The drama begins very shortly after the precipitating crisis. Ruth Putnam and Betty Parris are in a state of semi-consciousness following their participation in a seance and dance in the woods near the village. In the course of Reverend Parris' questioning it transpires that the evening involved superstitious and pagan rituals which point to a dark subterranean level beneath the apparently pious social order of Salem. Mercy Lewis' dancing and Mary Warren's watching indicate little more than frustration and curiosity, but the actions of two of the girls go far beyond adolescent hijinks. Ruth Putnam has been sent by her mother to commune with the dead, and Abigail Williams has tried to ensure the death of the wife of her lover, John Proctor. The bizarre encounter in the woods would probably have ended without incident had it not been discovered by Reverend Parris, who so frightened the girls that the youngest of them succumbs to some form of hysterical reaction. The play opens with the adults of Salem trying to ascertain the cause of the children's fits.

The opening act, which Miller calls an overture, introduces us to the principal characters in the play and establishes the pattern according to which Miller believes events unfold. The characters can be arranged rather crudely into three groups. First there are the representatives of the establishment, Parris and the wealthy Putnams. Next come the ordinary citizens of the village, the Nurses, the Coreys and Proctor. Finally there is the outsider, Hale, a representative of the higher authority of learning. It is soon evident that the village is split into factions based in part on wealth and in part on different attitudes to social obligations. On one side are Parris and the Putnams, both what we would call neurotic, both concerned with the maintenance of authority and both, in different ways, eager to blame others for their own limitations or shortcomings. At the other extreme is Rebecca Nurse, well-to-do, but as a result of earned, not inherited, wealth, naturally maternal, and aware that the community members should blame themselves rather than look outside for causes for their troubles.

Between these two factions stand John Proctor and Giles Corey. The latter is cantankerous and ready to blame the Devil for his litigious nature, but it is clear that Miller intends us to sympathise with this likeable crank. It is John Proctor, however, who is the central figure in the play, and his deeply divided nature is reflected in his relationships with his neighbours. The most fatal and mysterious of these relationships is his liaison with Abigail. Miller tells us that Proctor feels he has sinned against his own vision of decent conduct, but the farmer betrays no sign of such feeling in the opening scene. He appears unembarrassed by Abigail's presence and even smiles knowingly at her when he accuses her of being 'wicked'. He says their relationship is over (even going so far as to say they 'never touched'), but he admits he may have been drawn to her since she left his house. It seems clear that we are to attribute at least a little of Abby's 'wildness' and sensuality to her relationship with John, and to assume that the 'knowledge' which Proctor put in Abigail's heart is not simply carnal, but also includes some awareness of the hypocrisy of some of the Christian women and convenanted men of the community. This 'radical' side of Proctor's nature is further illustrated by his resentment of Parris' arbitrary use of his authority in calling in Hale without consulting the wardens, and by his opposition to the preacher's enforcement of discipline by hell-fire preaching. Proctor's is not a simple personality like that of Rebecca Nurse, but we are given only hints of his complexity in the first act.

In addition to introducing the characters, the first scene also illustrates Miller's analysis of the hysteria that affects Salem. The exact nature of the malady suffered by Ruth Putnam and Betty Parris is unclear. Betty presumably fainted in fright when she was discovered by her father, but since Ruth was at the seance at the behest of her mother, there is no reason for her to exhibit the same guilty reaction. Miller is less interested in the ultimate cause of the girls' fits, however, than in the response those fits provoke among the townspeople. That response he shows to be standard and constantly repeated. It begins with the victim of some misfortune or hostility attempting to place the blame outside himself. Ann Putnam blames witchcraft for the death of her children, Parris blames the Devil for his own unpopularity, Abigail blames Tituba for persuading her to drink the blood which she took as a charm against Elizabeth Proctor's life, and finally Tituba blames the Devil for her participation in the ritual. The last is most instructive since it shows so clearly how Tituba is first terrified by threats of whipping and hanging and then coached in her responses. Her 'confession' is further elicited by promises of forgiveness and security so the victim of the interrogation is offered release from fear and a considerable emotional reward for her co-operation. Part of Miller's point here is that this process goes on unconsciously so that neither the victim nor the interrogator is fully aware of the projection of guilt.

The second act takes place eight days after the arrival of Hale, and we learn that the Salem court has that afternoon passed its first death sentence. We also learn that Proctor had told Elizabeth that he would give evidence that would discredit the children as witnesses, but that he has delayed going to the court. Subsequent developments show that the delay was fatal. Miller intends the audience to view Proctor ironically. His lying to Elizabeth about his interview with Abigail, his reluctance to expose her, his rather hypocritical efforts to please his wife by praising the stew to which he has added extra salt, his lashing out at her in response to her criticism, all of these are the actions of a man who is rationalizing in order to avoid facing himself. Like many troubled individuals, Proctor is happier with external conflict than he is with inner strife. Proctor's opposition to Parris, his browbeating of Mary Warren, his threatening violence against the court clerk and his tearing of the Governor's warrant, all suggest a man of strong convictions. But they are more likely in this case the acts of a man who fears moral complexities and for that reason likes to reduce issues to black and white. Far from presenting Proctor as the one just man in a community of cowards, Miller is suggesting that at this point in the play Proctor is as guilty as any of projecting his own faults onto others. When Hale admonishes him by saying 'the world goes mad, and it profit nothing you should lay the cause to the vengeance of a little girl', Proctor accuses the minister of cowardice. But it is the cry of a man who knows his own paralysing fear. Hale continues, 'Let you counsel among yourselves; think on your village and what may have drawn from heaven such thundering wrath upon you all.' As Proctor knows, Hale might very well be speaking of his liaison with Abby, and he finally resolves to try to bring out the truth. But even at this point he attempts to avoid implicating himself. He threatens Mary Warren to force her to confess to the court that the evidence against his wife is fraudulent, but when Mary tells him that Abigail will charge him with lechery, he hesitates 'with deep hatred of himself'. He finally realizes, however, that he can no longer hide his true nature. The hypocrisy and pretence must be ripped away and he must appear naked to the world. The horror this thought inspires in Proctor is the key to his character. For it seems less the deed than the exposure of the deed that troubles him. In fairness, however, we should add that fear of nakedness is keenest in those who are deeply ashamed.

The third act dealing with Proctor's vain attempts to overthrow the court contains one of the most powerful scenes in Miller's work. Here the focus is once again on the public domain and on the officials and institutions of society. Proctor's inner drama is subordinated temporarily to the question of the general hysteria, and once again Miller traces the way in which self-interest corrupts the process of justice. Each of the officials upholding the court – Danforth, Hathorn and Parris – has a personal stake in its continuation. Only Hale seems capable of sufficient objectivity to judge the merit of the evidence submitted by the defence. And, as in the earlier scene, blunders and irrationality are the result of threatened self-interest. Danforth seems ready to listen to the critical witnesses until he is convinced that Proctor wishes to destroy the court and damage the Deputy Governor's reputation. From that point on, his prejudices blind him. Not only is he reluctant to let a lawyer argue on Proctor's behalf, but he is incapable of seeing through Abigail's rather obvious hypocrisy and evasion. Proctor understandably delays his own confession, hoping that Mary Warren's testimony will be sufficient to break the case against his wife. When he sees that Abigail is relentless and is about to destroy his witness, however, he attacks her and finally accuses her of lechery. But once again he has delayed too long, for he has already discredited himself in Danforth's eyes as an enemy of the court. When Abigail refuses to answer the charge, Danforth does not press her. Instead he calls in Elizabeth and asks her to testify. In a stunning reversal, Elizabeth lies to protect her husband, and Danforth eagerly accepts her word as proof of Proctor's deceit. Abigail leads the girls in an hysterical attack on Mary Warren who is terrified into turning against Proctor whom she accuses of being 'the Devil's man'. Finally enmeshed in the madness he could not overthrow, Proctor responds at first with anger, but then with insight.

> I hear the boot of Lucifer, I see his filthy face! And it is my face, and yours, Danforth! For them that quail to bring men out of ignorance,

> as I have quailed, and as you quail now when you know in all your black hearts that this be fraud – God damns our kind especially, and we will burn, we will burn together![2]

Here Proctor comes to see himself as partly responsible for the evil he has tried to oppose. Since he has just failed in one attempt to bring his fellow townsmen out of ignorance, he must here be referring to his initial reluctance to denounce the court as a fraud.

If the third act brings Proctor to a recognition of his complicity in the evil of Salem, the final act shows him coming to an acceptance of that guilt. Somewhat paradoxically, however, this act opens with Proctor at the lowest point in his spiritual development. He sits, reports the prison marshal, 'like some great bird; you'd not know he lived'. We are given no clue to Proctor's state of mind, but his subsequent appearance and his decision to confess suggest that he has lost all self-respect. From a reluctance to admit his own evil, he has come to complete self-loathing. His conviction that he is 'rotten' robs him of the pride necessary to maintain even the appearance of dignity. Somewhat characteristically, he looks outside for confirmation or denial of his worst fears. 'I would have your forgiveness', he says to his wife, hoping by securing it to reduce the load of guilt he feels. But Elizabeth realizes what he himself does not yet comprehend, that her husband must learn to forgive himself. 'It come to naught that I should forgive you, if you'll not forgive yourself', she says. But she does admit that she may have been partially to blame. 'You take my sins upon you, John... I never knew how I should say my love.'

Proctor's final quest is for some kind of truth that he can hold on to – a just evaluation of his life and of himself. As he refused to hand over his conscience to the court, he must not hand it over to his wife. But his sins against Elizabeth were real whereas the charges of Mary Warren were fraudulent. The inability of Proctor (or Miller) to draw clear distinctions between the two cases is one of the least satisfactory aspects of the play. The question of John's betrayal of Elizabeth seems to many to be side-tracked in the final moments and lost sight of in the rather melodramatic 'victory' of Proctor's defiance of the court. The stricter moralists among the critics would deny that Proctor's courage in dying for his innocence of the charge of witchcraft in any way cancels out his guilt on the charge of adultery. Of course Miller would agree. The impression of moral confusion that seems to hang over the final moments of the play arises from the fact that the playwright is not interested in the question of Proctor's guilt (his guilt is taken for granted) so much as in Proctor's acceptance of that guilt.

At first Proctor is overwhelmed by a sense of worthlessness. He agrees to confess because he feels unworthy to be ranked with the saintly Rebecca and feels that such a confession could not corrupt him more. On the other hand he is reluctant to confess to the wrong sins. His refusal to name confederates and to have his confession publicized stems from the same cause - determination not to further the cause of the corrupt court. Although he seems more jealous of his worldly reputation than of his credit with God, it is this last remnant of pride that saves him. The realization that in the end he cannot publish a lie about himself convinces him that he is not as evil as he thought. In the shadow of the gallows he comes to realize that, if he is not as good a man as he once thought he was, neither is he entirely evil. Like most human beings, he is a mixture with not much more than 'a shred of goodness'. But his triumph in the end is that he is able to act out of that small virtue rather than succumbing to the despair that threatened to overcome him when he confronted his larger evil. When Elizabeth says, 'He have his goodness now', she does not mean (as it might logically seem) that the venial John Proctor has been miraculously redeemed by the brave John Proctor. She means that he has found the true core of his nature which had been hidden beneath self-doubt and self-loathing.

The Crucible is a powerful play, eminently stageworthy, which has demonstrated repeatedly that it can have a very strong effect on an audience. Partly because of that power it is sometimes misunderstood. It has been seen as a criticism of the trial of accused spies Julius and Ethel Rosenberg, and as an attack on the HUAC. It has been dismissed as didactic melodrama, and praised as profound tragedy. It would be easy to attribute the confusion relating to the play to the political events surrounding its first production. But there are more fundamental reasons why the work continues to puzzle some readers and spectators. Foremost among these is the author's lack of complete objectivity. For while Miller intends us to be critical of Proctor, it is practically impossible not to see him as a martyr. There are many reasons for this, not the least of which is Miller's rather ambivalent attitude to the central characters.

This ambivalence is particularly evident in the second-act scene between John and Elizabeth where Proctor's self-justification is uncommonly convincing. His rather sensual nature is revealed attractively through his discriminating taste for food, and his love of the sights and smells of the countryside. Elizabeth, by contrast, seems narrow and pinched in spirit: a bad cook, a forgetful wife, and a woman who does not even seem to take pleasure in flowers. Given these two personalities and the nature of their quarrel it is hard not to sympathise with Proctor and to start to see things from his point of view. He is so convincing in pleading his 'honesty' that we tend to overlook the fact that he is continually lying to his wife. Furthermore, Abigail is portrayed as such an obviously bad piece of goods that it takes a clear-eyed French critic to point out that Proctor was not only twice the age of the girl he seduced, but as her employer he was breaking a double trust. Furthermore, the extent of Abigail's sexual awakening suggests that before her affair with Proctor she was a virgin. Miller's decision to omit detailed references to the early stages of the relationship has the effect of making Proctor's sense of guilt seem a little forced and perhaps not really justified.

A further difficulty some critics have with the play is what they see as its lack of religious dimension. It is perhaps inevitable that a twentieth-century author writing for twentieth-century audiences should portray the witch-scare in purely psychological and economic terms. But it is less understandable that Miller should fail to make some effort to show the support these Puritan martyrs gained from their faith. Apart from Rebecca and Elizabeth, none of the accused makes much reference to God. Indeed Proctor at the end is much more concerned about his 'name' than his soul. The fact that his actions will be judged in heaven by an all-seeing God, as well as in Salem by his very short-sighted neighbours, does not seem either to trouble or to comfort him.

Miller had been determined in *The Crucible* to emphasize the tragic victory of the protagonist. This victory does not consist in the defeat of the court, but rather in Proctor's triumph over himself. At the end of the play, Proctor, like the Puritan martyrs of old, knows who he is. Whereas the strength of the original Salem victims came presumably from their faith in God, Proctor's will comes from his belief in himself. Rejecting the claims of his wife or society (and by implication religion) to judge him, he stands at the end on the judgement of the only tribunal he acknowledges, his own conscience. The problem with the play is that too many of the proceedings of that tribunal are held *in camera*.

7
A Memory of Two Mondays (1955) and *A View from the Bridge* (1955)

In spite of the growing popularity of his plays both in America and abroad in the early 1950s, Miller came increasingly to feel that he was being misunderstood. *Death of a Salesman,* which he had written half in 'laughter and joy', had been received as a work of the direst pessimism. When, in his next play, Miller deliberately set out to create a more articulate hero, he had had little more success in communicating his ideas. Not one reviewer of the original production of *The Crucible* mentioned what to Miller was the central theme - the handing over of conscience to another. The sense of bewilderment and frustration resulting from this apparent incomprehension on the part of audiences led Miller to consider the limitations of conventional stage realism. English-speaking theatre had traditionally focused on the subjective lives of characters and tended to ignore the social context and economic forces that shaped those lives. What was needed, he came to feel, was not more subjectivity, but more self-awareness. Like Brecht, whose work he admired, Miller became convinced of the necessity to break through the surface of realism and reveal 'the pantheon of forces and values which must lie behind the realistic surfaces of life'.[1] The question was how to achieve this.

Writing to his friend, James Stern, in November 1954, Miller lamented, 'I am living under a certain curse; I can't see why one writes except to say what has never been said.'[2] In this unsettled mood, Miller was presented with the opportunity to write for the kind of audience that might be receptive to new experiments in dramatic form. Martin Ritt, a Group Theatre actor performing in a Broadway production of Clifford Odet's *The Flowering Peach,* had persuaded producer Robert Whitehead to allow him to use the theatre for a series of special Sunday night performances which he would direct. Intrigued by the prospect, Miller agreed, and in a little less than two weeks completed *A Memory of Two Mondays* – a one-act play based on a memoir he had written about his experiences working in a Manhattan auto-parts warehouse after leaving high school.

The play marks a radical departure from his previous style and reflects his efforts to find new ways of conveying the significance of the stories he tells. Instead of relying on the usual plot devices designed to enlist attention, Miller creates an almost plotless sequence of disconnected, and frequently incomplete, episodes. The scene is a large warehouse in which several employees carry out the routine tasks of finding, wrapping, labelling and shipping out automobile parts. The result is a 'play' as apparently formless as a scene caught on closed circuit television. From scraps of conversation carried out between trips to the office, washroom or other parts of the warehouse, we slowly piece together impressions of the lives of several of the workers. These include Larry, a thirty-nine year-old married man who has trouble supporting his family but who buys a car he cannot afford; Gus, sixty-eight years old, married to Lily whom he abandons on weekends to drink with his friend, Jim; Kenneth, a recent immigrant from Ireland with his head full of poetry and Irish songs; and Bert, a nineteen year-old high school graduate saving his money to go to university. Most of the first of the two Monday mornings is spent protecting Tom Kelly (who has arrived at work in an alcoholic stupor), from being seen by the boss. Just as Gus is threatening to quit if Tom is fired, he is called to the phone where he learns that his wife has died.

The transition from the first to the second Monday is accomplished in a scene in which Bert and Kenneth start to clean the filthy warehouse windows to let in the sun. Lighting effects indicate the change of seasons from summer to winter. During the interlude, the two men are alternately isolated and speak their private thoughts about their situations. Bert expresses his sadness at the repetitive routine of most people's existence, fearing that his life, like theirs, may turn out to be an endless 'riding back and forth across a great big room'. Kenneth complains about the expense and loneliness of life in New York with its streets full of strangers, not one of whom has read a book through or knows a song worth singing. On the second Monday morning we learn that Larry has been having an affair with Patricia, a young girl from the office, and has had to sell his car; that Tom, the alcoholic, has reformed; that Kenneth has taken to drink and that Bert has saved enough money to leave for university. In the afternoon, news arrives that Gus has gone on one final booze-up, spent most of the insurance money, and died. When Bert finally takes his leave, his co-workers are polite but indifferent.

Miller showed the completed script to Ritt who was delighted, but the playwright's agent, Kay Brown, together with the producer, Kermit Bloomgarden, felt the work deserved more than a single Sunday night performance and suggested that Miller write a curtain raiser for a full Broadway production. Digging into his files, Miller came across a work he had begun several years ago dealing with the betrayal of two illegal Italian immigrants by their relative. It was a story he had been unable to get out of his mind in spite of the fact that he had hitherto failed to shape it to his satisfaction. Now he saw how he could make the story clearer by separating the action of the piece from its generalized significance. He would do this by employing a device from ancient Greek tragedy – the chorus of objective observers who articulate for the audience the implications of the protagonist's actions which the hero himself is too blind to see. To conform with the modern setting of the play, Miller made the choral figure a lawyer who both participates in the action and steps out of the play's framework to address the audience directly. In just over a week, Miller completed the play as a one-act companion piece for *A Memory of Two Mondays.*

Characteristically, *A View from the Bridge* is a two-level play in which the psychological and social elements seem sometimes at odds. Eddie Carbone, a longshoreman in the Red Hook district of Brooklyn, and his wife, Beatrice, have been responsible for the upbringing of their niece, Catherine, since the death of her parents when she was very young. Catherine is now seventeen, and Eddie's affection for her as a daughter has developed into something much more powerful without either of them being aware of the change. Some hint of the possessive and unnatural form of his love is given by his reluctance to let Catherine wear high heels, but the full power of his passion does not emerge until Catherine wants to leave home to get married. At that point Eddie's jealousy brings him into direct and tragic conflict with his niece's boyfriend.

The social level of the play deals with the strict code of loyalty of the Sicilian-American community in which Eddie lives and with the tragic consequences of Eddie's infraction of that code. The crisis is precipitated by the arrival of Rodolpho and Marco, Beatrice's Italian relatives, who have been smuggled into the United States illegally. The Carbones take their relatives into their home where they provide them with food and shelter, but tensions between the visitors and their host build up quickly when it becomes apparent that Rodolpho and Catherine are beginning to fall in love. The antagonism reaches a climax when Eddie returns home early one day to find Rodolpho and Catherine in the bedroom. Eddie orders

Rodolpho to leave whereupon Catherine starts to go with him. Eddie grasps her arm and says,

> You goin' with him. You goin' with him, heh? (*He grabs her face in the vise of his two hands.*) You goin' with him! (*He kisses her on the mouth as she pulls at his arms: he will not let go, keeps his face pressed against hers.*)[3]

Unable to admit the true nature of his feeling for Catherine, Eddie converts his jealousy of Rodolpho into a conviction that he is a homosexual and only interested in Catherine as a means of obtaining American citizenship. He appeals to Alfieri, the lawyer in the district, for a legal means of stopping what he has come to consider Rodolpho's theft of Catherine. Alfieri, sensing the true cause of Eddie's torment but unable to make him see it, tries to tell him that 'Somebody had to come for her ... sooner or later'. He also warns Eddie against betraying Rodolpho to the immigration authorities, reminding him of the strict code against informers in the community. 'You won't have a friend in the world, Eddie! Even those who understand will turn against you.' Ignoring Alfieri's warning, Eddie phones the immigration officials who come and arrest Marco and Rodolpho as well as two other recently arrived immigrants. As he is led away, Marco spits in Eddie's face and, in front of his neighbours, accuses him of betraying them.

The final scene shows Marco returning for vengeance. We are told that he has prayed in the church, and since he carries no weapon it is unclear whether he intends to kill Eddie or simply punish him with a beating. Waiting for Marco, Eddie refuses to run and tries once more to separate Rodolpho and Catherine. Beatrice begs him to release Catherine, saying of Rodolpho, 'It's her husband! Let her go.' When Catherine and Rodolpho start to leave,

> (*Eddie lunges and catches her: he holds her, and she weeps up into his face. And he kisses her on the lips.*)
> EDDIE: (*like a lover, out of his madness*)
> It's me, ain't it?[4]

Marco finally arrives, and Eddie accuses them of stealing Catherine from him and of making his name 'like a dirty rag'. 'I want my good name, Marco! You took my name!' Eddie pulls a knife, but

Marco turns it on him, and he is fatally wounded. As he falls forward, he

> (*crawls a yard to Catherine. She raises her face away – but she does not move as he reaches over and grasps her leg, and looking up at her, he seems puzzled, questioning, betrayed.*)
> EDDIE: Catherine – why?[5]

The play ends with a speech by Alfieri which presumably sums up Miller's understanding of the 'generalized significance' of the story as he has come to see it:

> Most of the time we settle for half,
> And I like it better.
> And yet, when the tide is right
> And the green smell of the sea
> Floats in through my window,
> The waves of this bay
> Are the waves against Siracusa.
> And I see a face that suddenly seems carved;
> The eyes look like tunnels
> Leading back toward some ancestral beach
> Where all of us once lived. And I wonder at those times
> How much of all of us
> Really lives there yet,
> And when we will truly have moved on,
> On and away from that dark place,
> That world that has fallen to stones?[6]

This version of the play is a kind of Euripidean tragedy of passion in which the protagonist is overcome by an irresistible and self-destructive madness. The implication of the final speech is that such passion is essentially primitive, an aspect of human nature that belongs to a dead past, but which is still part of all of us.

There is some evidence that, even before the production of the play, Miller may have been dissatisfied with the solutions he attempted in it. A central problem was his inability to grasp the ultimate meaning of the story. When he first heard the tale from a waterfront worker in Brooklyn, he felt that the weaving together of the lives of the characters seemed almost the work of fate. But there are in fact two stories – Eddie's infatuation with Catherine, and his betrayal of his relatives. In dramatizing them he had been unable to define the relationship between the subjective love tragedy and the objective tale of betrayal and public disgrace. Consequently he felt that a certain mystery remained that he could not account for.

During the rehearsals for the production, Miller and the director, Martin Ritt, tried to achieve a non-naturalistic style of acting and design that would encourage a more objective response on the part of the audience so that their emotional identification with Eddie would not overwhelm their ability to judge his actions in the social context. To this end, excessive and arbitrary gestures were eliminated, and the set was designed to be suggestive of the classical parallels Miller saw in the story. The problem was that neither the director (a former member of the Group Theatre) nor the actors had any experience of this kind of staging. The two plays, under the collective title *A View from the Bridge*, opened in New York at the Coronet Theatre on 29 September 1955 to decidedly mixed reviews.

A second circumstance that dissatisfied Miller with the first version of the play was his discovery of his own personal connection with it. After seeing the production several times, he suddenly realized that the piece was, in some part, an analogy to situations in his own life. What those situations were Miller never explained, but perhaps he saw in Eddie's infatuation for Catherine a parallel to his own interest in Marilyn Monroe. He may also have seen similarities between Eddie's informing on his relatives and Elia Kazan's co-operation with HUAC. Whatever the nature of the new insights, when the opportunity arose to have the play produced in London, Miller felt he had to rewrite it to include them.

In the revised two-act version, the characters of Beatrice and Catherine are considerably enlarged, as is their role in Eddie's fate. Furthermore, the London production was conceived in a much more realistic mode (the set was a highly detailed reconstruction of the Brooklyn apartment with its surroundings of alleys and fire-escapes) and most of the poetry of the first version was eliminated or the ideas expressed in the vivid Brooklyn argot of the neighbourhood. The classically trained British actors were better able than their American counterparts to find an acting style that could move easily from the highly emotional to the sedately dignified.

Even more interesting than the alterations in form, however, are the changes Miller made in the central character, playing down Eddie's physical passion for Catherine and focusing instead on his relationship to Marco. In the concluding minutes of the play it is Marco's insult, not Rodolpho's rivalry, which is foremost in Eddie's mind. When

Beatrice attempts to make him confront his real motive, Eddie turns away from the truth.

> BEATRICE: Who could give you your name? ... if [Marco] goes on his knees, what is he got to give you? That's not what you want.
> EDDIE: Don't bother me!
> BEATRICE: You want something else, Eddie, and you can never have her! ... The truth is not as bad as blood, Eddie! I'm tellin' you the truth – tell her good-by forever.[7]

Confronted with this truth, however, Eddie cannot accept it and cries out his repudiation, 'That's what you think of me – that I could have such a thought?' When he goes out to challenge Marco shouting, 'I want my name', therefore, his concern is only superficially like John Proctor's. Whereas Proctor understood in the end that only he could pass judgement on his acts, Eddie still believes his name is in the custody of his accusers. In the revised version, however, Eddie dies in the arms of Beatrice, and Miller perhaps intends to suggest by this that he finally comes to some kind of acceptance of his nature and his strange love.

Alfieri's final speech in the two-act version is very different from the original. Paradoxically the emphasis seems to shift away from the universal and primitive nature of Eddie's passion to the unique qualities of the man.

> Most of the time now we settle for half and I like it better. But the truth is holy, and even as I know how wrong he was, and his death useless, I tremble, for I confess that something perversely pure calls to me from his memory – not purely good, but himself purely, for he allowed himself to be wholly known and for that I will love him more than all my sensible clients. And yet, it is better to settle for half, it must be! And so I mourn him – I admit it – with a certain ... alarm.[8]

The relationship of all this to the play and to Eddie's character seems extremely obscure. Alfieri is contrasting the sensible people who settle for half and the potentially tragic individuals who cannot let well enough alone. According to Miller's theory of tragedy, such individuals are driven to act when others would retire, and in so acting they cause the scheme of things to act with retributive violence against them. But in what way can Eddie's actions be interpreted as a challenge of the 'stable cosmos' and how do they lead to the discovery of new understanding or a moral law? What 'holy truth' has been pursued by this protagonist or revealed by his death?

Superficially it would seem that the evil in this play is not in the environment, but in Eddie, and in this respect the play is fairly traditional. In the revised version, however, Miller has introduced lines to suggest that he is contrasting the Sicilian-American code of revenge with Beatrice's plea for forgiveness, and that he intends to imply that the tragedy would not have happened if Eddie had acknowledged the dark side of his nature. But these themes (if indeed they are implicit) are overshadowed by the spectacle of Eddie's slide into madness. The strangely inappropriate nature of Alfieri's concluding comment suggests that Miller had still not fathomed the mystery at the centre of this story, and that its meaning still eluded him.

An opportunity to try for a third time to come to grips with the story of Eddie Carbone arose during rehearsals for a Paris production. Informed that no French audience would accept the notion that Eddie and Catherine could be unaware of the nature of the love between them, Miller wrote a third ending in which Marco refuses to kill Eddie. Isolated by his neighbours who make him realize that he himself is responsible for the loss of his good name, Eddie commits suicide.[9] This ending seems in many ways the most intellectually satisfying, although it is perhaps psychologically improbable.

When Miller prepared his plays for the collected edition of his dramatic works, it was the London version of *A View from the Bridge* that he selected to be printed. In the introduction to that edition, Miller returned again to a consideration of the play and what he had learned from the two very different productions. His original conception of the character of Eddie, he felt, was too objective. In the revision he was able to identify much more fully with Eddie and to make him more sympathetic to the audience. This made it more possible to mourn a man who, although guilty of serious offences, nevertheless has a certain dignity. Even more important than the insight into Eddie's character, however, were the lessons Miller learned about dramatic form. By comparing the receptions of the play in London and New York he became convinced that the ultimate test of a play's effectiveness is performance in the theatre. 'A play', he writes, 'ought to make sense to common-sense people ... It is their innate conservatism which, I think, is and ought to be the barrier to excess in experiment and the exploitation of the bizarre.'[10] Miller's choice of the second version of *A View from the Bridge* for inclusion in his *Collected Plays* suggests a repudiation of the 'distancing' effects he had experimented with at first. He had become convinced that, while ideas are a requisite part of drama, those ideas need to be expressed in ways that are accessible to a broad, popular audience.

8
Celebrity (1956-61)

In an attempt to win some privacy for themselves and to escape the prying attention of the press, Miller and Monroe decided to hold their wedding in Connecticut. Expecting no more than sixty or so correspondents to make the trip into the country, Miller was astounded on the morning of 29 June 1956 when some 400 journalists and photographers representing newspapers from all over the world flocked to his Roxbury farm, ominously situated at the junction of Goldmine and Tophet Roads. Hoping for a little breathing space before the ordeal of facing the reporters, the couple had arranged to have lunch at a neighbour's. However, a journalist from *Paris Match*, learning of their plans and hoping for a scoop, persuaded a photographer to drive her to the nearby farm. They arrived just as Miller and Monroe were leaving. On the way back to the Miller residence, the photographer missed a curve, crashing into a tree and killing the journalist. Unable to cancel the press conference, the couple went through the proscribed ritual, but with a heavy sense of foreboding. In the evening, they were married in a civil ceremony in a court house in Westchester County, and two days later in a Jewish ceremony at the home of friends. Thus solidly joined, they moved into a luxurious New York apartment on East 57th Street.

A few days later, Miller finally received his passport but, since he still refused to supply names to HUAC, on 10 July he was cited for contempt. Still free to travel, he and Monroe flew to London where they were met by Laurence Olivier and his wife, Vivien Leigh, and a media reception even more frenzied than the one they had faced in Roxbury. Monroe revelled in the attention, but Miller was distinctly uncomfortable. He began to realize that the quiet intimacy they had shared during their (relatively) secret courtship was now a thing of the past. Trapped in their public images and struggling to promote their separate careers, Miller and Monroe started to confront the differences between them. Miller, who had been accustomed to spending long hours alone at his desk, was unable to escape the tensions of the film world. Monroe, insecure at the best of times and intimidated by what she considered

Olivier's condescending attitude, expected Miller to defend her. Increasingly the playwright found himself caught up in disagreements involving Monroe, Olivier, Paula Strasberg (brought along as Marilyn's acting coach) and Milton Greene. Temperamentally inclined to see both sides of an argument, Miller proved to be a half-hearted advocate, not the all-loving, protective father figure Monroe had dreamed of. More catastrophically, some time during this period Marilyn read an entry in her husband's notebook in which he expressed some disappointment in her. The incident was traumatic and made her more ready to see betrayal in her husband's behaviour. In spite of these distractions, however, Miller was able to complete a short story based on his experiences in Nevada which he called *The Misfits*. He also worked with the British director, Peter Brook, on the production of the two-act version of *A View from the Bridge* which opened at the Comedy Theatre in London on 11 October 1956.

On their return to America the Millers attempted to settle down to a less harried life, renting a summer house in the ocean-front town of Amagansett on Long Island. There Miller wrote in the mornings and in the afternoons drove with Marilyn to the beach where they walked along the dunes or fished in the surf. But they could not escape the outside world for long. Miller had to face his trial for contempt of Congress which came before the House on 14 March 1957. In his defence, his lawyers pointed out that the prosecution of the playwright appeared to be vindictive since some thirteen individuals, most of them in more sensitive positions than Miller, had also refused to name associates known to be Communists and yet not one of them had been cited for contempt. After a relatively short debate, in which only some half-dozen Congressmen spoke in defence of the dramatist, Congress voted overwhelmingly against Miller. On 19 July he was fined $500 and given a one-month suspended sentence.

By that time, however, the couple was back on Long Island enjoying what was probably the happiest period of their married life. Marilyn cooked, did the housekeeping, and went for long walks on the beach where she rescued the 'junk' fish discarded by the fishermen, carefully returning them to the sea. More importantly, they were expecting their first child, a child that Marilyn had been desperately longing for. In the autumn, however, this tranquillity was destroyed. One morning Marilyn began experiencing severe cramps and, after an agonizing four-hour ride into a Manhattan hospital, she had to be operated on for an ectopic pregnancy. Devastated by his wife's sad vulnerability and wanting to give her something to hope for, Miller promised to write a film script for her.

When they moved back into Manhattan, however, she became severely depressed and once again Miller had to act as nurse and guardian.

Intending, perhaps, to put his first marriage completely behind him, Miller had sold the Roxbury property shortly after his divorce. Since then, he and Marilyn had been looking for another farm in the area, and early in 1958 they found what they wanted – an eighteenth century, white farmhouse just a little further along Tophet Road. Marilyn wanted to tear down the old building and build their own dream home on the site and she commissioned Frank Lloyd Wright to come up with a design. Possibly understanding his client's extravagant romanticism, Wright proposed a mansion with a sixty-foot, circular living room, seventy-foot pool, but only one bedroom. Miller balked at the price tag, and they decided instead to remodel the existing house. At Marilyn's suggestion (and probably with her money) they also purchased an additional 315 acres of adjoining property.

Work proceeded on the renovations during the spring and summer while Miller worked on his promised screenplay – a film adaptation of his short story, *The Misfits*. Neither Marilyn nor his agent much liked what he produced, but Miller's friend and editor, Frank Taylor, persuaded them that the script might interest the film director, John Huston. Before reaching a decision on the project, however, the Millers left for Hollywood where Marilyn had agreed to appear in *Some Like it Hot*. Once again Miller was forced to act as a buffer between his emotionally volatile wife and her irascible producers. To complicate matters still further, Marilyn discovered that she was pregnant. Partly as a result of her behaviour on the set, filming dragged on until December at which time she had a miscarriage.

During this period Miller continued to write, but the demands made on his time and nervous energy by his wife's career were beginning to tell. He was still wrestling valiantly with the play that started out in 1952 as *Plenty Good Times* (and became known by Kermit Bloomgarden as Miller's *Third Play*), and by early 1959, had produced more than 3000 pages without finding a satisfying meaning or structure. In a letter to Kenneth Rowe, his old drama professor, however, he described the scope of his ambition and the nature of his hope for the work. It will, he said, 'sum up everything I know I am and ... combine everything into an image of what man is and might become'. His aim was to arrive at a style which would 'infuse intelligence with passion, and visceral action with a kind of speech and construction'. He hoped to project 'not only heat but light into the audience's heart' and to 'change the direction of our stage'.[1] In the meantime, however, he still had to complete his film project.

By the summer, John Huston had expressed interest in *The Misfits*. In the meantime, however, Marilyn had agreed to fulfill a Hollywood commitment by co-starring with Gregory Peck in *Let's Make Love*, the script of which she had not even bothered to read. When Miller pointed out that her character appeared in only three scenes, she asked him to enlarge her part whereupon Peck withdrew from the project. As a replacement, Miller suggested Yves Montand who had appeared in the Paris production of *The Crucible*. When the producers agreed, the Millers returned to Hollywood where Marilyn began rehearsals. By this time, however, their marriage was in serious trouble. Marilyn's behaviour on the set was even more erratic than usual. Increasingly barbiturate-dependent and hostile to Miller, she nevertheless still depended on him for comfort through sleepless nights. Then during the filming, she became emotionally involved with her co-star, Montand, and her reckless lack of discretion led to the affair being picked up and blown out of proportion by the popular press. Miller refrained from comment, but found it difficult to maintain his dignity with his private life the subject of international gossip.

It was in these circumstances that the filming of *The Misfits* finally began on 18 July 1960. Although they tried to maintain appearances, the Millers were hardly speaking. They shared the same hotel suite, but travelled to and from the set separately. Once again Marilyn's nerves made her unreliable at work and Miller was forced to sit with her through countless sleepless nights and to oversee her intake of medication until he himself was on the verge of a nervous breakdown. Midway through the shooting Marilyn had to go into hospital to be treated for barbiturate dependence and exhaustion. On her release she admitted that 'it's all over' between her and Miller. What had begun so hopefully as a gift for Marilyn after her first miscarriage had somehow turned into a horrible, soul-destroying nightmare.

When the film was finally finished, the couple returned to New York on separate planes and Marilyn announced her plans to seek a divorce. 'I had wanted some calmness, some steadiness in my life', she told a reporter, 'and for a time I had that with Arthur. That was a nice time. And then we lost it.'[2] As for Miller, he told John Huston 'Neither of us reproaches the other and there is no one else to blame.'

Whether or not the troubled marriage of Arthur Miller and Marilyn Monroe might have survived away from the maelstrom of public attention no one will ever know. In the years since the divorce, there have been literally hundreds of attempts to pierce the mystery of this most romantic, most unlikely of liaisons. Since her death in 1962, Monroe has been eulogized and patronized, praised and dismissed, pitied and condemned until she has become an iconic presence – larger than life. She is now a screen upon which the compassionate, the lonely, the abused, as well as the frustrated, the envious, and the salacious project their fantasies and dreams. Behind the thousands of photographic images that have survived remains the enigma. Prominent among the many who have sought to unravel that enigma was Miller himself. For the memory of his golden, free-spirited, tormented child-wife would haunt him until the end of his days.

9
The Misfits (1956-61)

The most chameleon-like of Miller's works, *The Misfits*, exists in three very different forms. The first is a Hemingway-like short story that appeared in *Esquire* magazine in 1956. The second is a film, directed by John Huston and starring Marilyn Monroe, that premiered in 1961. The third is the published version of the screenplay put out by Viking in 1961. In an introduction to this latter, Miller explained that the sense of the story depends very much on 'the nuances of character and place' which the 'diagrammatic manner of screenplay writing' (and by implication the highly concentrated and graphic method of film making) cannot convey. To compensate for the limitations of the film medium, therefore, he invented a form of fiction - neither novel, play, nor film script - in which he attempted to supplement the moving image with 'the reflective possibilities of the written word'.[1]

The constantly metamorphosing *Misfits* evolved over a period of four years and is the only major work Miller produced during his years with Marilyn Monroe. The story is based on his experiences in Nevada during his six-week residence in that state waiting for his divorce in the spring of 1956. As an urban Easterner he had been struck by the startling contrasts in this western setting: between the harsh landscape and the stubborn vitality of the human and the animal inhabitants; between the futility of the casinos and the divorce court on the one hand, and the rugged lives of the rodeo riders and itinerant ranch hands on the other. During that time he had accompanied two cowboys on an excursion to catch wild mustangs. Although attracted by the sympathy and directness of these men and by the vast emptiness in which they tried to make their home, Miller initially felt that their world was too distant from his own to provide material for his creative imagination. Later, however, by a characteristic imaginative transferral of some of his own background into the situation, he felt he knew more about their lives than he had suspected.[2]

The resulting short story, which he wrote in London later that year, tells of Gay Langland, Perce Howland and Guido Racanelli. These three itinerant cowboys eke out a precarious living doing odd part-time jobs to allow them to retain a false sense of independence and avoid the humiliation of holding down a permanent job. The work that gives Gay and Guido the most satisfaction, and the labour by which they like to define themselves, is the hunting of wild mustangs. Once an honourable occupation needed to supply riding ponies and breeding stock for the farms and ranches in the region, the hunt has degenerated into a sordid pursuit of the small remnants of the once vast herds to sell to the processors of dog food. The three men view the hunt differently. Guido, a callous veteran of many bombing missions during the Second World War, takes pride in the technical aspects of the hunt – the pursuit by plane and truck and the use of heavy tyres to capture the horses – all of which are his inventions. Gay insists that what he is doing has not changed, but that society has demeaned his labour. Perce, the youngest, is the only one to respond to the suffering of the horses themselves, or to perceive any vestige of tragedy in their destruction. But they all agree that the hunt is 'better than wages', and somehow convince themselves that it represents an honourable alternative to enslavement by a commercial society. In the end, even Perce's scruples are quelled as he agrees to accompany the others to Thighbone Mountain to ferret out the last survivors of the wild herds.

Miller's portrayal of this pathetic group of 'misfits' is brilliantly ambiguous. On the one hand, they represent the last of a dying breed of men whose courage and spirit of independence recall the days of the American frontier. Huge as it was, that frontier had a sense of community and common purpose which had even then been destroyed in other parts of America. In the west, the community transcended family. It was an 'endless range ... and it connected [a man] sufficiently with his father and his wife and his children... [Gay felt that] he had neither left anyone nor not-left as long as they were all alive on those ranges.'[3] In such a world, family life is pleasant (Gay remembers his home as the best part of his life), but it is essentially limiting – 'a stake to which [one is] pleasurably tethered'. On the other hand, Miller shows with a restrained irony the limitations of these 'heroes'. Since the death of his wife and baby, Guido has lost his ability to love and the sense of 'loose gaiety' he feels is a symptom of his lack of a sense of purpose. Gay is immature, with boyish facial features and an adolescent's need to do things which he cannot explain or justify logically. Perce is also young, with a young man's sensitivity, but totally lacking in ambition and willpower. These men have refused to accept the conventional role of wage-earner that American society attempts to impose on its members.

But they have not found a way to live as responsible adults. Instead they have themselves become victimizers, enslaving and destroying the mustangs to avoid their own enslavement by the capitalist system. The story ends with a long and detailed description of the captured horses.

> From time to time the stallion caught the smell of the pastures [in the mountains] and he started to walk toward the vaulted fields in which he had grazed; but the tire bent his neck around, and after a few steps he would turn to face it and leap into the air with his forelegs striking at the sky, and then he would come down and be still again.[4]

The 'misfit' horses are obviously symbolic of the misfit men, and by focusing on them at the end of the story in this way Miller seems to imply that both are powerless to control their own lives.

Rejected by several magazines as being too long, *The Misfits* first appeared in a cut version in *Esquire* in May 1957. When, later that summer, Marilyn lost the baby she was carrying, Miller promised to write a film for her and resolved to adapt his short story for the screen. Doing so, however, proved difficult and he worked intermittently on the project for the next two years. The problem involved expanding a sharply focused, tautly written account of a one-day mustang hunt into a more lengthy narrative including as a central character a figure mentioned only peripherally in the original. What had started out as an action story was transformed into a romantic comedy, but one that lacked most of the characteristics of the genre. With virtually no obstacles (such as disapproving fathers or social barriers), the three cowboys become lovesick rival suitors, all attempting to win the girl by demonstrations of *machismo* which she finds either frightening or abhorrent. The result is a kind of inverted western in which the catalyst for change is not the stranger in the white hat, but a woman whose sensitivity and gift for life succeed in domesticating at least one of the previously independent, but irresponsible, cowboys.

The focus of the extended film version of the story is the relationship between Gay Langland and Roslyn Tabor. Filling out the details of the short story, Miller shows Roslyn obtaining her divorce, meeting Guido and Gay in a Reno bar, moving into Guido's unfinished house with Gay, travelling with him and Guido to Dayton to find a third hand for the hunt, attending the rodeo where they team up with Perce Howland, and finally joining the men in their excursion to find mustangs. These scenes leading up to the film's climax establish Roslyn's personality as hypersensitive, excessively alarmed by violence and cruelty, and suffering from an almost overwhelming sense of being lost. The character is clearly a portrait of Miller's wife, combining what he saw as Monroe's greatness of spirit and gift for spontaneity with her depression, nervousness, paranoia, insecurity and panic attacks. But the portrait of Roslyn is more than just a character in a film. It appears that Miller hoped through creating the proper role for his wife he could strengthen their relationship; that he might not only demonstrate what she meant to him, but also get her to step out of herself and see her own worth.[5] To this end, it became important to him to present a couple able to forgive each other's faults and so provide a model for their own reconciliation. This intention affects the resolution of the story, however, and Miller kept altering the script even while the film was being shot.

The movie version differs from the story in that Roslyn (Monroe) persuades Perce (Montgomery Clift) to release some of the tethered mustangs. When Gay (Clark Gable) sees what they have done, he tries single-handedly to recapture the stallion. In the original version of the film he is unsuccessful and is left lying exhausted in the sand. For Miller, who conceived the story in a mood of hopefulness, however, such a resolution was unsatisfactory.[6] In the final version, therefore, Gay succeeds (altogether improbably) in recapturing the animal and tying it to the truck. Having done so, however, he comes to realize that this kind of life is finished. While he has remained the same, the world has changed. Far from living the heroic, independent life he has supposed, he has in fact been 'ropin' a dream' and he will now have to find another way to prove he is alive. If Gay has been brought to see through his self-delusions by Roslyn, Roslyn, in her turn, has been changed by Gay. His kindness gives her a sense of self-confidence and the necessary courage to face life in its harsh reality. Overcoming her anxiety, she learns to accept the interrelationship of death and life, and to understand that kindness and cruelty can co-exist in the same heart. With their new knowledge, Gay and Roslyn look forward with hope to an uncertain future.

Miller's trouble with the film's ending was partly a result of his deep personal involvement in the story, but it may also have been a consequence of his ambivalent feeling towards the medium itself. Fundamentally unsympathetic to the world of film, he resented the time he had to spend on the screenplay when he would rather have been writing a play. He soon found himself in conflict with the director, John Huston, who (understandably) was more concerned with images than dialogue. Miller also had to face the resentment of his wife who felt that the role of Roslyn failed to allow her to shine as the serious dramatic actress she longed to be. The result was a picture that was the product of almost daily script conferences and rewrites as Miller and Huston tried to shape the film to reflect their own separate visions.

What Miller objected to primarily in film was its tendency to eliminate context, blocking out background with close-ups, and wiping out the symbolic implications of objects. A good example is the mustang hunt which is so strong visually, and so obviously cruel and senseless, that it is difficult for many viewers to see anything at all heroic in the cowboys' activity. And yet we must feel sympathy for the men if we are to have the necessary respect for Gay's former life. There are other examples, too, where what Miller calls the 'effect of documentation inevitable in photography' fails to convey his vision. The shots in the film of the Dayton crowds do not unequivocally convey the impression of a society 'enslaved by its own will' as Miller describes it in the printed version. Similarly, the film cannot capture the symbolic resonances Miller sees in the story. He had set the rodeo scene in a small town where he had noticed a somewhat dilapidated church. The cross atop the steeple was tilted and in danger of falling to the ground, 'a reasonable symbol' he wrote later, 'of what he was after in the film'.[7] But the church doesn't appear in the film. Owing to a shortage of water for the large production crew, the scene had to be shot in a different location.

Miller spent hundreds of hours working with Huston on the film before and during the ninety days of shooting, but felt that he had little power over the results on the screen. He tried to compensate for this in the published version of the script[8] where he carefully spells out the psychological and metaphysical dimensions of the story. The result is one of Miller's least successful prose works. Not only is the tone uncharacteristically sentimental, but the style is correspondingly overheated, possibly because Miller's own emotional engagement in the various transformations of *The Misfits* from short story to film to novel. What began as a project he hoped might bring him and Marilyn closer together and provide them with the chance to live and work in partnership,[9] ended in recriminations and separation. By the time Miller saw the final rough cut in November, 1960, he lamented, 'I still don't understand it... I made a present of this to her, and I left it without her.'[10]

10
Refuge (1961–68)

Returning alone to New York in early November of 1960, Miller picked up some of his belongings from the 57th Street apartment and checked into the Chelsea Hotel. While the country was excitedly anticipating change with the election of the young John F. Kennedy, Miller tried to come to terms with his past. He blamed no one but himself for the tragedy, but how was he to go on without remorse or bitterness? On 20 January, Monroe flew to Juarez, Mexico, where in a special night session arranged by judge Miguel Gomez Guerra, she successfully filed for divorce on the grounds of 'incompatibility of character'.[1] Two weeks later, the opening of *The Misfits*, the film on which Miller had pinned such hopes, was darkened by news of the recent death of its leading man. Clark Gable, perhaps the most popular and respected film actor of his time, had collapsed and died of a heart attack shortly after completing the picture. As Miller and others knew, Gable's death was probably hastened by his participation in the strenuous action of the film.

In March tragedy struck again, this time closer to home. Miller's mother had been in ill health for some time suffering from diabetes and heart disease. Lately she had had the extra burden of caring for her husband, stricken with prostate cancer. She finally managed to get him into hospital for surgery on 6 March, but on returning home she collapsed and was rushed to the Jewish Hospital of Brooklyn where she died later that night. Miller's relationship with his mother was probably the most formative of his life. Always her favourite, sharing her imagination, her love of books and music, even for a time her spiritualism, Miller had long felt 'cramped' in expressing his feelings towards her. But at her funeral, looking at her casket and remembering her as a young woman full of expectation and pride for her children but never for herself, the tears finally came.[2]

In the spring, feeling he had to get away from New York, Miller moved out to the place in Roxbury to which, thanks to Marilyn's generosity, he now had sole title. There he hoped to find the uninterrupted stretches of time necessary to regain his feet as a writer. He began work on a long short story, planted 2000 trees, and tried to put his life back together.[3] For a time it seemed that he could neither face nor flee the despair he felt. But among the many talents he had inherited from his mother, not the least was the ability to move on. He realized that he could not survive alone, and began to make plans for the future.

Central to those plans was a petite Austrian woman he had met in Nevada while filming *The Misfits.* Ingeborg Morath, a photographer with the Magnum agency, had travelled by car from New York with her mentor, Henri Cartier-Bresson, to record the making of the film. There she had found the tension between Miller and Monroe so great she had had trouble getting them close enough together to take their photos. Miller had told her some of his marital problems, but not wanting to console a 'Marilyn Monroe victim', Morath just wanted to get away.[4] Miller had seen her occasionally in New York during the winter, but now he resolved to act more decisively.

Inge was then taking still photos on the set of a film version of *A View from the Bridge* being shot by a French company in Paris. Miller decided that this provided him with the opportunity he needed. He flew to Paris to be with her and, following the assignment, the two of them travelled to Austria, visiting Hitler's birthplace at Linz and, just outside it, the Mauthausen concentration camp. Miller found the experience profoundly disturbing. While he identified with the victims, he also realized that he would have done anything to have avoided ending up in their place. Suddenly he could almost sympathize with the bystanders who had watched the trucks as they carried their human cargo to the ovens. As an Austrian, Inge reacted to the visit more viscerally but with an understanding born of her own experience.

Born in Graz, Austria, in 1923, she had grown up in a liberal Protestant home with her parents, both of whom were scientists. Studying languages at the University of Berlin, she had refused to become a Nazi supporter and, as a consequence, was drafted to work in an assembly plant at the Templehof Airport along with Ukrainian prisoners of war. Since the airport was a prime target for allied bombing, the posting was practically a death sentence. In 1945, however, she managed to escape. Determined to return home, she set out to walk to Austria. On the way as she passed scenes of wanton, unutterable destruction, she almost gave way to despair and, had she not been saved by a soldier who stopped her from jumping in a river, would have taken her own life. With her unknown saviour she travelled on to Salzburg where, miraculously, she found her parents alive.[5] If Miller was a product of the Depression, Inge Morath had been formed by her wartime experiences in Berlin. They had made her clear-eyed and understandably suspicious of any sentimentality about the inherent goodness of humanity. But she was not a pessimist; she welcomed the good in people despite expecting the worst. Standing outside the high-walled Nazi prison, Miller found her spirit remarkably complementary to his own.

Back in New York, however, the playwright got caught up once again in the undertow of his old life. In October an opera based on *The Crucible* opened at the New York City Opera; in January the film version of *A View from the Bridge* played to unfriendly reviews. Even when he married Inge Morath in a quiet ceremony before a justice of the peace in Milford, Connecticut, on 17 February 1962, the shadow of his past hung over them. Inge felt she was resented for having replaced Marilyn in Arthur's life,[6] a resentment that became more pronounced after the news of Monroe's death from an overdose of Nembutol on 5 August. Overwhelmed by the inferno of publicity surrounding his former wife's demise, Miller took refuge in escape, refusing to attend the Los Angeles funeral which he feared would be a 'circus'. He even declined to send flowers.

Just what Miller felt during those semi-hysterical days (Monroe's death got more coverage than the Cuban missile crisis) it is impossible to fathom. There is no question that it constituted a critical turning point in his life. In death, Monroe had finally been captured completely by the media – an icon now forever young, forever vulnerable. Whatever hope Miller might have had of trying to reach some kind of mutual understanding, of meeting to 'talk sensibly about all the foolishness they had been through'[7] was finally dashed. The dialogue he would carry on until the end of his life was now to remain one-sided.

If the past was inescapable, however, it could perhaps be thrown off the scent. So Miller and Inge decided to transform the circumstances of their lives. Both by nature urban and sophisticated, they resolved to move permanently to the country. Although Miller had had property near Roxbury since 1947, his principal residence had always been in the city. His first Connecticut house, located some three hours from New York on a country road rarely ploughed in the winter, had served primarily as a summer refuge to escape the Brooklyn heat while the children were growing up. The second house, bought with Monroe and deeded in her name, had been intended as a more luxurious rural residence. The rather ostentatious visions of Frank Lloyd Wright having proved impractical, the house, though modernized, was left much as it was. Beautifully situated on 340 acres in a lovely New England landscape of hilltops, pastures and well-kept stone walls, it was comparatively isolated and totally lacking the cultural amenities that both Arthur and Inge enjoyed. The nearest town, Roxbury, was a small community of 2100 incorporated in 1796, with a general store, library, school and some hundred colonial houses, barns and other structures over 200 years old. What it did provide was an escape from the constant media attention which had become a torment, and the quiet essential for their creative work.

As permanent residents, Arthur and Inge became part of the local community, employing local craftsmen, running for the school board, shopping in the local hardware store. For both of them, their country home came to represent a safe haven of a kind they had never known. So, while they continued to travel internationally and to follow successful professional careers, they now had a place where they could start their new life together. Over the next few years, they began what for Arthur was a second family, one that was to be blighted by secret tragedy. Their first child, a daughter born 15 September, 1962[8] they named Rebecca Augusta after Arthur's mother. At forty-six and feeling more like a grandfather than a parent, Miller doted on the girl. When sometime later Inge gave birth to a boy, the couple were initially elated and Miller phoned Robert Whitehead to share his excitement. The following day, however, the boy was diagnosed with Down Syndrome and Miller confided to Whitehead, 'He isn't right. I'm going to have to put the baby away.'

The decision divided the parents. Inge was reluctant to part with her child, but Miller prevailed and the baby, now called Daniel, was hastily placed in a home for infants in New York City and his birth hushed up.[9] When Daniel was older, Inge wanted to bring him home, but Arthur refused and a compromise was found. At age four, Daniel was moved to a facility just a ten-minute drive from Roxbury. There in the Southbury Training School, a home for the developmentally disabled, Daniel was to spend his youth and adolescence, provided with room and board, some limited education and programmed activities such as farming. Inge visited her son weekly; Miller almost never did. Nor did the author anywhere in his published work acknowledge his son's existence.[10] Until almost the end of his life he acted in public as if Daniel did not exist.

Whatever secret sorrow the Millers shared in private they did not trumpet to the world. Indeed to most observers their relationship seemed not only remarkably harmonious but mutually supportive. Miller appeared to benefit from his contact with the very different sensibility of his wife. Not only did her European outlook widen his perspective, but her less abstract, more down-to-earth point of view offered a healthy counterbalance to Miller's philosophical proclivities. Her work as a photographer helped him as a playwright, prompting him to visualize scenes more than he had before.[11] He also collaborated with his wife, producing four illustrated travel books: *In Russia* (1969), *In the Country* (1977), *Chinese Encounters* (1979) and *Salesman in Beijing* (1984).

As the 1960s proceeded and the Vietnam war dragged on, Miller came to feel more and more alienated from mainstream America, suspicious as he was of the wild experimentation and unapologetic self-indulgence of the time. As a delegate to the Democratic Convention in Chicago in 1968, he was appalled by the violence against the protesters, but realized that he could no longer share the passionately held convictions of either side, neither the belief in a democratic crusade in Vietnam nor the faith that America was being revolutionized by youth or black movements. His confidence in the progressive momentum of history had been shattered and he was groping for a belief to replace it.

One of the few credos that survived the general collapse was his belief in the redemptive power of art and the importance of its free expression. Consequently, when asked in 1965 to assume the presidency of an international association of poets, essayists and novelists, he accepted. Established after the First World War in the hope that an organization of writers might help prevent another war, PEN had gradually lost its effectiveness in a world of hostile ideologies. Miller agreed to attend a PEN Congress in Yugoslavia where he found that his international reputation helped persuade Soviet observers to consider joining the organization. When he visited Russia to conclude the arrangements, however, it became clear that the Soviets would never abandon their censorship of art, and the negotiations collapsed.

During all this time, their Roxbury home was the base from which the couple launched their sorties into the larger worlds of politics and art. Miller's contact with the professional theatre remained his primary concern and source of his major discontents. After a nearly nine-year absence from Broadway, he was anxious to reestablish his flagging reputation with another New York hit. Things began hopefully in 1962 with the announcement that the new Lincoln Center for the Performing Arts would include a permanent repertory company under the co-direction of Robert Whitehead and Elia Kazan. To be patterned on the great repertory companies of Europe, the troupe would include actors and theatrical craftsmen dedicated to the theatre as art rather than entertainment. Such at least was the hope of the two directors when they approached Miller in October 1962 to secure his commitment to let them produce his next play. Miller and Kazan had not worked together since their estrangement in 1952. A reconciliation of sorts had been effected since that time, partly by Marilyn Monroe and partly by Miller's mellowing attitude brought about by his increased awareness of the complexity of the issues he once thought so clear.

The prospect of performance by a genuine repertory company and the pressure of an imminent deadline encouraged Miller to return to his 'third play' on which he had been working since the early 1950s. Drawing heavily on his own experience, it dealt with individuals who had lived through the 1930s and found their ideals in conflict with the course of post-war American life. In his sketches he had been trying to break out of conventional realism by using 'Shakespearean' techniques of juxtaposing characters and incidents. Now he began to add material from his more recent past - his divorce, the death of his mother, and his trip to Europe with Inge. By the autumn of 1963 the script, now titled *After the Fall*, ran for five hours. Rehearsals began on 24 October and lasted some three months during which time Miller continued to shape and rewrite. The play opened in January, not as had been hoped in the Vivian Beaumont Theatre in Lincoln Center (still incomplete), but in the ANTA Theatre, a temporary structure hastily erected to house the company in Washington Square.

Reaction to *After the Fall* was sharply divided. While audiences enjoyed it and extra performances had to be scheduled by the company, many critics were outraged by what they considered to be Miller's self-justifying presentation of his relationship with Marilyn Monroe. Although the dramatist stoutly denied that the play was any more autobiographical than his other works, the general perception was that the scenes between Quentin and Maggie were almost embarrassingly documentary. This public display of a private quarrel (as it was widely regarded), questionable enough at any time, seemed to be particularly tasteless in view of the relatively recent, and widely publicized, suicide of the popular actress. Once again, Miller appears to have completely misjudged the effect his play would have on its audience. So preoccupied had he become with the general issues in the drama that he lost sight of its personal relevance. According to Robert Whitehead, three months before the play was ready to go into rehearsal Miller phoned him to say that it had just occurred to him that audiences might mistake Maggie for Marilyn.[12] It is scarcely surprising, therefore, that Miller felt that the reaction to the New York production of the play was distorted, and that the real issues raised by the drama never received the discussion they deserved.

During the summer of 1964, in a period of some five weeks, Miller dramatized a story he had first heard in 1955. *Incident at Vichy* is set in a police waiting-room during a round-up of suspected Jews in southern France during the Second World War. It tells of an Austrian aristocrat who is brought to an awareness of his complicity in the Nazi evil, and who attempts to atone for his guilt by helping a Jew to escape. It is a rather transparent moral fable on Miller's favourite themes of guilt and responsibility, but skilfully crafted and written with passionate conviction. The play opened on 4 December 1964 to generally favourable reviews.

The following year saw Miller's reputation continue to rise, due in part to the revival of two of his earlier plays. In 1965 the National Theatre of Great Britain mounted a production of *The Crucible* under the direction of Sir Laurence Olivier, which was the finest performance of the play to that date. Later in the same year, Ulu Grosbard staged a highly successful off-Broadway revival of *A View from the Bridge*. By the mid-1960s, therefore, it seemed that Miller had come through the apparent 'slump' of a nine-year absence from the New York stage to become once more a powerful force in the American theatre.

The New York successes of 1964–65 were, however, slightly deceptive. Both *After the Fall* and *Incident at Vichy* had been performed as part of a repertory season, and given only fifty-nine and ninety-nine performances respectively. *A View from the Bridge* achieved a longer run, but it was in the less commercial atmosphere of off-Broadway. The most ominous sign of the times, however, was the failure of the Repertory Theatre of Lincoln Center to realize the ideals of its founders. Some of the actors who had made financial sacrifices to belong to the company began to suspect that not everyone had been equally altruistic. The management, too felt underfinanced. Finally, the tension between Robert Whitehead and the Board of Directors erupted when it was discovered that the Board had been searching for a new General Manager. Since he had not been informed of the move, Whitehead resigned, and Kazan and Miller left with him, convinced that the Board had no intention of honouring its commitment to support a true repertory system. Whatever hopes Miller might have had of becoming part of a dedicated ensemble of theatre people comparable to the best repertory companies of Europe were shattered. Henceforth, he would have to tilt with the Broadway monster on his own.

Just how difficult that could be became apparent during preparations for the production of his next play, *The Price*. The original opening, scheduled for the autumn of 1967, had to be delayed because of casting problems. Rehearsals finally commenced in December with Ulu Grosbard directing; in the course of rehearsals, however, Jack Warden, the original

Victor, became ill and had to be replaced in the role by Pat Hingle. This postponed the out-of-town premiere in Philadelphia, and then, two days before the New York opening, David Burns had an emergency operation and his understudy had to step into the role of Solomon. To complicate matters further, Miller and Grosbard disagreed on the production, and the playwright took over direction for the last week of Broadway previews. When the play finally opened, it was hailed as Miller's most successful work in many years, playing for 425 performances in New York after which it transferred to London for another year.

11
After the Fall (1964)

After the Fall was the culmination of Miller's many earlier attempts to combine detailed psychological portraiture with a criticism of society and a search for ultimate meaning. In his determination to get as close to 'reality' as possible, Miller has once again (as in *Death of a Salesman*) gone inside the head of his protagonist to dramatize Quentin's subjective life. In the process, the objective world virtually disappears, to be replaced by a fluid, timeless 'consciousness' into which memories come and go at the prompting of will or passion. The story of the play, therefore, is less concerned with Quentin's actions in the world than with his inner search for some pattern in his existence, some 'law' that would explain the disaster of his life.

Because of the nature of this search, the figures in Quentin's recollections are both vividly individualized and at the same time mythic. Quentin is partly Arthur Miller painfully reviewing incidents in his own mental and emotional development; but he is also Everyman looking for a way to survive with dignity in the modern world; he is Cain wandering in the desert. In the same way, Louise and Maggie bear certain resemblances to Miller's first two wives, but they also embody opposing attitudes to sex that can be said to go to the roots of the western Judaic–Hellenistic tradition. Because of the complexity of the work and the seemingly sensational nature of its revelations, *After the Fall* provoked widely differing responses when it opened early in 1964.

That opening was singularly propitious. The play not only marked the beginning of the Repertory Theatre of Lincoln Center, it brought together, for the first time since *Salesman,* the theatrical talents of Miller, Elia Kazan and Jo Mielziner. By general agreement, however, the collaboration did not repeat their triumph of some fifteen years earlier. The scenic problems presented by the script and the auditorium proved insurmountable. The large open stage and wide amphitheatre of the ANTA-Washington Square Theatre were ill-suited to the intimate and subtle requirements of *After the Fall.* Miller had wanted to create a theatrical 'stream of consciousness' in which memories and associations follow one another in quick and bewildering succession. The new theatre, however, dictated that actors had either to make long entrances across the wide stage or else remain immobile, but continuously in view as part of the action. Mielziner's design, a large, craggy, free-form setting, provided acting areas for individual scenes or a series of 'niches' from which the various characters from Quentin's past could assail the protagonist. Centrally located at the back of the set, a realistic concentration-camp tower brooded symbolically over the entire play.

Kazan's direction, characteristically, drew from the actors vividly realistic and emotionally true performances. In the case of newcomer Barbara Loden who played Maggie, this realism was seriously distracting. Amounting almost to an impersonation of Marilyn Monroe, her performance drew undue attention to the autobiographical basis of the play. As Quentin, Jason Robards Jr gave a subtly varied portrayal which was widely praised. But even the accomplished Mr Robards could not raise Quentin's private anguish to the level of universal import. Consequently, too many of the spectators (and critics) saw little in the play beyond its superficial relationship to Miller's private life.

While it is probably true (as Miller later maintained) that the New York critics never discussed the themes he was dealing with, the fact is not altogether surprising. For the play makes quite extraordinary demands on its audience. Miller is here attempting to present the kind of psychological detail that may well be beyond the scope of drama, in some respects a relatively blunt instrument. The associations and cross-references in the text are frequently too subtle to be caught in a careful reading let alone a first viewing. Furthermore, the absence of a strong narrative line deprives the play of what has been called the drama's soul. It is sometimes difficult to determine, not only what is happening, but why it is 'happening' when it does. At certain moments Quentin acts in an external world, speaking to a Listener, lighting a cigarette, moving in an objective time and space with past and future chronologically fixed. But this 'objective' reality is shadowy. We do not see the Listener, nor do we hear his (her?) words although we can deduce from Quentin's responses what they must have been. Compared to *Death of a Salesman*, for example, the real world hardly exists in this play, as Quentin's memories constitute almost the entire 'action'.

If Miller has abandoned almost completely any attempt to create a realistic context for Quentin's subjective life, his dramatization of that life seems sometimes baffling or inconsistent. For example, Quentin is sometimes a character in his own memories, sometimes a superego standing apart from those incidents. Similarly, the other characters in the play are sometimes actors in the drama of the past, sometimes accusers in the dialectic of the present. A more disturbing problem is the inconsistency of the level of Quentin's awareness. It is not at all clear how certain insights gained into his own actions in the past affect his memory of various characters in the present. His recollections of his early happiness with Maggie are curiously unclouded by his knowledge of what subsequently happened. In other words, the incidents in the play are only partly released from their continuum in time. The strict chronological treatment of some parts of the past seems sometimes at odds with the convention of a universal present in the speaker's memory.

A related problem is the whole question of sequence in the drama. Do 'events' in the play follow one another according to any understandable principle, and if so what is it? That part of Quentin which we see is poised between the external, public, social, objective world and his own internal, unexpressed, scarcely understood needs and desires. His quest (like that of so many of Miller's heroes) is to reconcile the one with the other, to square what people tell him with what he knows, to align what his eyes say he must believe with what in his heart he wants to believe. Here the difficulty for the reader, let alone the spectator, is formidable. While it is just possible to puzzle out a coherent line of action for the Listener based on Quentin's replies, it is extraordinarily difficult to comprehend the workings of Quentin's unconscious. When he is surprised or puzzled by the associations his unconscious makes, has he been repressing that knowledge? How do we determine how accurate Quentin's recollections are? When is he rationalizing to avoid issues he cannot face? Is there genuine change at the end of the play, or will Quentin simply begin his habit of repression and rationalization all over again? Questions like this indicate something of the complexity and range of what Miller has attempted in this play.

The core of *After the Fall* is Quentin's relationship with his second wife, Maggie, which is treated in a compressed but chronological way in the last two-thirds of the drama. Embroidered around this story are memories from Quentin's childhood and later maturity. The juxtaposition of similar events from different periods of his life allows Quentin to generalize about his own experience, and draw from it conclusions he believes to be applicable to all human existence. This leads him to see parallels that extend still further into universal myths that are the expression of mankind's experience as a whole. The pattern of the myth – in this case the loss of Eden – helps him to understand his own nature and the nature of man. Gradually Quentin's life comes to seem to him to be that of a modern Cain wandering in a spiritual wilderness.

Unlike his Biblical counterpart, Quentin has forgotten his own crime, and has only dim memories of existence in a paradise where he had no consciousness of himself, nor any knowledge of sex or of his separateness from others. In the course of the play he re-enacts in his own experience the 'fall' of his parents. He discovers his exile from Eden, his difference in nature from his brother, the destructive intoxication of sex, and finally his capacity for murder. His eyes have been opened, but he has barely the courage to go on living with the burden of his knowledge.

It is easier to describe the nature of Quentin's spiritual and psychological education than to identify the specific stages along the way. He begins as a deeply divided individual with a profound sense that he has become a 'stranger' to his life. He cannot recognize himself in his actions, by which he means (or at least reveals) that the image he has had of himself can no longer be squared with what he has observed about his impulses and actions. In this state of psychic disorientation he tries to reconcile what he knows with what he feels. Emotionally he has always thought of himself as someone special, an individual capable of realizing extremely high standards of love, altruism and self-restraint. Intellectually he knows, and has known for a long time, that he has not always lived up to his own ideals. This has resulted in an acute sense of guilt and finally in the feelings of a pointlessness and unworthiness that have paralysed him prior to his visit to the Listener.

The problem with the play is that Quentin's progress from ignorance to awareness is by no means distinctly charted. Nor is it always easy to know when Miller is being ironic. It is apparent from the context of the play as a whole, for example, that Quentin is deluded when he sees Maggie as a kind of innocent pagan saint, but the strength of his affirmation of sexuality when he first takes her to bed may leave the spectator temporarily puzzled. Similarly, it is too easy for the audience to become involved in the personal dialectics of the drama without realizing that the other characters have no objective reality. The relative guilt or innocence of other figures (especially Louise and Maggie) is not really at issue. What is of concern is Quentin's changing attitude towards these figures in his past. He begins by blaming others (the 'goddamned women' who have injured him), but ends accepting his own culpability.

The first half of the play, therefore, constitutes a kind of prelude. Psychologically it represents a somewhat reluctant skirting of issues. The figure of the dissolute, drug-sodden Maggie is repressed, and only memories of the carefree meetings before their marriage are allowed into Quentin's consciousness. A start has been made towards self-knowledge, but Quentin remains essentially bewildered – genuinely unable to admit his own guilt and seeking to find explanations for his life in external causes. A concomitant of Quentin's inability to accept his own fallen nature is his continuing faith in moral absolutes. The failures of his mother, Mickey, Elsie and Louise to live up to his ideal of connectedness and love do not, in his mind, invalidate the ideal. On the contrary, Quentin seems to feel that, although others have 'sinned', a state of innocence is attainable. The ending of the act is heavily ironic as Quentin reluctantly faces the memory of his dead wife, understanding that sooner or later he will have to confront her accusations.

The second act begins with Quentin prepared to go more deeply into his own unconscious. 'I think I can be clearer now', he says. 'I am bewildered by the death of love. And my responsibility for it.' The contrast in his mind between the hopes he felt at the time of his marriage to Maggie and the sad destruction of those dreams has made him feel that he is incapable of love. His life seems to him to be little better than a treadmill on which he is doomed to repeat the mistakes of his past. As he contemplates entering into a new relationship with Holga, his fear and guilt make him look back on his marriage with Maggie with self-recrimination. The relationship is shown cyclically from their first ecstatic intimacy to their last sterile embrace before Maggie's attempt at suicide. In the aftermath of shock and depression, Quentin can see only his egotism in the affair and nothing of his love. The movement of the second half of the play takes Quentin from a sense of overwhelming guilt to one of acceptance and responsibility.

Quentin's present interpretation of his relationship with Maggie (as opposed to what he thought at the time) is that it was motivated entirely by a desire for power. Paradoxically, however, the power he wanted was the power to protect Maggie from her own unhappiness. Quentin's sense that he had such power is derived from that feeling of being special, 'a light in the world', that he has acquired from his mother. Quentin's bewilderment stems from his feeling that he cannot live up to his special status. In comparison to his brother Dan's genuine altruism, his own unselfish gestures seem fraudulent. The Listener tries to get him to see the love in his acts as well as the vanity, but so great is Quentin's sense of guilt that he finds it difficult to regard his feelings for Maggie as anything but dishonest.

The supreme irony of their early attraction for one another is that Quentin perceived Maggie's apparent lack of shame and natural sexuality as a kind of innocence. He believed (wrongly as it turned out) that he could be open with Maggie in a way he could not with Louise. She inspired in him a desire to 'live the truth', but he has trouble in determining what that truth is. He suspects subconsciously that his apparent altruism is either a desire for power or possibly a reaction to his feeling of having been betrayed by his mother as a boy. But the sense he once had of seeing himself clearly is gone, and he goes over and over his relationship with Maggie in an effort to sort out the love from the guilt or innocence.

The heart of Quentin's problem is his ambiguous attitude to sexuality. His temperament and training lead him to regard Maggie with 'contempt' and to be ashamed of his desire for her which he suspects is nothing but lust. Because of this he has to rationalize his behaviour; he finds a 'principle' to justify his going to bed with Maggie, adopts a posture to excuse his selfishness. Even as he remembers his first intimacy he cannot call it 'love', but defines it as 'living in good faith'. He admits he is not 'innocent' or 'good' (as those words are understood by his family), but claims that he is at last 'saying yes to a truth'. In this sequence Miller sees Maggie as a kind of apotheosis of pagan sensuality, an identification which is made even more strongly in the TV version where Maggie is compared to Venus who 'knows the worst and the best ... swallows it all like the sea, and it all becomes beautiful'.[1] But Quentin's attempt to embrace paganism is doomed from the start. Even at the climax of physical love he is conscious that the 'truth' he wishes to celebrate is unspeakable, contemptible, covered with slime, blind and ignorant. But whether Quentin is here recalling how he actually felt at the time he was making love to Maggie, or whether he is distorting the past because his bitterness makes him cheapen the truth, seems impossible to determine. All we can say for certain is that Quentin's attempt to escape from the world of intellectual abstractions by plunging into the world of blind sensuality fails miserably. And the climax of the play records the nature of that failure.

Because Quentin is secretly ashamed of Maggie, he unconsciously tries to change her while at the same time protesting that he adores her as she is. For a long time he believes that his love can reconcile their differences, but ironically and inexorably those differences kill his love. Maggie's demands on his time and nervous energy first affect the spontaneity of their relationship. As their sexual life deteriorates, it becomes evident that Quentin is more emotionally attached to his daughter than he is to his wife. Quentin believes that he can remain loyal out of a sense of duty, but gradually realizes that even loyalty is limited and, in the end, self-preservation takes precedence over all else. The cycle ends where it began, in Maggie's bed. But in this last embrace there is nothing but self-disgust on Quentin's part. Not even Maggie's appeal to his 'humanness' can rouse the pity which was once the feeling that allowed him to overcome his shame.

When Quentin is brought to understand that he is a separate person, that he is not capable of limitless love, that in certain circumstances he might even be brought to commit murder, he must face what to him is the ultimate horror – that his most profound beliefs about the world and his own nature have been false. Contrary to what he had thought, neither socialism nor love is a cure for man's potential for evil. Even more disillusioning, he has been forced to acknowledge that he is not special, that far from being the 'light' of his mother's expectations, he is just like everybody else.

Characteristically, Quentin's reaction to the knowledge that he is no better than other men is to conclude that he must be worse. The final movement of the play traces Quentin's emergence from the despair in which he finds himself at the beginning of the interview. Faced with the fact of his 'original sin', Quentin has in effect two choices. He can despair and choose the escape of suicide chosen by Lou and Maggie, or he can face the truth and go on living. In choosing the latter, Miller implies, Quentin does the harder thing.

There are many weaknesses in *After the Fall*, but not as many as some critics and spectators have charged. The work has provoked an astonishing amount of hostility towards the playwright, and there are still some who have never forgiven Miller for what they consider to be the naked exploitation of his relationship with Marilyn Monroe and the tasteless strain of self-justification in the play. For many, the play's message seemed to be little more than the summation of the reviewer from *Time* magazine, 'When things get tough, find a new woman and start again.' This is clearly a monstrous distortion of the work. But that such critical confusion could arise is at least partly the fault of the playwright. The form in which Miller has chosen to express himself in *After the Fall* is cumbersome and excessively demanding. Drama conventionally presents an 'objective' view of reality which enables the audience to distance itself from the protagonist by comparing his actions with those of other characters around him. The hero's self-delusion and the author's ironic viewpoint can be conveyed by juxtaposition and contrast. In *After the Fall*, no such distancing devices exist. The play presents only Quentin's experience, and there are few unambiguous signposts to show where Miller's view as playwright diverges from Quentin's as protagonist. This difficulty is compounded, of course, by the disconcertingly autobiographical nature of the play. Consequently, it is extraordinarily difficult for an audience, or even a careful reader, to achieve the kind of detachment from Quentin that is essential if we are to view the play as art and not as true confession.

The obstacles to easy comprehension presented by the formal peculiarities of the work are compounded by the nature of its content. The play is not only about ambivalence, bewilderment and self-deception; it is an attempt to dramatize those very mental and emotional phenomena. But just as a play about boring people must not bore, so a play about confused people should not confuse. Much has been made of the rather 'forensic' nature of Miller's work. The plays are full of judges, courts, lawyers, briefs, and the format of many of the dramas resembles that of a trial or court of enquiry. This often seems to reflect a judicial view of life on the part of the author, a view that not only tends to see all issues in terms of right and wrong, guilt or innocence, but also assumes that it is easy to see the difference between the two. In *After the Fall* that comfortable assurance is gone. Indeed the play is largely about the loss of faith in the very possibility of passing judgement. In a world in which everyone is guilty, it is senseless to speak of 'innocence'. The whole apparatus of dialectic distorts the truth. Reality (and especially subjective reality) cannot be divided into categories of black and white, bad and good. Love does not exclude selfishness, betrayal or even hate. Moral absolutes, if they can exist at all, are possible only in a fabled Eden.

12
The Price (1968)

Like most of Miller's plays, *The Price* is about an individual's confrontation with his past. It shows the gradual stripping away of habitual excuses and illusions until the protagonist comes face to face with truths he has been reluctant to admit. The device linking past and present, subjective and objective, in this play is the sale of the contents of a New York brownstone mansion scheduled for demolition. The solid, outsized furnishings which had been purchased in the 1920s now seem of dubious value and beauty. The inevitable disagreement between the dealer's assessment of what the furniture is worth and the family's feeling of what they should get for it underlines the subjective nature of value and truth.

Miller's shift from representing the past entirely through the eyes of one character, as he did in *Salesman* and *After the Fall*, to showing it through the conflicting memories and attitudes of Victor and Walter Franz has certain strong advantages. It enables the audience to judge Victor more critically and to recognize the role that self-deception has played in his understanding of himself and the world around him. But it has made the exact nature of the past more shadowy. Motives, and even facts, are uncertain and it is difficult for the audience or reader to choose between the different interpretations of the two brothers. Indeed, it appears that Miller has deliberately exploited this ambiguity.

The play takes place in the attic room of a New York brownstone mansion to which the Franz family retire after the crash of 1929. Not long after the loss of the family wealth, Mrs Franz dies, and Walter leaves home to attend medical school. His younger brother, Victor remains behind with their father and all the family furniture which they have unaccountably crowded into the attic with them. About 1934, Victor begins university and shortly thereafter meets Esther, his future wife. In 1936, at about nineteen, Victor feels he can no longer finance his own education and also support his father and so he goes to his brother Walter, then in medical practice, and asks for a loan of $500. His request is refused. Feeling that he cannot abandon his responsibilities, Victor gives up his plan to become a doctor, joins the New York police force, and continues to support his father until the old man dies. Because of his resentment, Victor has been unable to communicate easily with his brother and the two drift apart. When it becomes necessary to sell the family furniture because the building is about to be torn down, Victor tries unsuccessfully to get in touch with his brother. Finally he contacts a used-furniture dealer to come to the apartment to negotiate the sale of the estate.

When one tries to reconstruct the past in this way from the bits of exposition in the play, it is evident that several important pieces in the puzzle are missing. When, for example, were Esther and Victor married and what was the connection between this decision and Victor's decision to give up university? How did Victor pay for his first years of higher education? Who owned the house in which Victor and his father lived, and who got the rent for the rest of the building? Such questions seem petty at first, but they are a consequence of Miller's method. The play is a continuation of the debate begun in earlier works such as *After the Fall* about the ethics of survival. To what extent should the individual allow the welfare of another to jeopardize his own chance of success? The answer to the question as Miller has formulated it seems to have to do with the extent of the other's need. We cannot know if the price Victor paid to keep his father from ending up on the grass was too high unless we know first if it was a fair one. If, as Walter maintains, the same end could have been achieved by selling the furniture, dipping into the old man's savings, or even forcing him to go out to work, then the ethical dilemma raised is not a true one. Much of the power of the argument is weakened if there is no way to choose between contradictory interpretations of the facts. We are left with Victor's satisfaction with his actions, but no objective standard by which we might determine whether or not his sense of values corresponds with our own.

The action of the play proceeds in two movements which could be described as 'setting the price' and 'accepting it as fair'. Gregory Solomon, the furniture dealer, arrives at the crowded attic and after considerable delay offers $1100 for the furniture. Just as Victor accepts Solomon's terms and has some of the money in his hand, his brother walks in and begins questioning the appraiser's offer. The play ends with Victor taking the balance of the money to close the deal. In their responses to Solomon the three characters reveal their different natures: Victor trusting, naive, incapable of bargaining; Walter questioning, aggressive, unable to settle for the status quo; Esther caught between her love for her husband and her desire for more of the things that money can buy. Walter and Esther try to persuade Victor to go along with a dishonest but legal income tax dodge which would net them about twelve times what Solomon had offered them. Faced with the opportunity, however, Victor cannot seize it and he begins to try to understand what separates him from his brother, and what he has really done with his life.

Each of the characters in *The Price* has reached a crisis which has precipitated an intense self-examination. In the course of the play Walter and Victor are made to confront facts which they had 'known' about their lives but never before dared to face. The catastrophe is the now familiar reaction to insight upon which Miller has focused in earlier plays. The action of the drama itself consists of the gradual peeling away of 'fantasies' until each of the characters is forced to look upon the truth. The characters not only interact with one another on a realistic level, but they also bear certain symbolic relationships to each other and to the central meaning of the play. The central figures, of course, are Victor and Walter who might be Biff and Happy twenty years later. They are the archetypal brothers we find in several Miller plays – one selfish and materialistic, the other idealistic. Both brothers are a product of the Depression, but they have reacted to that catastrophe in opposite ways. The spectacle of his father's ruin inspires Walter with a kind of terror that haunts all his subsequent life. The fear of finding himself 'degraded and thrown down' as his father had been drives him to seek the kind of financial and social security that would render him untouchable. In the process he gives too little time to his wife and family, and loses them through divorce and alienation. Following a nervous breakdown, Walter comes to understand the driving force at the root of his existence and succeeds in living a slower-paced, more outgoing life after his recovery.

Victor too has been shaped by the catastrophe that hit his family, but in a much more complex way. His perception that the world is merciless leads him to reject the rat-race and to assert the importance of love, loyalty and kindness. But his eligibility for a pension after twenty-five years in the police force brings on a crisis somewhat like Walter's nervous breakdown. After a quarter of a century planning a new life Victor finds, when the opportunity comes, that he is unable to make a decision. He has begun to doubt that the values he chose as a young man are, in fact, as valid as he had believed them to be. Having started out believing that life is more important than the rat-race, he discovers that only money is respected. No longer sure what it was he was trying to accomplish, he looks back to see nothing but 'a long, brainless walk in the street'.

Part of the reason for Victor's uncertainty is his realization that his dream of starting again in another career at fifty is an illusion. But he is also unsettled by his wife who has come to resent their poverty. Esther too had been forced to choose before she knew what was involved and, now that their only son has left home for college, her relationship with Victor no longer seems enough to satisfy her. Not only has she started to drink, but envy of Walter's financial success is translated into dreams of a more secure life with Victor in a higher paid, more respected job. This vision is dependent, in her mind, on realizing a substantial profit on the sale of the furniture and Victor's refusal to accept Walter's offer of a job and money seems wilful and perverse to her. Her anger with her husband is prompted by his apparent surrender when the means for combat are at hand.

Central to the debate between Walter and Victor (and to Esther's final allegiance to her husband) is the question of clear-sightedness. 'What is the point?' Victor asks Solomon when the latter tells of his marriage at the age of seventy-five and the question lurks beneath the entire play. What is the 'truth' in any situation? Is it better to believe what you see or to invent yourself in order to act with conviction? There is no 'reason' for Gregory Solomon at age eighty-nine to continue working except that he loves it. There seemed to be no reason why the elder Franz should have given up when he lost his fortune except that he didn't have the heart to go on. More fundamentally, do the reasons for having done something in the past remain valid indefinitely? At the beginning of the play Victor is not sure. He says of his life 'I know all the reasons, and all the reasons, and all the reasons, and it ends up – nothing.' By the end of the play Victor's uncertainty is removed.

The heart of the drama is the searing confrontation between Victor and Walter which takes place in the second act. At the beginning of the argument each man is self-deluded. Walter has come to believe that Victor deliberately chose to become a policeman in order to avoid the rat-race (just as later Walter chose to work at a slower pace in order to give more time to his friends). This belief is based on his conviction that Victor could have financed his education if he had really wanted to. He comes ostensibly to tell Victor that he admires his courage, but really to assuage the unadmitted guilt he feels for having refused to lend Victor the $500 he needed to finish his degree.

Victor claims to believe that Walter owes him nothing and that his decision to stay and support his father was his own choice. It is clear, however, that he harbours a bitter resentment against his brother, whom he secretly blames for abandoning his responsibility. When Walter offers him a substantial cash settlement for the furniture and a job in the new hospital, it would seem that all of Victor's dreams could come true. But something makes him hesitate. He cannot overcome the feeling that he is being bought off and refuses to let the issue drop.

He begins by disabusing Walter of the comforting notion that he chose to give up science. In his opinion he was forced to abandon college for economic reasons, the principal one being that his father needed financial support and Walter was paying only $5 a month to help out. Walter denies that their father really needed help, and says that Victor was exploited. The violence of Victor's reaction to this suggestion shows that it expresses his own secret opinion. But Victor can neither express exactly how he views the situation nor confess his real resentment, so it is Esther who brings up the subject of the loan. It is Walter's refusal to lend Victor the $500 he needed to complete his degree which is the real obstacle between them, and Walter tries to justify what he knows in his heart is unjustifiable. Victor knows that Walter is trying to make up for the past by offering him a job and money, but he also understands that time has made that impossible.

> You can't walk in with one splash and wash out twenty-eight years. There's a price people pay. I've paid it, it's all gone, I haven't got it any more... This is where we are; now, right here, now.[1]

Furthermore, he sees and resents the implication that his life has been a failure and his sacrifice needless. Walter betrays his own deep ambivalence by admitting that while he might admire the decision to forgo the rat-race, he cannot respect poverty. In his own eyes, he is offering to save Victor by giving him the money and opportunity which he denied him twenty-eight years ago. When Victor returns to the accusation that Walter walked out on his responsibility, the elder brother reveals that their father, in fact, had money in the bank all during the Depression. This revelation stuns Victor and makes him re-examine what he really 'knew' about his father during this period. It turns out to be more than he then or subsequently ever admitted. In response to the probing of his brother, Victor has to acknowledge that he suspected that his father did have money, but he was reluctant to challenge him. When Esther realizes that Victor may have known his support was not needed, she can think of nothing but the sacrifices they have made:

> To stick us into a furnished room so you could send him part of your pay? Even after we were married, to go on sending him money? Put off having children, live like mice.[2]

To Esther, the father seems nothing but a calculating liar and Victor an accessory because in his heart he knew the truth. Gradually Victor comes to see that his decision to stay with his father was not dictated by economic factors so much as by a psychological need. When he saw the unemployed men in the park and comprehended that there was no mercy in the world, he felt it necessary to make a gesture affirming love and loyalty to prove to his father that things were not falling apart. Walter presses in to remove even this last illusion by pointing out that there was never any love in the Franz household.

> There was nothing here but a straight financial arrangement. That's what was unbearable. And you proceeded to wipe out what you saw... We invent ourselves, Vic, to wipe out what we know.[3]

Walter claims that the two brothers escaped from the same trap by different roads, and that their animosity is an illusion. Victor is prepared to acknowledge the 'unreality' of his hatred for Walter and to accept responsibility for his own choices, but he wants Walter to do the same. And he knows that Walter's offer of reconciliation has not been made in good faith.

> You came for the old handshake, didn't you! ... And you end up with the respect, the career, the money, and the best of all, the thing that nobody else can tell you so you'll believe it – that you're one hell of a guy and never harmed anybody in your life![4]

Victor refuses to grant his forgiveness, not because he harbours any resentment against Walter, but because he knows that Walter must forgive himself. This Walter is unable to do, because he cannot face his past. Like other Miller characters, he sees the evil in his soul but looks away. Consequently he leaves the apartment convinced that Victor has 'sacrificed his life to vengeance', deliberately giving up a medical career in order to make his brother feel guilty.

The resolution of *The Price,* although conventionally moral, offers little consolation or inducement to virtue. Victor and Walter remain unreconciled and we are not intended to imagine much change in their outward lives. Victor will not apply for his pension, but will continue walking his beat. Walter in a very short time will be as busy and successful and rich as ever. The changes that have occurred are all internal. Victor has come to see that his support for his father was not forced upon him, but was an expression of his own nature and his love. 'I just didn't want him to end up on the grass and he didn't.' He also realizes that he was foolish to have imagined that his sacrifice could have brought any reward, or sense of forgiveness. Virtue is its own reward. As for the worldly view that the price he has paid for his father's security is too high, that too is a matter of viewpoint. In the end Victor seems satisfied with the deal he has struck with his life. Walter's inner development is more difficult to measure. His response to the crisis of 1929 was selfish rather than altruistic, and consequently impossible to justify in moral terms. It is clear that he is ashamed of his action and cannot accept his own guilt. In another Miller play we might expect him to flee from his conscience through suicide or drugs.

The play ends, not with any of the members of the Franz family, but with Gregory Solomon. Left alone with the furniture he is oppressed and worried by the challenge it presents. Almost distractedly he puts on the laughing record which Victor had played in the opening scene. Within minutes Solomon is reduced to helpless laughter and the curtain descends on his mirth.

The significance of this final action is ambiguous, and perhaps deliberately so. Without the benefit of the detailed stage directions an audience might well mistake Solomon's outburst for the laughter of triumph, the satisfaction of a successful dealer who has outwitted an honest client. Or it might be seen as an echo of the evasive laughter of the elder Franz when Victor asked him if he had money in the bank. Almost certainly, however, Miller intends the laughter as a symbol of hope and courage, the qualities most necessary to overcome despair. For Solomon (as his name suggests) is not only the oldest, but also the wisest character in the play. And it is significant that the knowledge he brings has nothing to do with the themes of selfishness and altruism. Solomon's wisdom relates to the more fundamental question of belief itself. What Miller seems to admire in Solomon is his realism. As Esther expresses it, he believes what he sees. He can look at the past without sentimentality or regret. He mourns the loss of his daughter who committed suicide, and he understands the implication that her death is in some ways his fault.

> I had a daughter ... she took her own life... But if it was a miracle and she came to life, what could I say to her? [5]

Solomon's strength is not that he has found hope in some conventional creed, but that he can face life with courage. His daughter's suicide, we are told, was caused by her despair at losing her ability to believe in anything. Solomon says to Victor,

> Let me give you a piece advice – it's not that you can't believe nothing, that's not so hard – it's that you still got to believe

> it. *That's* hard. And if you can't do that my friend – you're a dead man![6]

In other words, it is easy to become disillusioned and see the world as meaningless. What is difficult is to see the meaninglessness and still act with hope. It is Solomon's ability to act in the midst of chaos that makes him a symbol of Miller's deepest convictions in this play.

The Price is one of Miller's most balanced achievements, a skilful amalgam of the playwright's principal themes and technical resources. At first glance it seems to be a return to the claustrophobic Ibsenism of *All My Sons.* But this is realism with a difference. The cluttered attic apartment bears a resemblance to such symbolic settings as the Eckdal attic in *The Wild Duck,* but it is more generalized in its application than most nineteenth-century symbolism. *The Price* shows the influence of contemporary dramatists such as Beckett, Ionesco and Pinter whose stage settings are often theatrical metaphors for the human condition itself. The Manhattan attic where Victor and his father lived is a symbol of an attempt to arrest time. The careful preservation of these remnants of a vanished prosperity reflect the inability of Victor or his father to give up the 'dream' the furniture represents. In its sad disarray, the room epitomizes an ideal that collapsed with the stock market in 1929. On another level, the room evokes the metamorphosis of time. Furniture, clothing, records that had seemed beautiful in their time, now seem awkward or bizarre; ideas and actions from the past suffer a comparable transformation. Confronted by the evidence of former feelings and actions, the characters find them incomprehensible. One's past is dead, like a daughter who committed suicide, and it is impossible to bring it back to life. The setting is as specific as the Keller backyard in *All My Sons* or the Salem of *The Crucible,* yet at the same time as universal in its implications as the placeless and timeless setting of *After the Fall.*

The action of the play also unites the universal and particular in an especially successful way. The Franz family shares the usual similarities with Miller's own. But the individuals comprising that family have been abstracted to enable Miller to focus on two concerns which have formed the core of his work. The framework of the action is provided by the two 'father' figures in the play. Mr Franz, dead sixteen years but still very much a presence in the play, epitomizes defeat. Having espoused the values of free-enterprise capitalism, he could never recover when that system failed him. He is a close relative of Willy Loman. Diametrically opposed to Mr Franz is Gregory Solomon who seems to be the very spirit of life. Solomon has recovered after at least four depressions and gives every sign of being unstoppable. Not improbably, these two figures embody something of Miller's own ambivalent attitude to life – his sympathy with the defeated and despairing, and his admiration for the courageous and hopeful.

The central characters, Victor and Walter, represent in an even more obvious way the conflicting sides of human nature that Miller has always been concerned with. These can be described as altruism and selfishness, socialism and capitalism, spiritualism and materialism. What sets his treatment of the Franz brothers ahead of his studies of the Keller or Loman brothers, or his comparison of Dan and Quentin, is his greater sympathy for the materialist. He now recognizes that 'as the world now operates the qualities of both brothers are necessary'. Walter is the more conventional of the two brothers with his oppressive sense of guilt and his need for forgiveness. In earlier plays, Walter would have been the central character and the play would have focused on the nature and consequences of his antisocial behaviour. Typically the drama would have shown the purging of guilt through expiation (*Sons*), insight and expiation (*The Crucible*), blindness and expulsion (*View*). In *The Price,* Walter's story is not only subordinated to that of Victor, but it is left more or less unresolved. It is true that Walter too has paid a price for the abandonment of his responsibility to his father. He has divorced his wife, lost touch with his children, and suffered a nervous breakdown. But at the end of the play he claims to have overcome his sense of shame and to have exorcised his feelings of guilt. He will presumably return to his medical practice which has brought him not only wealth but considerable personal satisfaction. It may be that he will find no rest from the accusations of his conscience, but it is probably a little sanguine to think so.

No doubt Miller intends us to see Victor's story as something of a triumph, but the nature of his success is difficult for many to grasp. *The Price* is the most uncompromisingly moral of Miller's plays in that it rejects all the easy, and therefore popular, solutions. Virtue in *The Price* is not made attractive; it is given neither the sanction of martyrdom nor the blessings of prosperity. It has no reward but itself. True we are asked to believe that Victor walks out with a pure heart; but many will see his victory as hollow and catch in Solomon's laughter the justified derision of the flexible pragmatist for the stiff-necked idealist. Perhaps the most difficult lesson of this play is that there is no external arbiter of moral values. Each man must set his own price on his actions and then learn to accept the consequences. This explains the disturbing ambiguity that many find in the ending. Viewed from the perspective of the average middle-class, moderately acquisitive spectator or reader, Victor is a fool who sacrifices a personal advantage for an abstract principle. His action and motives can hardly be understood in a society which has come to believe that value is a synonym for price.

13
Alienation (1968–2000)

Following the success of *The Price* (1968) Miller had little financial cause to concern himself about the reception of his work. He was earning a respectable living on royalties from domestic and foreign productions of his plays, and paperback sales of *Death of a Salesman* alone had reached more than a million. His reputation was firmly established, his personal life peaceful at last and, as he confided to James Stern, life was 'the best it's been'.[1] And yet the hunger remained: the hunger to write plays, the hunger to have them seen in the only place that seemed important – a Broadway theatre. But Broadway was changing. Costs were rising, the number of productions beginning to decline, and producers were becoming more cautious as higher ticket prices were driving away the lower middle-class audiences. The New York commercial theatre had ceased to be the nursery of new plays it once was and had become (in Miller's opinion) a playground for visitors run by real estate lawyers for profit,[2] making Broadway increasingly inaccessible to serious playwrights.

Miller's first attempt to return to the New York stage after *The Price* took place in 1972 in association with Robert Whitehead, one of the few Broadway producers still willing to sponsor serious work. The play was a whimsical version of the Book of Genesis called *The Creation of the World and Other Business*, and preparations for its production were plagued by problems from the beginning. Some of these related to the choice of Harold Clurman as director. Clurman was then nearly seventy years old and two generations away from some of the young actors in the cast. The rehearsal period was marked by misunderstandings and tensions brought on by the leading actress' determination to challenge the authority of the author by improvizing her lines, and by the refusal of the leading actor to take directions from Clurman. At first Miller tried to work in the new 'democratic' way, taking the cast into his confidence and even adopting some of their ideas (although not the suggestion that Lucifer be the father of Cain). Finally in the fourth week he asserted his prerogative and insisted that Barbara Harris learn her lines, whereupon she and Pat Hingle resigned. The play opened in Boston to unfavorable notices, and Miller felt that more revisions were needed. Further previews were scheduled in Boston and New York before the official opening on 30 November 1972. Critics who had come to expect a certain kind of social realism from Miller were baffled by this excursion into mythology, and the play closed after only twenty performances.

Miller's second undertaking with Whitehead, *The Archbishop's Ceiling* (1977), was similarly plagued. Because Miller failed to meet his deadline for finishing the play, tryouts that had been scheduled to begin at the small Long Wharf Theatre in New Haven had to be transferred to the much larger Eisenhower Theatre in the Kennedy Center in Washington. There reviews were so negative the producers decided to close the show rather than risk taking it into New York. *The American Clock* (1980) fared marginally better. Sponsored by the Harold Clurman Theatre, the production previewed in New York, moved on to the Spoleto Festival in Charleston, South Carolina, where it underwent revisions before opening at the Biltmore Theatre on Broadway where it lasted a mere twelve performances.

During the next two decades, Miller's new work continued to meet with indifference and even hostility as he tried repeatedly to duplicate earlier successes. Two one-act plays which he himself directed for a six-week season at the Long Wharf Theatre, *Two-Way Mirror* (1982), went no further; a revised version of *The Archbishop's Ceiling* for the Bolton Theatre in Cleveland (1994) failed to interest a Broadway producer; the stage version of his TV adaptation of *Playing for Time* appeared at the Studio Theatre in Washington but nowhere else; two further one-act plays, *Danger: Memory!* (1987), played at the Vivian Beaumont Theatre (then part of the non-profit Lincoln Center Theatre); and *The Last Yankee* appeared in a twenty-minute version in the Marathon One-Act Play Festival at the New York Ensemble Studio Theatre (1991) and as a two-act work at the Manhattan Theatre Club (1993). It was not until 1994, fourteen years after his last appearance on Broadway, that Miller finally made it back into the charmed circle with a new play, *Broken Glass*, at the Booth Theatre. Then in 1999, after an off-Broadway production of *Mr Peters' Connections* at the Signature Theatre in New York, he returned in relative triumph with *Ride Down Mount Morgan.*

As Miller's new work languished in America, however, it continued to find enthusiastic supporters overseas. In London, directors such as David Thacker at the Young Vic and Richard Eyre at the National championed his work. Classically trained British actors responded to the demotic, yet literate, dialogue; audiences (more accustomed than their

American counterparts to political drama) enjoyed his serious engagement with social issues. Nor was admiration confined to theatrical circles. In 1989 the University of East Anglia opened an Arthur Miller Centre for American Studies. British Television produced not one, but two, profiles of the playwright in 1991, and in 1999 a survey of 800 playwrights, actors, journalists and other theatre professionals cited Miller more frequently than any other dramatist, ahead of Pinter and Beckett.[3] By 2000, the National Theatre had produced more plays by Arthur Miller than by any other dramatist except Shakespeare. Impressed by the high standards and low costs of production in London, Miller for the first time in his career, decided to open one of his plays, *Ride Down Mount Morgan* (1991), in a theatre outside the United States. Thereafter his plays were produced in England shortly after their first appearance in America, invariably to greater public and critical applause. As he became more familiar with the theatre culture in Britain, Miller grew steadily more caustic about conditions in the commercial theatre in his own country.

Behind Miller's frequently hectic public existence during these decades there was a quieter private life that remained less well known. In the years after taking up permanent residence in Roxbury, he and Inge had put down solid roots in the community. As the area attracted more and more New York celebrities, the Millers managed to bridge the two worlds, dividing their time between the New York theatre and publishing worlds and the pursuits of rural Connecticut. Arthur developed a tree nursery and built furniture in his woodworking shop. Inge gardened, swam, practiced yoga and did the cooking. A vegetarian herself, she put Arthur on a low fat diet, but served goulash at their frequent dinner parties. When Rebecca was old enough, they enrolled her in the local school. Inge cut back on her travelling to look after her daughter, and spent time tramping about the countryside capturing the pictures of the area which would appear in the volume, *In the Country*, which she published with her husband in 1977. Gradually Miller lost touch with his theatre acquaintances of the 50s and began to mingle instead with painters and writers.

During these years, Miller also continued to engage with the world at large. As former President of PEN, he campaigned on behalf of imprisoned writers, and frequently travelled abroad. He and Inge visited China in the 1970s and again in the 1980s. But increasingly he welcomed the peacefulness of the country where he could write in the morning, spend the afternoon reading or listening to music, and visit friends in the evening. As his critical reputation declined in America, it continued to grow in England where he was fêted at the National Theatre on his eightieth birthday and regularly flattered with honours, including a Chair in Contemporary Theatre and an honorary degree at Oxford. Finally in the 1990s, recognition, grudgingly withheld during the previous decade, was granted to his work in America. He was given a Tony Life Achievement Award in 1995 and a PEN birthday celebration at the New York Public Library in the same year.

Nineteen ninety-five was also a year of personal reconciliation. Relations with his elder children after his divorce from Mary Slattery had been strained. Jane, particularly, had found it difficult to forgive her father until she herself married in 1970. Thereafter she maintained closer contact with her family and her much younger half sister. Robert had seemed to repudiate his father's somewhat conservative lifestyle, living for a time in a commune, travelling to England with the unmarried mother of his baby, finally settling on a career in television and film which took him to New York and Hollywood. In the early 1990s, however, he had persuaded his father to adapt *The Crucible* for film and to allow him to produce it. Shooting began late in 1995 and was attended by both Miller and Rebecca who, shortly after the completion of the movie, married its star, Daniel Day-Lewis.

The most unsettling incident in Miller's private life that year, however, was his unexpected encounter with his own son, Daniel. The meeting took place in Hartford where Miller was the featured speaker at a conference. After his address, Miller was stunned when Daniel emerged from the audience to embrace him.[4] Following that meeting, Daniel continued to live apart from his parents in a shared apartment with the help of social workers. At their urging, Miller agreed to attend a review of Daniel's progress and was astounded to find that his son was able to live independently and keep a job. If thereafter there was slightly greater contact between Daniel and his father, there was apparently no question of bringing the young man to live in Roxbury. Indeed, Daniel spent his holidays, not with his parents, but with an elderly couple whom he had met after being released from Southbury Training School. Inge, Rebecca and (one Christmas) Joan would visit Daniel for part of the day before returning for celebrations with the rest of the family.

The sudden rediscovery of his long 'lost' twenty-nine year-old son on that September day in Hartford must have had a profound effect on Arthur Miller. And yet he seems to have been unwilling or unable to deal with the matter in public. A little more than a month later, in conversation with a Reuters reporter, he remarked 'I don't know how to regret things. It's part of a growth system. You cannot be right all the time'.[5] It would be almost a decade before he could finally take his life in his arms.

14
The Creation of the World and Other Business (1972)

Miller's relationship to the Bible was longstanding, going back to his first discovery of Genesis in Hebrew at the age of six or seven, and continuing through many years during which he kept a copy of it by his writing desk. The playwright was by no means religious in the traditional sense, but he felt that a need to search for 'an ultimate sanction beyond our wits' end' was part of human nature,[1] and that the stories collected in the Bible represented primary examples of that search.

In retelling the account of Adam, Eve, Cain and Abel, Miller follows the original in general outline: the creation, the temptation, the Fall and expulsion, God's preference for Abel's offering, Cain's killing of Abel and subsequent banishment. But he elaborates the basic story in a variety of ways. To begin with, he solves the problem of evil in a monotheistic world by bringing Lucifer into the tale as a sort of Iago figure, capable of befriending God but dedicated to his overthrow. When God asks Lucifer's advice, the angel suggests that the reason the newly created humans are not multiplying is because their sex drive is not strong enough and that they need to lose their innocence. God is shocked at the idea, but Lucifer succeeds in persuading Eve to eat the apple and she forces Adam to do the same. Discovering their disobedience, God drives them from the Garden. When Eve finally becomes pregnant, Lucifer takes credit for the fact. He argues that disobedience can be useful and indeed is the complement to, not the enemy of, the good. He suggests that he and God should reign jointly, thereby demonstrating that God can love evil; this would, in his opinion, eliminate self-loathing and guilt. God is struck by the idea, but insists on the eternal separation of good and evil. He banishes Lucifer, but is then beset by doubts.

The story of the first murder is elaborated even more extensively than is that of the Fall. Miller has said that Cain is the 'first personage in the Bible who can be called human'[2] and in the second part of the play we are introduced to a very human family. Eve, pregnant, is visited by

Lucifer who warns her of the pain she will have to endure, and offers to kill the child within her in revenge for God's injustice in making her suffer more than Adam. She refuses, but when she wakes she feels estranged from Adam who now finds her unattractive and wants to kill the creature marring her beauty. They are finally reconciled, however; Eve gives birth to Cain, and God warns the couple to protect the innocent child from the evil of their murderous impulses.

Sometime later, God feels that the human family (now including Abel) is drifting away from Him, and in an effort to reawaken their reverence, sends a dream of death to remind them of their mortality. Cain is disturbed by the vision of Abel dead, and begins to question his parents about their decision to leave Paradise. When he learns that they were in fact expelled for disobedience, he comes to the conviction that they are not innocent and blessed as they had imagined, but in need of God's forgiveness. He begins to quarrel with Abel, resenting his easy life as a shepherd and the fact that he is his mother's favourite. Sensing that God wants Cain to murder Abel so that he will feel guilty and seek forgiveness, Lucifer tries to reconcile the two brothers. But Cain decides he needs to give something to God to win back His blessing. He prepares an offering of his crops. Not to be outdone, Abel sacrifices a lamb. The deity who appears at the altar, however, is not God but Lucifer in the shape of a man with the head of a bull offering to abolish guilt and grant them total freedom. Adam recognizes Lucifer as the Devil, but Eve embraces him saying, 'This God is Mine – For only this one frees me of my sin.' She and the two boys engage in a wild dance with Lucifer when suddenly God appears, putting a stop to what has turned into an incestuous orgy. Lucifer once again tries to terminate the war between good and evil by proposing that he and God share Heaven – Lucifer reigning as the god of what-they-are, with God in charge of their improvement.

God ignores Lucifer and turns to the altar to sample Cain's vegetables. He finds them agreeable, but not as succulent as Abel's lamb which He praises as the best He has ever tasted. In gratitude for His favour, Eve acknowledges God as the only God, and the family departs leaving Cain with Lucifer. Lucifer tries to mollify the young man by urging him to be indifferent to his perceived slights and to stifle love. At that moment, however, Abel returns to summon his brother to God's presence and, in a jealous rage, Cain kills him. When confronted by his crime, Cain blames it on God's injustice in having contempt for his offering. God is dumbfounded, explaining that he likes lamb better than onions and, in any case, has never used the word 'justice'. Lucifer then accuses God of precipitating the murder with his dream of death. God explains that the dream was a test to see if Cain's love would restrain him from violence. Confronted with the triple failure of Adam, Eve and Cain, He despairs of future generations saying that the only way for them to choose the way of life over the way of death will be for them to develop a moral conscience, 'the eye of God in the heart'. When the humans continue to blame others for their aggression and appear only to want anarchy, God starts to leave. Eve cries out that she cannot live with the man who murdered her son, but Lucifer offers neither judgement nor consolation, leading Adam to realize that the angel does not love them as God does. The loving but judging God banishes Caïn, but puts on him a protective mark – a frozen smile behind which his agony will forever be concealed.

Miller has called *The Creation of the World and Other Business* 'the clearest expression of his religious beliefs that he's come to'.[3] The clarity of this expression has been anything but evident to most critics and audiences. This is almost certainly because the burden of argument is much too heavy for the rather slight vessel in which it is launched. Long passages of Jesuitical reasoning or theological disputation are difficult for the reader in the study let alone an audience in a theatre. This problem is compounded by the whimsical tone of the play which shifts erratically from lyrical to farcical, to folksy, to ironic so that the seriousness of the author is always in question. Miller moves rather quickly from a fairly harrowing presentation of childbirth to a celebratory dance of life involving God and the Mother of Mankind, to a scene in which Eve, with some embarrassment, removes the apple from Cain's offering to God. Unlike anything Miller had written previously, the play most resembles those medieval mystery dramas with their mixture of spectacle, crude comedy, naive narrative and simple homiletics produced to inculcate faith in an illiterate audience. Miller is no preacher, but it is interesting to observe his use of one of the common techniques of allegorical drama – symbolic characterization.

Perhaps the most striking use of such archetypal representation is the figure of Cain. Miller is clearly fascinated by the Biblical representation of primal sibling rivalry. The image of Cain sent to wander the world imprisoned behind a frozen smile is one of the most moving in the play, and a powerful symbol of timeless human alienation. The treatment of the other human characters, while less startlingly original, is nevertheless noteworthy. There is no effort in this play to mitigate Eve's primary guilt in the story of the Fall. Uninfluenced by feminist sensibilities, Miller has Eve literally force the apple down Adam's throat thereby virtually absolving him of blame. Not for Miller the Miltonic view that greater intelligence demands greater responsibility and that Adam's fault is therefore greater than Eve's.

Once out of Eden and reduced (elevated?) to human state, Miller's first family has been compared to an immigrant Jewish family trying to do their best for the kids in a new country.[4] It is a family, indeed that bears a striking resemblance to the Lomans with Adam as the dreamy husband, longing for Paradise, childishly enthusiastic about his sons' plans, blindly loyal to a kind of Uncle Ben God, and Eve as the more down-to-earth, practical and protective wife. Where Adam and Eve differ from the Brooklyn couple is in their attitude to sex. Nobody in this play believes in sinless sex, (unlike the Puritan Milton in *Paradise Lost*). Miller seems to regard the knowledge gained by eating the apple as strictly carnal. As Lucifer explains: to serve its function sex must be made not just good but terrific. It has to have the same sort of holiness as religion – 'the hope that is never discouraged and never really fulfilled'.[5] And while it is supposed to be Adam who is to be put into a condition in which he can think of nothing but sex, it is Eve who turns out to be the more interested of the two. As the first to eat the apple, she is the more sexually aggressive and the more attracted to pleasure and sensuality. But pleasant as it is, she knows perfectly well that multiplying is 'not something you do in the Garden'.

It is not the human characters, however, who carry the major symbolic weight in this play, and Miller's handling of God and Lucifer is of particular interest. Astonishingly, God is portrayed as an almost comic character. Slightly bumbling (some of his creations such as the furry fish prove to be failures), and less intelligent than Lucifer. God is a sort of harried single parent unable to control his rebellious children. This is due in part to his creative temperament, but almost as much to his indecisiveness, alternately attracted by and violently rejecting Lucifer's advice. He acts primarily on instinct or feeling rather than from a clear notion of fairness or justice with calamitous consequences for the family.

The most original and fascinating of the mythic characters is Lucifer. Absent from Genesis, Lucifer was only later associated with the snake in the Garden by Jewish and Christian commentators who identified him with Satan, the adversary of God. Such a figure is necessary in a monotheistic cosmos to explain the existence of evil which cannot be an attribute or creation of God. The origin and nature of evil are two of the central mysteries addressed by the world's religions, and a principal preoccupation of Miller himself. As a secular rationalist, however, he seeks his answers in the human condition rather than sacred scripture and uses the play to draft a theology more reflective of that condition. His experience has taught him to be equally suspicious of absolute, self-righteous authority and of anarchy passing itself off as freedom. To explore this problem, he opposes to an indecisive God, a 'devil' of frightening persuasiveness. Lucifer is presented as the embodiment of modern, scientific rationalism. He proposes that morality should be based on a factual analysis of what man is, not a prescription of what he 'should' be. Acceptance of the Deist principle that 'whatever is is right' would eliminate the concept of evil, bring an end to notions of injustice, put a stop to wars and, best of all, get rid of ideas of guilt and innocence. In Lucifer's view, it is the existence of a totally innocent righteous God and the attendant failure of humans to live up to such an impossible model that is at the root of the human problem. As long as people feel guilty for their shortcomings and seek forgiveness for these 'sins', then they will remain enslaved. Only a deity who can love the 'evil' as well as the good, who makes no distinction between sin and innocence, a God of infinite permission and total freedom, can bring peace and happiness to Mankind.

As in *Paradise Lost*, Satan's arguments are compelling and there is always a danger that some critics will miss the author's irony. Miller makes clear his rejection of this specious celebration of anarchy by having his human characters finally choose God's love over Lucifer's indifference. But the play ends with the departure of God and His adjuration to the first family to seek Him in their hearts. Eve remains troubled by God's lack of fairness to her and her two sons, ignorant of why Abel had to die, and of who or what rules the world. Cain in his blindness refuses to face his own hostile feelings or even acknowledge his own acts, continuing to maintain his innocence. Only Adam seems to have developed a true conscience and a recognition of his responsibility to follow its dictates. One out of three is not an impressive score, and Miller is all too aware that in a secular age the percentage of people moved by a genuine love of God is certainly much smaller.

15
The Archbishop's Ceiling (1977)

In the decade following 1965, Miller's horizons were considerably broadened by his close association with PEN, the association of poets, essayists and novelists, of which he was President from 1965–1969. Personal contact with writers from all over the world at the annual congresses, and participation in campaigns to free imprisoned authors dramatically raised his awareness of the persecution experienced by authors unprotected by the American Bill of Rights. But it was his travels to countries behind the Iron Curtain that brought home to him the paradoxes of censorship and state oppression. In Russia he saw how writers were seduced by the system to collaborate in State repression of their fellows;[1] how rules were applied arbitrarily by an untouchable bureaucracy; how the writer was regarded as State property, accountable for his attitude.[2] At the same time, he could understand the Russian writers' fear that their way of life might be destroyed by unrestricted individualism. He had to admit that the obsession with sex and commerce characteristic of much writing in the west was a poor advertisement for a free literature. Still influenced by a sort of residual attraction to the socialist ideal, however, Miller imagined that he saw in Russian society of the late 1960s a deep patriotism and an aspiration for communal brotherhood born of a profound suffering.

If questions of freedom of expression were complicated in Russia, they were doubly so in Czechoslovakia. Miller made two trips to that country – first in 1968 shortly after the invasion by Warsaw Pact troops, and again in 1973. There he saw how the hopes of the 'Prague Spring' – that an egalitarian, socialist economy could be opened to humane values, individual liberty and freedom of expression – were ruthlessly crushed. State police were free to enter writers' homes and confiscate manuscripts; some 152 Czech writers were forbidden to publish anything within the country and, though not imprisoned, were denied access to education and good jobs. In order to survive in such conditions, some writers recanted on television, others wrote what the state demanded, many emigrated.[3] But a few found something within them that did not allow them to conform. What, Miller wonders, was the source of such defiance? Was it ideology? Pride? Egoism? Or something beyond all these? Between 1973 and 1976, the playwright wrestled with these ideas as he worked on a new play.

The Archbishop's Ceiling is set in an Eastern European city, almost certainly Prague, to which an American writer, Adrian, has returned to reestablish contact with friends he had met two years earlier. He is alternately attracted and repelled by a society he regards sometimes as a kind of Jerusalem and sometimes as a haunt of demons. His pretext for returning is that he is doing research on a novel. On his first evening in the city he dines with his friend, Sigmund, who tells him about his own novel which he has been forced to keep concealed for fear of the Secret Police. The next night, in the sitting room of a luxurious flat owned by Marcus, one of the country's most prosperous and officially admired writers, he meets Sigmund again, along with Maya, a former actress and poet who has given up serious literary work and now writes for a breakfast radio program. Gradually we come to understand something of the memories, old rivalries, and deep suspicions that bind the three Europeans. Maya, it seems, has not only been romantically involved with both Sigmund and Marcus (most recently as the latter's mistress), but has also had a brief affair with Adrian during his last visit to the city (which is perhaps the real reason for his return). The sexual tensions caused by this three-way romance give way to more immediate concerns, however, when Sigmund announces that his novel has been discovered and confiscated by the police. Gradually the crisis resolves itself into a conflict between Sigmund on the one hand, and Maya and Marcus on the other. In their different ways the latter two have made their own accommodation with the State and fear that Sigmund's increasingly strident criticism of the regime will endanger them. The situation is complicated by the fact that the three friends, once close, have over the years gradually drifted apart. Maya has been replaced in Marcus' bedroom; Marcus, once the leading novelist in the country, has lost that pre-eminence to Sigmund. Now unable to write, Marcus makes his way by shrewd collaboration with a regime he considers slightly more benign than the one that preceded it. It is with seriously mixed motives, therefore, that Maya and Marcus try to persuade Sigmund that the confiscation of his manuscript is a sign that the State intends to prosecute him along with his friends, and that it would therefore be better for all if he left the country. For a variety of reasons, not least of which is the fear that he would not be able to write abroad,

Sigmund is extremely reluctant to do this. When the astonishing news arrives that the authorities intend to return his manuscript, Sigmund begins to feel he is in less danger than Marcus had been suggesting, and that it would be safe for him to remain. Apprehensive about how this will affect his own career, Marcus accuses Sigmund of deliberately seeking confrontation with the authorities in a search for notoriety or martyrdom. Maya, convinced that Sigmund's remaining in the country would lead to the loss of the only job she has been able to secure, also begs Sigmund to leave. In this she is joined by Adrian who offers to help Sigmund find a place teaching at an American University where he would be able to carry on with his own writing. Feeling that he could not write deprived of the sound of his own language, but deeply sorry for the trouble he may be bringing on his friends, he asks forgiveness. The play ends with the return of the manuscript and the resumption of the endless struggle between state power and the creative spirit.

The play has generally managed to baffle audiences everywhere (although somewhat more profoundly in America than in England where there is a tradition of political and philosophical discussion on stage and more familiarity with life behind the Iron Curtain). On the face of it, the work would seem to be conventional fare for Broadway (where it has yet to be produced). The sitting room setting, the copious bar, the curious intruder, an unsolved crime, all these might suggest an Agatha Christie mystery. But as is almost always the case with Miller's plays, the realistic surface hides depths of psychological and metaphysical ambiguities. To plumb these depths requires more attention than the average audience is willing, or indeed able, to devote to the task. Because the characters are not always entirely candid, it is difficult or impossible on a first hearing in the theatre to separate truth from falsehood. This is particularly true with regard to the presence (or not) of a listening device supposedly planted in the ceiling of the sitting room which may (or may not) be transmitting everything they say to the authorities. The uncertainty about this and other aspects of plot and motivation contribute to an unsettling experience for spectators expecting an evening in the theatre to end with the solving of the crime and the identification of the criminal.

At one level, *The Archbishop's Ceiling* is a variation of Miller's familiar story of sibling rivalry. There is the successful entrepreneur, skillful at playing the system, charmingly ruthless in advancing his career, and not particularly scrupulous. Opposed to him is the stubborn idealist, uninterested in financial gain, highly focused, unwilling to make a bargain with Fate or compromise with his nature and ready to accept the consequences of his choices. Not only are the characters of Marcus and

Sigmund reminiscent of the Franz brothers in *The Price*, but they also play the same kind of psychological games. Marcus has returned from London where he claims to have learned from a state agent that the authorities plan to put Sigmund on trial for his opposition to the regime. It turns out later that this may have been a lie cooked up to frighten Sigmund into leaving the country. Marcus' feelings are deeply ambivalent: admiring, even loving on the one hand, but at the same time resentful, envious, and fearful that his own success may be compromised by his support of the younger writer. The complexity of such emotions is underlined by Adrian's querying whether 'anything we think really determines what we're going to do. Or even what we feel.'[4] In other words, at a deeper level the play is about the unconscious, the ultimate grounds for moral choice.

The play is set, in a former Episcopal Palace, once the luxurious residence of a Prince of the Church, which has become the somewhat less opulent quarters of a privileged State artist. Whereas the former ecclesiastical tenant provided access to the Church and reassurance of the existence of God, its present occupant is an influential intermediary with the State bureaucracy, but indifferent to any higher truth. The possible existence of a listening device in the ceiling (affirmed by Maya, denied by Marcus), therefore becomes an ambiguous symbol of the possibility of communicating with a higher power. The play ends, with the return of the stolen manuscript. But the further problem of Sigmund's willingness to submit to Party discipline remains unresolved. Unless he does submit, Maya fears that she will lose her job and that Marcus will be imprisoned and possibly executed as a result of conversations overheard through the ceiling. So the final moments of the play deal with the dilemma that has been at the core of many of Miller's plays, if not of his own life - how can an individual weigh the claims of others against those of the self?

Sigmund faces two alternatives - the death of his talent if he emigrates, and quite possibly his own death if he refuses to submit. Because Maya and Marcus are urging him to leave, he believes they have been destroyed by the system and, like Judas, are preparing to deliver him over to the authorities for their own profit. Marcus accuses Sigmund of moral blackmail. Maya argues that Sigmund's desire to preserve his talent is no less selfish than her desire to keep her job or Marcus' wish to retain his privileges. Apparently in genuine distress, Sigmund cries out that he doesn't know what drives him, but that he cannot leave, even though he knows his actions will hurt others. Looking up to the ceiling, he finds no answers, but seems to be able to draw his strength from the example of other writers who have dared to challenge Power. Standing, not in his own name, but in the spirit of creativity, he seems less self-righteous than some of Miller's earlier self-justifying heroes. Asking Adrian to safeguard the 'relics' of his faith (letters from other writers who have dared to speak to Power), Sigmund turns to face the new demands of the State as the curtain falls.

The problem with *The Archbishop's Ceiling* is that the context in which Miller has chosen to explore his ideas is remote from the experience of the average playgoer. Even in England where sympathy for, and understanding of, the problems of artists under Communist rule is more widespread than in America, the play proved puzzling. The intellectual chess game Miller has devised is much too complex to follow in a single viewing. Furthermore, the semi-allegorical form he has adopted and the symbolic import of the hidden microphone are unduly confusing. (Miller's ruminations about the bug's effect on one's identity, and about its similarity to God, or to conscience shorn of moral distinctions, do little to clarify the matter).[5]

16
The American Clock (1980–86)

Sometime in the early 1970s, Miller discovered Studs Terkel's recently-published oral history of the Great Depression called *Hard Times*. It comprised a great many interviews with survivors of the period plus a few with members of a younger generation who were almost totally ignorant of what their parents had gone through. What struck Miller was that the interviews shattered many of the clichéd assumptions about the time. Not all of the financiers were grasping, not all those who rode the rails or stood in bread lines were selfless. Terkel recorded without comment the prejudices, self-deceptions and rationalizations of the interviewees so that the contradictions and inconsistencies of history and human nature were vividly exposed. When the interviewer did introduce his own opinions, it was in a 'Personal Memoir (and parenthetical comment)' at the beginning of the volume. There he alternated his own recollections of the Crash with general comments about their significance and wider context. At a time when the neo-conservatives seemed determined to dismantle as much of the New Deal legacy as possible, Miller felt it was important to show how Roosevelt's solutions to the economic problems of the 1930s were the basis of much that remained valuable in post-war America. Terkel's introduction to *Hard Times* suggested how it might be done.

The American Clock is Miller's most autobiographical drama. It tells of the young Lee Baum (Arthur Miller) who, with his parents Moe and Rose, must give up a luxurious Manhattan apartment and move into a cramped house in Brooklyn when the family loses its money in the collapse of the stock market in 1929. Lee witnesses the gradual discouragement of his parents as his mother is forced to pawn her jewelry and his father must work for others instead of running his own business. Lee's bicycle is stolen. He has to go out to work. But finally he manages to save enough money to get himself into university. After graduation, he applies to the writers' project at the Works Progress

Administration. Meanwhile, his mother becomes more and more despondent as the pressures of poverty almost overwhelm her, and she reflects on how so many of the public figures she admired have turned out to be criminals or frauds. The play ends in the present with Lee, a successful sportswriter, heartened by the memory of his now-dead mother who, in her contradictions, hopefulness and vitality, seems to him to embody the spirit of the country itself.

Accompanying and interspersed with this biographical material are scenes illustrating the social context of the period drawn from the interviews in *Hard Times*. These show the almost blind faith in the market which was widespread in the 1920s as well as the bewilderment and suicides that followed its collapse. They also show the hardship in the rural hinterlands, from a farm auction in Iowa to the destitution suffered by the poor along the Mississippi. Glimpses of urban hardship reveal how the failure of the financial system had affected people at all levels, from financiers forced to seek welfare to dispossessed farmers begging in city neighbourhoods and reluctant welfare applicants fainting from hunger. Miller's purpose in combining the story of a single family with a panoramic view of the country is to replicate in the theatre the effect of a mural where, although individual faces can be identified, they are not presented as intimate portraits but as part of a large, thematic picture.[1]

In structure, therefore, *The American Clock* is much more sweeping in scope than most of Miller's earlier works, combining as it does a psychologically realistic domestic story with a series of newsreel-like mini documentaries. It takes the form of a memory play, something like *After the Fall* or *The Glass Menagerie*, in which the central character speaks directly to the audience and then participates in the re-enactment of his own recollections. In the original version, two contrasting spokespersons, rather like the interlocutors in a minstrel show, comment on the causes and effects of the historical scenes from opposite points of view. This results in a running debate between a sixty year-old Lee and an equally elderly financier by the name of Arthur Robertson who discuss politics and economics and then doff their grey wigs to become part of the dramatic action. The difficulty with this arrangement is that it fails to strike a balance between the epic elements and the intimate lives of individuals and families.[2]

The original play opened at the Spoleto Festival in May 1980, to tepid reviews but reasonable audience response. Uncertain that he had solved the structural problems of the play, Miller allowed the producers to talk him into revising the work for Broadway. But when the play moved into the Biltmore Theatre in New York in November of 1980, the critics were no kinder (one specifically deploring the changes made to the original script),[3] and the production closed after only twelve performances. Miller was beginning to find, however, that a play's death in New York was not necessarily terminal. There *is* life after Broadway and *The American Clock* went through two further transformations before it reached its final form at the National Theatre in London.[4]

In England the tradition of non-realistic entertainments, from the annual Christmas 'pantos' to the plays of Brecht and the collective creations of Joan Littlewood, was alive and well. Consequently, when the National Theatre decided to mount *The American Clock* in 1986, director Peter Wood felt much freer than had his American counterparts to experiment with the staging. Instead of employing the two 'interlocutors', Wood created a 'choral area' at the back of the stage where the nineteen performers sat in full view of the audience when they were not involved directly in the action. He placed a five-piece jazz band on one side of the stage and played individual scenes on a bare acting area with minimum props and furniture moved into position by the actors themselves. Music – some forty popular songs of the period – was used extensively to provide transitions between scenes and to set the tone or comment ironically on the action.

In this production, the function of introducing and commenting on the action was taken over by the non-participating actors in the choral area. This contributed to the presentational nature of the experience by drawing attention to the reality behind the illusion. Wood used a variety of distancing techniques such as choral speaking, pantomime, and dancing when he wanted to draw attention to a general situation, or prevent the audience from empathizing too strongly with an individual character. These succeeded in better integrating the scenes of intimate psychological revelation with those of social comment. The production was a great success. The critic for the *Times* called it 'nothing short of magnificent' and characterized it as 'part variety show, part drilled spectacle in the presentational style of the 1930s'.[5] Audience response prompted the management to shift the production from the small Cottesloe Theatre to the larger Olivier auditorium for an extended run for which it received a nomination for the Olivier Award as best play of the season.

Much of the polemic concerning the evils of capitalism and the salvation brought about by Roosevelt's New Deal has been removed from the final version, so it is more difficult to say exactly what Miller is driving at or why he has decided once again to revisit his already well-scrutinized past. In part it is to speak to a generation ignorant of the benefits they had inherited from the 1930s; in part it is a defence of the achievements of the New Deal from the attacks of the neo-conservatives. Partly, too, it is a tribute to those who had survived the Depression and gone on to help build a new society, or else to die in one of America's wars defending it. It is also an attempt by an aging playwright, no longer convinced of the certainties of his youth, to turn back the clock in search of the feelings that once ruled his life and had been stolen from him by time. Like many of his contemporaries, like his family in the 1920s, he had been a profound believer in the American Dream and when it shattered, part of his identity was lost.[6]

What is interesting is how Miller's beliefs and attitudes have mellowed. The presentation of the Depression as a national catastrophe affecting both rich and poor is not original, but like Terkel, Miller avoids stereotypes. There are humane financiers as well as grasping ones, generous and selfish individuals of all classes. Adversity does not always breed sympathy, nor mutual misfortune trust. The novel twist to a balanced but conventional picture of the Depression is the character of Theodore K. Quinn, a self-made millionaire who resigns from the position of President of General Electric one day after having been appointed to the post because he objects to the monopolizing tendencies of the corporation. Based on a character of Miller's acquaintance, Quinn was a product of the 1930s, but his message seems designed for the much later age of merger mania.

In the end, however, *The American Clock* is less a social or historical play than a *bildungsroman*, the story of the growing up of a young man who, in spite of the familiar details, is remarkably different from the Arthur Miller we have come to know from other sources. Lee is a rather phlegmatic character, very different from his friend, Joe, and his cousin, Sidney, both of whom are passionate in their interests in politics and music. It is Joe who is the Marxist at university not Lee, who seems uncommitted. After graduation, instead of pursuing his ambition to become a writer, Lee drifts around the country, seeing the desolation in the south, and getting to know something of the injustices facing the blacks. Back in New York, he connives with his father to get the papers necessary to qualify for relief payments through the WPA. We see nothing of his struggle to succeed as a writer, and are surprised towards the end of the play to discover that he has become a successful journalist. There is nothing in this portrait reminiscent of the strongly-held convictions and fierce determination to succeed that characterized Miller in his youth. Indeed the Lee we meet in the play is almost a temporizer, indecisive because too able to see both sides of an argument.

The theme of belief is central to the work. Some people achieve things (trans-Atlantic flights, home runs) because of their beliefs; others are ruined because they believe in the wrong thing. In the depths of the Depression, Roosevelt kept alive the American dream of Washington and Jefferson, and gave people back their belief in the country. Lee seems conflicted. While he can cheer up his father with fantasies of a better future, he knows himself that there is a long, bad time ahead. So instead of acting, he waits, with no hope 'for the dream to come back from wherever it had gone to hide'. He seems to lack any part of the young Arthur Miller's firm conviction of the historical inevitability of socialism.

The play ends with a much older Lee recalling with his cousin, Sidney, those of their family and friends who have died, committed suicide, or been killed in wars. Of them all, the one he remembers most vividly is his dead mother who seems to him so much like the country itself. Contradictory, inconsistent, changeable, obsessed by money but wanting a free life, she clings to a fervent conviction that the world was meant to be better. It was undoubtedly what she taught her son to believe as well.

17
Incident at Vichy (1964) and *Playing for Time* (1979–85)

Late in 1978 Miller was approached to write a TV adaptation of a recently-published memoir of the Holocaust. Although he knew well the perils of dealing with this controversial subject, he was attracted to the project by the extraordinary nature of the author's experiences. Fania Fenelon, a French singer and pianist, had survived internment at Auschwitz by playing in a women's orchestra in the camp. Thirty years after her liberation she decided to publish her recollections which appeared in English as *The Musicians of Auschwitz*. So remarkable was the story, so balanced and clear-eyed the author's observations, that Miller agreed to revisit a subject that had haunted him for years.

Miller's pre-occupation with fascist anti-Semitism grew out of his own experiences in New York in the late 1930s, experiences reflected in his 1945 novel *Focus*. It was only later, however, as a result of visits to Germany and attendance at Nazi war trials in Frankfurt, that he confronted the full horror of the Nazi Final Solution. That horror remained somewhat abstract in *After the Fall*, symbolized by the omni-present concentration camp guard tower. But in *Incident at Vichy* the playwright brings it vividly to life. The play is based on a story told to him by a Viennese psychiatrist who had lived in the Unoccupied Zone of France during the Second World War. It concerned an individual who was picked up by police working for the Vichy government during a roundup of suspected Jews. Taken to a police station where his identity was certain to be discovered, the man was saved at the last minute by someone he had never seen before who gave him the pass to freedom he had received at the end of his own interrogation.

In dramatizing this anecdote, of which he could remember only the bare outlines, Miller had to invent believable characters and provide credible motivation for the climactic act of astonishing self-sacrifice. The central character, Prince Wilhelm Johann Von Berg, he based on an aristocratic Austrian friend of Inge's who had been forced to do menial labour in

France during the war. The man who was saved he modeled very loosely on the person who had told him the story, Dr Rudolph Loewenstein. In an effort to universalize the incident, he chose a dramatic form reminiscent of medieval morality plays in which characters are types or personifications rather than individuals. Apart from the Prince, none of the people in *Incident at Vichy* has a first name and several, such as the detectives, the waiter, the gypsy and the old Jew, are merely generic. There is very little action, the characters waiting helplessly as one by one they are taken from a queue into an inner office where they are interrogated and then detained or released. After initial confusion about the reason for their arrest, followed by a futile discussion of the possibility of escape, the prisoners resign themselves to the possibility that they are being selected for transportation to the death camps. The play then becomes little more than a debate about stratagems to deal with the situation in which they find themselves.

As the grim reality dawns on them, each individual tries to cling to some vestige of comfort or hope. In some cases these are material – the gypsy's pot (which he may or may not have stolen), the Old Jew's bag (which turns out to contain nothing but feathers). In others, hope takes the form of faith – in Communist ideology, in reason, in law, in humane ideals. In the face of senseless violence, however, all their strategies fail. One by one, the characters are stripped of their possessions and their illusions. The Communist must face the fact that a large number of the working class support the Nazis; the music-lover must acknowledge that an appreciation of art is not incompatible with murder; the rebel advocate of solidarity finds to his horror that to save his life he would abandon his comrades. In the end, the debate is carried on by three individuals – a German major who claims to be as much a prisoner of the system as the detainees; Leduc, a Jewish psychiatrist, who maintains that defiance of evil is possible; and Von Berg, who protests his innocence of any animosity towards the Jews.

The climax is reached when Leduc accuses Von Berg of being a collaborator because he did not attempt to stop his cousin, a Nazi, from persecuting Jews in Vienna. Stunned by this accusation, Von Berg acknowledges that he had known of his cousin's activities and since he had made no objection he could, perhaps, be considered an accomplice. When Leduc sees that he has awakened a sense of guilt in the Prince, he protests that, 'It is not your guilt I want, it's your responsibility.' At that moment Von Berg is summoned into the inner office leaving Leduc alone in the waiting room. When Von Berg emerges a few minutes later, he is carrying his pass to freedom. Instead of leaving the police station, however, he hands the pass to Leduc and tells him to go. Confronted with this agonizing choice, Leduc '*backs away ... in the awareness of his own guilt*' and walks to freedom. The play ends with the police discovering the exchange and raising the alarm. Left alone on stage, the German Major and the Viennese Prince face one another - the one a reluctant collaborator, the other a heroic martyr - '*forever incomprehensible to one another*'.[1]

Not surprisingly, perhaps, their incomprehension is shared by many readers and spectators. Does Von Berg lay down his life in the name of his ideals or because he feels guilty for his role in the persecution of the Jews? Does his sacrifice redeem him and, if so, is the price demanded excessive? As for the German Major, if he is being condemned for refusing to disobey orders, is he more or less guilty than the French detectives who seem to carry out their duties with particular relish? The play seems to make no distinction between sins of commission and sins of omission and to imply that there is no such thing as an innocent survivor. As in *After the Fall*, Miller's concern here is not so much to identify and condemn the perpetrators of evil, as to ensure that the ground from which they spring will never again be so fertile. To that end, he seeks to expose the process by which such a culture develops and in so doing perhaps provide a lesson for the future. Like Leduc, Miller appears to believe that the real danger is that Man is unwilling to accept 'that he is *not* reasonable, [and] that he is full of murder'. Until such time as mankind as a whole reaches that level of awareness (a time that Leduc at least appears to believe is coming), the world will remain a dangerous place.

Misunderstood by many who did not share his belief in universal brotherhood (or Good Samaritans), Miller subsequently tried to make himself clear. In an article in the *New York Times* a month or so after the opening of the play at the ANTA Theatre, he explained that the work was less about Nazism than about evil and the individual's relationship with injustice and violence.[2] While disclaiming to know why anyone would sacrifice himself (any more than why he would commit suicide), Miller nevertheless suggested that Von Berg acts as he does because he is unwilling to pay the price of his own survival which would be the 'authenticity of his own self-image and his pride' thereby adding Von Berg to a growing list of his dramatic heroes who die to preserve their name.

Fifteen years later Miller was astonished to find in *The Musicians of Auschwitz* what seemed to him confirmation of his earlier surmises. As a camp survivor and first hand witness, Fania Fenelon exhibited a skeptical, but humane, intelligence very much like his own. Her ability to see the frailty of human nature without losing either her empathy or her optimism, he found inspirational. As a result, he took scarcely a month to prepare a TV film-script which was ready in early 1979. If he had hoped to avoid the controversy that plagued his earlier Holocaust productions, however, he was disappointed. When it became known that Vanessa Redgrave (a vociferous supporter of the Palestine Liberation Organization) had been cast as Fania Fenelon, there was an outcry from several Jewish groups. The author herself was flown to New York by the Simon Wiesenthal Center for Holocaust Studies to express her outrage to the executives of the CBS television network. As a result of the controversy (and the somber nature of the subject matter), several advertising agencies withdrew their support. In spite of this opposition, however, the film was made and broadcast to glowing reviews and universal admiration for Miss Redgrave's performance.

The Musicians of Auschwitz is the extraordinary story of the all-female orchestra in the Birkenau women's prison at Auschwitz; an unsentimental, and unusually objective account of the bewildering contradictions, ironies and complexities of life in a Nazi concentration camp. As Fania Fenelon rather remarkably understood, it was a system that imprisoned jailers and inmates alike – the former in a rigid ideology and coercive hierarchical command structure; the latter in terror of the guards, as well as in a life-and-death struggle with one another. For the system could only work with the active collaboration of a large number of prisoners who, in exchange for privileges or temporarily prolonged life, provided many of the services, from cooking meals or deputizing for the guards in the prison blocks, to leading the condemned to the gas chambers and putting the bodies in the ovens. The camps became an arena for the playing out of the central Jewish dilemma (which is also a human dilemma) – 'How much can one compromise with the dominant group and still remain a Jew?'

Five years after it was presented on television, Miller adapted the piece for the theatre. The stage version, called *Playing for Time*,[3] retains the fluidity of its predecessor with scenes following one another on a stage bare except for essential furniture and properties. Changes of location are made in full view of the audience, and offstage action is described by Fania Fenelon, as narrator, speaking directly to the audience. In style, it is very similar to *The American Clock* except that, instead of drawing attention to the 'staginess' of the play, Miller here seeks to engage the audience's emotions as fully as possible.

The action begins, as it were, immediately after *Incident at Vichy*. Inmates from a French prison are herded into a boxcar and taken to

Auschwitz where they are separated into groups, relieved of all their possessions, shaved, and put into cell blocks where they must sleep several to a bed. Fania learns that, since she had decided to walk from the station to the camp instead of travelling in what appeared to be a Red Cross truck, she had escaped being transported directly to the gas chambers. A little later she is again preserved when she is recruited for a camp orchestra. The bulk of the play recounts her experiences in the curious limbo inhabited by this privileged, yet highly compromised, group of women. Better housed, slightly better fed, spared the rigours of the work details and the terrors of the 'selections', the musicians have to live with the respect (even admiration) of their captors and the contempt and hatred of their less fortunate fellow prisoners.

The world of the orchestra is a microcosm of Europe. French, German, Polish, Belgian, Romanian, Dutch and Ukrainian prisoners are united in their plight, but frequently separated by national, religious, racial and political antagonisms. The hierarchy of power includes not only the SS Guards, but also a number of Aryan Polish prisoners who carry out their orders. There are German prisoners as well as German officers, and some of the inmates are more brutal than the Nazis. All seek a strategy to survive in an insane world. Miller has included most of the characters Fenelon has drawn in her memoir: Mandel, the chief of the women's camp, who becomes attached to a small Polish boy and mothers him for a short time before sending him to his death in a gesture of 'sacrifice' and an act of high German discipline; Marianne, the innocent young French girl who, in return for gifts of food, becomes no better than a prostitute, turning against those who had first protected her; Mala, the Jewish translator who escapes from the camp, is captured, beaten and executed as an example to others; Alma-Rose, the German-Jewish violinist and conductor of the orchestra who is murdered by an envious Nazi supervisor.

Fenelon's original memoir had explored most of the questions raised by life in this nightmare environment. Primary among these was the problem of integrity. What could she salvage of herself from the wreckage of civilization around her? Was there a limit to what she would surrender? The test came when, as the daughter of a Catholic father and a Jewish mother, she won the right to remove one half of the star of David on her prison uniform. She found that she was unable to do it. Something made her assert a common humanity with her fellow prisoners. The same instinct allowed her to identify in part with her captors. Rejecting tribalism and ideologies that stereotype whole groups, she insisted on looking at the facts, astonishing or unpleasant as they may be. For her the problem was not that the Nazis were monsters; the problem was that they were human.

With all this Miller was very much in agreement, so there was no need, as there had been with *Incident at Vichy*, to invent characters or provide motivation. The one significant addition he made to the play was the expansion of the role of a Polish prisoner who enters the women's quarters occasionally to do electrical work. In the TV version, this figure is presented as somewhat odd – 'perhaps deranged, perhaps extraordinarily wise'.[4] By the end of the film, he has become almost otherworldly, seeming '*to blaze in an unearthly luminescence ... Staring in a sublime silence ... he lifts his arms in a wordless gesture of deliverance, his eyes filled with miracle.*' The character in the stage version is considerably more corporeal, but his repeated directions to Fania not to turn away from the horrors confronting her, and his urgent insistence that she live to report them remain and underline her mission as witness and memorialist.

Miller's two Holocaust plays show the playwright struggling to make sense of one of the central mysteries of the twentieth century. Although he himself had no direct experience of the events he dramatized in *Incident at Vichy*, he nevertheless felt that he could flesh out the story by drawing on his own knowledge. He also seems to have believed that he could evaluate the behaviour of his characters on the basis of that knowledge. In *Playing for Time*, however, because of the nature of the source, Miller's interpretive role is much smaller. It consists almost entirely of hinting at some kind of spiritual source for Fania's strength and compulsion to bear witness (an implication that is all but removed from the final version for the stage). In the years between 1964 and 1985, Miller had grown less eager to apportion blame and prescribe cures. If, in the interval, he had not altogether lost hope for some kind of ultimate explanation, he seemed much more content to live in the moment. Referring to his musical *Up From Paradise* in 1979, he had told a reporter from the *New York Times* that the work provided 'no possible rational ground for any hope whatsoever. And that's wonderful. There is nothing to do but go on living as happily as possible.'[5] *Playing for Time* communicates something of the same stubborn optimism.

18
Four One-Act Plays (1980–87)

During the early 1980s, Miller turned briefly to the writing of one-act plays. In general, these works seem more personal and enigmatic than most of his longer work. Like short essays, they are dramatic reflections on certain experiences and ideas that interested him at the time. But whereas the personal elements in earlier plays were often transparent, these works are both more private and more mysterious.

This is especially true of the earliest, *Elegy for a Lady*, written in just two-and-a-half days in 1980, and springing directly out of the author's subconscious.[1] As he tried to explain in retrospect, the play was an attempt to explore the way in which grief affects our perception of the world. 'There is an anguish,' he wrote, 'based on desire impossible to realize, that is so unrequited, and therefore so intense, that it tends to fuse all people into one person.'[2] Structurally the play is an attempt to reproduce the way the mind creates objective reality.[3] It is unclear whether the action takes place entirely in the unnamed man's mind, or 'in the space between the mind and what it imagines'.[4]

The experience presented is that of an older, married man trying to understand the nature of his relationship with a younger lover who may or may not be terminally ill. The action seems to take place in a gift shop where the man, with the assistance of the proprietress, is trying to choose a present. In the course of their conversation, the man reveals that he is not sure whether or not his lover is actually dying since she has refused to see him and won't tell him in which hospital she is to have her operation. It also transpires that he knows little of her likes and interests, and is therefore afraid that each gift he considers – flowers, plant, book, kerchief, negligee, sweater or bed-jacket – might send an inappropriate signal. His indecision and uncertainty are perhaps understandable since he has never hitherto bought a present for his lover during their two- (or possibly three-) year relationship. The situation becomes more mysterious when the proprietress not only seems to intuit the lover's feelings, but even takes on certain characteristics of the young woman. When the two embrace, and share 'a deep familiarity', the proprietress seems to have become fused in some way with the man's loved one. Under the guidance of this mysterious stranger-lover, the man comes to accept his role as friend rather than lover. He concludes that the young woman will probably survive, and has deliberately avoided deepening her relationship with him during this crisis. He finally chooses an antique watch as a gift which he hopes will tell her to be brave each time she looks at it.

The play is puzzling, in part because of the ambiguous character of the proprietress, but also because of the extremely shadowy nature of the relationship between the man and his lover. The woman never emerges in clear outline, and seems to exist only in her relationship with the man. It is *his* guilt, doubts, insecurities and frustrations that take centre stage, and (as is so often the case in Miller's dramas) these are assuaged by an ardent female admirer. The result is a rather solipsistic view of love, possibly a consequence of the deeply personal nature of the feelings on which the play is based, not impossibly related to the memory of Marilyn Monroe.

A similar sense of semi-confessional revelation characterizes the second one-act play of this period. *Some Kind of Love Story* also deals with an adulterous relationship, this time between an older married man and a young woman who suffers from serious psychological problems. The two are involved in a complex murder mystery in which a young boy has been convicted of a crime he did not commit. The woman, Angela, has evidence to prove the boy's innocence, but refuses to give it to the detective, Tom Dooley, who has been working for some years to overturn the conviction. The situation is complicated by Angela's remarkable promiscuity which has involved her in sexual relationships not only with the detective, but also with at least two of the State officials taking part in the murder investigation.

In its general outline, the plot of *Some Kind of Love Story* closely resembles a similar case of wrongful conviction that Miller himself had been drawn into some ten years earlier when he had helped establish the innocence of the accused. The details have been altered and the focus shifted from the action of the police to the rather strange and intense relationship between the detective and a reluctant witness. It is the prolonged, late-night encounter between these two that constitutes the only action of the play. Ostensibly the interview is about the murder investigation and Angela's fears that her life is in danger because of her inside knowledge of police involvement in the murder and their subsequent cover-up. In reality, it is part of an ongoing strategy on Angela's part to retain Tom's interest and attention. While Tom is still attracted to Angela physically, he realizes that to revive their sexual relationship would jeopardize his pursuit of justice which seems to be his driving motivation. In an extended psychological struggle (in which Tom employs a mixture of flattery and threats to leave, and Angela escapes into multiple personalities to avoid unpleasant subjects or threatening confrontations), the identity of the killer is finally revealed. But Angela refuses to relinquish the incriminating letters she possesses thereby depriving Tom of the evidence he would need to bring the case to trial. The play ends, not with the triumph of justice, but with the *status quo ante* – with Tom still in Angela's power and seemingly helpless to break her hold over him.

What is odd about the play is the conjunction of elements from an actual police case and a 'love story' that seems from an altogether different context. Describing these two one-act plays, Miller explained that he had been interested in how our 'objective reality' is really a product of our mind, and as such is affected by what our needs require it to be. In a comment that seems to be particularly relevant to *Some Kind of Love Story*, Miller maintained that we are sometimes forced to make decisions that we know are based on illusion and the power of desire.[5] Seen as an exploration of the wilder shores of love, the story is perhaps improbable. As a metaphor for the mind-forged manacles of irrational sexual attraction, however, it is penetrating and unsentimental.

Two or three years after the completion of *Love Story*, Miller returned to the murder mystery genre. Once again, the action in *Clara* consists of a single long interview between a police detective and an unco-operative witness, but the focus is very different. In this play the playwright deals much more explicitly with the process of denial which he seems to think lies at the root of our faulty perception of reality. The play takes place in the apartment of the murdered girl, Clara, where the victim's father, Albert Kroll, is being interrogated by the detective, Fine. Still in a state of shock after viewing his daughter's body, Kroll finds it difficult to remember details of the past, and especially the name of the most likely suspect, a Puerto Rican ex-convict who had been imprisoned for murdering a former girlfriend and whom Clara had befriended. Kroll's memory loss is largely owing to his sense that he has been partly responsible for his daughter's death. He is afraid that his own early idealism and antiracist convictions may have instilled in her an unrealistic set of values and lack of a proper sense of danger. He also regrets that he did not try to stop his daughter developing a romantic attachment to the criminal because of his sense of relief to discover that she was not a lesbian. One of the police officers, going through Clara's record collection, discovers an early recording of Kroll singing and suggests that they play it. When Kroll hears his voice as a young man, it brings back a memory of how he had saved several black soldiers from a lynch mob, and how, as a young girl, Clara had been inspired by the story. In that recollection he realizes how proud he is of his daughter's fatal idealism and of her stubborn adherence to values he has himself abandoned. The realization unlocks his memory and he is able to name the suspect.

In *Clara*, Miller employs a technique he had used before to dramatize a character's memories. The dead Clara materializes at different points in the play as Kroll, like Willy Loman, struggles to connect past hopes with present reality. The climax is reached when he relates her social conscience with his own youthful instincts, and sees in her death a tragic working out of his own lost aspirations. If the mood is less despairing than that of Beckett, it is nevertheless more ambiguous than is usual in Miller's plays. For while Kroll's youthful values of equality and altruism are extolled, they have proved fatal to Clara and been abandoned by all the other characters in the play. So, undermining the affirmation of humane values is the question of whether they can survive in a world ruled, as the detective maintains, by greed and race.

A similar ambivalence underlies Miller's treatment of serious issues in *I Can't Remember Anything*. The work differs from the other short pieces in that it is rooted much more firmly in real life. Miller has said that the play is a loving tribute to his long-time Roxbury neighbours, Alexander and Louisa Calder. The painter and sculptor, 'Sandy' Calder had moved with his wife to rural Connecticut in the Depression, and Miller had known them since the 1940s. He had come to admire their love of life, their 'sure instinct for decency' and their 'unpretentious simplicity'.[6] The play grew out of Miller's recollection of their voices 'going at one another' and the play is a sort of fictionalized memoir to show something of their spirit. The meeting between Leo (in his late sixties) and Leonora (twelve years older) takes place in the living room-kitchen of Leo's house on a back country road. Since her husband's death ten years earlier, Leonora has come to believe that she is useless, and has lost her sense of life's purpose. She betrays little interest in her son who has moved to India from where he writes only very occasionally. Her memories are of the 'more precious life' before the war, the parties attended by hundreds of people, the many dead friends. More recent events she can't remember and when reminded of them can only excuse her forgetfulness with the expostulation, 'What difference does it make?' Convinced as she is that the country is being ruined by greed and ignorance, she is puzzled and irritated by Leo's continued optimism.

For his part, Leo is content with his own small accomplishments, and is not afraid to face his inevitable death. He rejects as sentimental any suggestion of purpose in the universe, and accepts with equanimity his ultimate dissolution into the chemical components that make up his body. And yet he refuses to succumb to the sort of apathy and discouragement that afflicts Leonora. He makes plans to donate his body to Yale Medical School, and cannot lose his Marxist faith that some incredible improvement is imminent. He tries in vain to get Leonora to take an interest in life instead of wasting her time in regret. When they finish their dinner, Leo puts on the record that Leonora has just received from her son. Instead of the expected Indian music, it turns out to be a samba. Energized by the rhythm, the two dance awkwardly. This unites them briefly, and they join in conspiratorial laughter. But their differences are not reconciled, and they part temperamentally distinct and mutually mystified.

The one-act plays represent a change of pace for the dramatist, allowing Miller greater freedom to explore aspects of his craft than the longer works. In *Elegy for a Lady*, for example, he creates a puzzling and disorientating world not unlike that of some of the plays of Harold Pinter. But, significantly, he avoids the extreme manifestations of theatrical experimentation such as surrealism, expressionism or their more recent derivatives. Although he spoke often of his search for dramatic forms appropriate for his themes, that search took him almost exclusively in one direction - towards a means of exposing the workings of the unconscious mind. Why people believe the things they do, and how to break down the walls of denial they build to hide the truth were subjects that fascinated the playwright all his life. In his youth, Miller believed that enlightenment would reveal a universal truth. As he matured, however, that youthful conviction was replaced by a more sober awareness of the powerful quarrel between reason and the heart's desire. If he came at last to accept the collapse of his early convictions, he found it more difficult to renounce the hope they had engendered. In the one-act plays and the works that follow them, Miller attempted to affirm that hope against increasingly hostile odds.

19
The Ride Down Mount Morgan (1991–2000)

In the concluding moments of *The Creation of the World and Other Business*, God and Lucifer compete for the allegiance of the first human family. Lucifer offers a world of total freedom from which sin, innocence and guilt will be banished, but where appeals for consolation will be met only with indifference. God promises a world of love, forgiveness and mercy reserved for those with an awareness of good and evil and a sense of responsibility. Adam and Eve choose God's way; Cain, in refusing to accept blame for the murder of his brother, casts his lot with Lucifer and is condemned to wander the earth an outcast, a fixed smile concealing his loneliness and anguish. During the 1980s, prompted in part by the increasingly materialistic and narcissistic mood of Reagan's America, Miller kept returning to the conundrum presented by the competing claims of individual liberty and social responsibility. Attempting to investigate what he described as 'the immense contradiction of the human animal'[1] Miller worked intermittently on a play in which he explored those contradictions. By early 1987 he had accumulated about one thousand pages of dialogue, but was still uncertain that he would be able to complete the work.[2]

The story he had devised involved the amatory adventures of Lyman Felt, son of an immigrant Albanian merchant and his Jewish wife. From his mother, Lyman has acquired the characteristics of a judge and a lawyer; from his father, the temperament of a rebel. He early proves a disappointment to his harshly critical father, an importer of East European specialty foods who fails to show any interest in Lyman's modest literary success, and he struggles to escape the old man's disapproval. At nineteen, he meets and marries Theodora, a clergyman's daughter with strong moral convictions and an optimistic view of small-town American life. With Theo, Lyman abandons his literary ambitions, takes a job with an insurance company, and becomes a considerable financial success and respectable member of the community.

In his mid-forties, however, two crises occur; his father dies leaving him with a heightened awareness of his own mortality, and he meets a twenty-one year-old Jewish insurance executive by the name of Leah with whom he falls passionately in love. Buying out her company, he sets up an office outside New York to cover his absences from his home in that city, and begins an affair which ultimately leads to Leah becoming pregnant. Against her better judgement, Leah agrees to keep the child when Lyman promises to marry her. In spite of his bravado, however, Lyman finds that he is unable to confront his wife, so by the time the baby is born, Leah has become reconciled to raising it on her own. About this time, Lyman takes his wife and married daughter, Bessie, on a trip to Africa where, on a safari, he confronts an approaching lion, risking death and facing down his own feelings of cowardice and guilt. He also learns from Tom, the family lawyer, that bigamy, 'a victimless crime', is seldom prosecuted in the United States. Sometime after his return from Africa, therefore, Lyman takes Leah to Reno where he pretends to obtain a divorce and goes through two (bogus) marriage ceremonies, one civic and one Jewish. In his new pseudo-bigamous condition, Lyman takes on a second personality. For nine years, during which time his son, Benjamin, grows to idolize him, he lives a double life, never able to be completely honest with anyone. The arrangement falls apart when Lyman sets out one night in a sleet storm and crashes his car on a ride down Mount Morgan. When he is hospitalized, both families are notified and Lyman's lies are finally exposed.

The story has obvious dramatic possibilities but Miller was to spend a long time trying to discover what obsessed him about it so that he could find a solid central order of events.[3] As it turned out, that order of events proved elusive and it was not until 1991 (some ten years after he had begun it) that the play was finally ready for production. By that time, *The Ride Down Mount Morgan* had developed into one of the most complex (and possibly most baffling) of Miller's later plays. Using techniques he had worked out in *Death of a Salesman* and *After the Fall*, he combined objective 'reality' with the subjective experiences of various individual characters. Whereas previously Miller had focused on the inner world of a single person, however, here he dramatizes the thoughts and recollections of four. He does this in a conventional plot of 'ripe circumstance' which begins very near the end and reveals the past through extensive exposition.

The action itself covers little more than twenty-four hours from Lyman's admission to hospital after his near-fatal accident to the departure of the two women he has deceived. Shortly after Theo learns of her husband's betrayal, she phones Tom, the family lawyer, who drives up from New York and acts as an intermediary between the various potential litigants. He tells Leah that her 'marriage' is invalid, comforts Theo, and tries in vain to get Lyman to acknowledge the wrong he has done the two women. One by one, Theo, Leah, and Bessie also challenge Lyman to explain, or accept responsibility for, his actions, but none of them is able to elicit much more than grudging admissions qualified by vigorous denials and protestations of innocence combined with counter-complaints of victimization. Convinced, finally, that Lyman is incapable of thinking of anyone but himself, the three women leave him to face the future alone.

This brief action in the present provides a framework for a series of memories, dreams, hallucinations and visions that fill in portions of the past and reveal glimpses of the fevered, and occasionally tormented, mind of the central character. A major problem of the play is the complexity and ambiguity of these departures from strict realism. To begin with, the 'flashbacks' are not the product of a single consciousness, but rather the dramatized recollections of four different minds, who (like the characters in the Japanese film *Rashomon*), disagree in their interpretations of events. While these contradictory recollections illustrate the difficulty of reconstructing the past, the problem for the audience is that there is no 'objective' truth against which to test the reliability of any particular witness.

Even more puzzling is the nature of Lyman's imaginings. A distinction between sleep and reason is indicated by a change of lighting or by Lyman (as a spirit?) leaving his bandage-encased body on the hospital bed to participate in other people's memories, or to utter his own secret thoughts. These visions and dreams, experienced as Lyman drifts in and out of consciousness, are awkwardly incorporated into the play as a whole. The scene in which the two women first meet is the physical representation of Lyman's imagination, but it ends without any transition back to 'reality'. Even more jarring are the dramatized fears and fantasies of the central character. One of these is the ghost-like figure of Lyman's father whose relentless criticisms presumably explain the son's insecurities and whose ominous presence symbolizes Lyman's fear of death. Equally bizarre are the grotesque images of Lyman's relations with his wives, sometimes appearing as mutually satisfactory and at others as dangerously destructive. Although these surrealistic episodes represent the repressed anxieties of Lyman's unconscious, they clash in style with the rest of the play.

The density of the work's texture, far from contributing to a richer and more meaningful theatrical experience, presents an obstacle to an audience's easy understanding and demands a careful and prolonged reading. This difficulty of interpretation is compounded by the distracting nature of the material Miller has used for his story, material drawn from his own experiences of marital discord in the mid 1950s. The character of Theodora shares with Mary Slattery a sharp intelligence, interest in literature, radical ideas, and a rather prim propriety. Lyman's dilemma is strikingly similar to Miller's own problems during his affair with Marilyn Monroe while he was still a married man. His increasingly risky encounters with Monroe in New York during the summer of 1955, his evasive encounters with the press, his decision to wed Monroe (rather than simply keep her as his mistress as Elia Kazan did), his Reno divorce, his encounter with the 'lion' of the HUAC, his double wedding (one civil and one Jewish), the resentment of his daughter, Jane, after the divorce, and her subsequent marriage to an artist, as well as his own sense of liberation with his new wife, all find a place in the story of Lyman Felt.

But it would be wrong to consider the play nothing but autobiography, or to look for insights into the characters of Monroe or Mary Slattery in the personae of Leah and Theo. One of the themes of the play is the impossibility of knowing another person. As usual, Miller has used details from his life to explore a broad moral issue – in this case the relationship between one's responsibility to one's self and the responsibility one owes to others, a theme this play shares with *All My Sons.* Whereas Joe Keller's conscience is awakened to greater self-knowledge, however, Lyman's remains untouched. When Tom suggests that the ride down Mount Morgan was an unconscious attempt to commit suicide brought on by a sense of shame, Lyman explicitly denies it, saying that it was made in an effort to revive his passion for Leah. Lyman seems the quintessential sensualist for whom a woman's warmth is the last (and only?) sacredness. Indeed Lyman's dirty mind sets him apart from most of Miller's earlier characters, and is even remarked on by the nurse. As a dramatic creation, Lyman seems less a believable person than an epitome of the conscienceless psychopath. Incapable of feeling love, he is condemned to imitate it, all the while inhabiting what he calls his own dark cave 'searching for another ... hoping to touch and afraid; and hoping and afraid'.[4] The life of this salesman combines the lovable charm of Willy with the ruthlessness of his brother Ben. The women likewise are less real people than foils for the central character. For in common with many of Miller's works, this play presents reality from a predominantly male perspective. While we are given considerable insight into Lyman's psyche, the women remain opaque. Their pleas for explanations, apologies, or understanding are met only by belligerent self-justification. Any irony intended in Lyman's vigorous defence (by character or author) is difficult to detect.

Partly because of his despair with Broadway, and partly because of the interest of two British producers, Miller agreed to open *The Ride Down Mount Morgan* in London. The play premiered on 11 October 1991 to uncomprehending reviews. Miller was unhappy with the London production, which he thought was miscast, but there was no opportunity to return to the play until several years later when it was finally produced in the United States at the Williamstown (Massachusetts) Theatre Festival in 1997. This revival led Miller to produce a revised and tightened version of the play which was staged at the Joseph Papp Public Theatre in 1998 and two years later on Broadway where it ran for 120 performances. The New York Production brought out more humour in the work than was evident in London, prompting a description of the play as a 'seriously discomfiting comedy'. Like the English critics, however, the New York reviewer felt that Miller has made Lyman's case stronger than that of his wives. This inherent lack of balance was exaggerated in New York by Patrick Stewart's charm in the central role which made Lyman's stunning amorality nearly reasonable.[5]

Miller has given many explanations of the themes of the play and a few reasons for his obsession with them. Perhaps the most revealing, however, is one that hints at the necessary ruthlessness of the creative artist, a subject he had touched on in *The Price* and *The Archbishop's Ceiling*. He explained that Lyman 'is intent on not suppressing his instinctual life, on living fully in every way possible ... He will confront the worst about himself and then proceed from there ... He manages to convince himself, and I believe some part of the audience, that there is a higher value than other people and that value is the psychic survival of the individual.'[6]

20
The Last Yankee (1991–93)

In June 1991, the Marathon One-Act Play Festival, an annual presentation of the small Ensemble Studio Theatre in New York, featured a new play by Arthur Miller entitled *The Last Yankee.* It was a twenty-minute piece about two men who meet in the waiting room of a large state mental institution where they have come to visit their wives. Apparent strangers, John Frick and Leroy Hamilton attempt to size up one another through a series of conversational probes and the exchange of guarded confidences. Frick turns out to be a wealthy capitalist with interests in several businesses. He earns a substantial income and has provided a good home for himself and his wife who nevertheless has recently succumbed to irrational and disabling fears. Leroy is a struggling carpenter with seven children who has been supporting his wife through periodic attacks of depression for twenty years. About the only thing the men share is mystification over the cause of their wife's mental illness.

Misled by the tweed jacket and slacks, Frick is surprised to learn that Leroy is a carpenter. When he discovers that it is Leroy who has built the new altar in a local church, Frick is impressed, but still cannot conceal his social condescension. Tension between the two is heightened when Frick recalls a newspaper report that Leroy is a direct descendent of Alexander Hamilton, one of the signatories of the American Constitution. Frick is astonished that Leroy is not only working in a relatively lowly occupation, but that he has made no effort to maintain contact with his distinguished relatives or to make use of their influence.

Finally Leroy can contain himself no longer and demands in exasperation, 'Am I supposed to be ashamed I'm a carpenter?' adding, 'Well what's it going to be, equality or what kind of country?' When Frick expresses bewilderment at this outburst, Leroy apologizes and blames it on the strain of worrying about his wife. But it is clear that he is referring to the paradox that, while the Declaration of Independence asserts that all men are created equal, the competitive nature of American life ensures that success is unequally distributed and that it is the financially successful who are respected. The scene ends in mutual incomprehension.

This short version of *The Last Yankee* bears certain resemblances to Miller's other one-act plays. It is a seemingly realistic 'slice of life' conversation with no more apparent meaning than a photograph. Yet it is richly suggestive of the contradictions in American society and of the hopes and disappointments that have tormented Americans at all social levels.

A longer two-act version of the play, which opened at the Manhattan Theatre Club in New York on 21 January 1993, and five days later in London at the Young Vic, explores those themes more fully. An added second scene introduces the wives the two men have come to visit. Karen Frick, in her sixties, has only recently been committed for an illness which has long gone undetected. Unconcerned by financial worries, she has nevertheless had to bear the weight of her husband's continuing disapproval. This has recently been added to by the death of her mother who died leaving the family farm to a cousin. The combination of the depression brought on by these double disappointments, together with the effect of the pills prescribed to cure it, have left Karen in a deeply confused state.

By contrast, Patricia Hamilton seems almost normal. She has stopped taking her medication and has resolved to try to return home. Still attractive at forty-four, Patricia had been a beauty queen in her youth and shared with her brothers a feeling of natural superiority and entitlement. Disappointed of these unrealistic expectations, both of her brothers committed suicide and Patricia has lived since with barely contained bitterness. During the past twenty years she has sought relief in medication, prayer, and resentment of her husband's failure to provide her with the trappings of material success which she feels are her due. From her Swedish father, in addition to her sense of superiority, she has inherited a residual antipathy towards the Yankees who mistreated Swedish immigrants to the area in the nineteenth century. From her mother, she derived a sort of innocent sensuality, and it was her death two years before that led to the worsening of Patricia's mental condition and her hospitalization. Because the family cannot afford a private room, she shares her bedroom with another patient who seems to be in a catatonic state, neither moving nor speaking during the course of the play.

When Leroy enters, he is delighted to see a marked improvement in his wife's appearance and mental condition. His pleasure is soon dampened, however, as the old feelings of resentment and suspicion that have poisoned their relationship in the past soon resurface. In a variety of ways Patricia shows her disappointment in Leroy's failure to assert himself, and her conviction that he has not had the life that he might have.

On his part, Leroy tries to make his wife understand that he is content with his lot, and that she must learn to accept life as it comes. When Karen returns from the waiting room with her husband, she surprises Leroy with her account of how positive and encouraging Patricia has been to her. Partly at Patricia's urging, she agrees to demonstrate her tap dancing in the costume her husband has brought to the hospital. She dances, hesitantly at first, but then, prompted by Patricia's encouragement, with more and more passion. She is brought to a sudden stop, however, by an outburst of combined embarrassment and anger from her husband, and the dance ends amid general discomfort. When Frick leaves, Patricia and Leroy try to encourage Karen to continue, but after a few steps she stops and leaves the room.

Seeing how Frick's disapproval has destroyed his wife's spirit, Patricia finally realizes the effect she has been having on her husband, and is newly grateful for his patience and loyalty. She also begins to accept what he has been telling her – that she must learn to love the world even though it is not as she might want it to be, and that blaming her husband will not make things wonderful. The two prepare to leave the hospital, with Patricia temporarily reconciled to her straitened circumstances and looking forward with new hope.

The critical reviews were respectful but somewhat tentative. There was general admiration for Miller's style (likened to a late Matisse sketch)[1] and characterization 'drawn with economical strokes'.[2] But this is an art that, in concealing art, obscures meaning and several reviewers neatly avoided any explication of the text. The *New York Times* called it a 'glancing play' in which the 'motives were never satisfactorily explained'. We were assured that Miller was interested in these lost souls 'exclusively for their symbolic value' without being told what that value was.[3] It was a woman, however, who noticed what a rarity this work was – a Miller play that treated love romantically, that honoured marriage, glorified steadfastness, and asserted that 'the values on which this country was founded deserve to be cherished'.[4]

Miller attempted to clarify his intentions in an introductory essay in the second edition of the play published in 1994.[5] There he explained that his aim was to explore the 'sickness of the soul' which had manifested itself in the widespread incidence of depression in the western world. The root cause of such depression, he maintained, was what he called 'the success mythology ... the endless advertising-encouraged self-comparisons with others who are more or less successful'. The cure of such depression, he felt, was insight and conversion to some more healthy mythology. In Patricia Hamilton's case, the agent of recovery is her husband, with his 'incredibly enduring love for her, for nature, and for the world'.[6]

On one level, therefore, *The Last Yankee* is a love story, but below the surface realism the action is 'overtly stylized'. The inert patient in the next bed represents those unable to resist their illness; Patricia's Swedish ancestry is perhaps an indication that the immigrant is particularly susceptible to the lure of success; Karen's dancing is a symbol of the natural sensuality that has been repressed in a materialistic society; Leroy's stubborn independence is a disappearing healthy alternative to destructive competition. The danger of such a split vision embracing both psychological realism and what Miller calls 'thematic selectivity' is that it occasionally leads to contradictions. Depression may sometimes result from disappointment or failure, but it is also a disease with a recognized pharmacology. Not all sufferers are able to dispense with their medication by a simple act of will. Furthermore, Patricia's release from chemical dependence comes, not from a recognition of the ills of consumerism, but because she stops blaming her husband. Only later does she come to realize that his steadfastness, self-reliance and willingness to take life on its own terms are the values she must learn to embrace if she is to be cured of her disease.

But she learns a second lesson from her observation of Frick. She recognizes in his treatment of his wife a mirror of her own frequently expressed disappointment in her husband, and comes to understand what he has had to endure. This is a second insight on her way to a cure. Leroy Hamilton is the 'last Yankee' in two senses then. He is representative of those New England values which contributed so importantly to the idealism of the Founding Fathers. But he is also the last Yankee whom Patricia, as a Swedish immigrant, will blame for historical injustices.

Like Miller's other short plays, *The Last Yankee* is written in a spare, almost cryptic style. The dialogue is life-like in that it replicates the incomplete sentences, meandering thoughts, and veiled implications of real conversation. It is a style which one critic described as a refinement of Miller's 'best artistic tendencies'.[7] It is literary in its demands on the auditor and its deceptive simplicity. It constitutes a kind of distillation of Miller's ideas that go back to *Death of a Salesman*. But whereas in his youth, Miller looked for some kind of social revolution, in his later years he seems to have settled for personal (or perhaps joint) salvation.

21
Broken Glass (1994)

Broken Glass tells the story of the Gellburgs, an unhappily married Jewish couple living in Brooklyn during the 1920s and 30s. They had met during the First World War when Phillip, just out of accounting school and only 22, had got his first job. Sylvia, two years younger, was already a head bookkeeper. Shortly after their marriage, Sylvia gives birth to their son, Jerome, but when she says that she would like to return to work and decides she doesn't want any more children, relations between the two begin to fray. Feeling that his authority and ability as a provider are being challenged, Phillip insists that Sylvia stay home with the baby. Obedient but resentful, Sylvia lets her dissatisfaction be known, thus increasing the tension between them to the point where Phillip becomes impotent.

As his marriage disintegrates, however, Phillip's career flourishes. Working steadily through the Depression, he rises to be manager of the Mortgage Department in his company, and evinces growing satisfaction with his position as the only Jew in the company and a personal friend of the President. Phillip's determination to succeed in the WASP world of business is accompanied by other strategies to repudiate his Jewish roots. In an effort to escape the Brooklyn stereotype, he sends his son to West Point where he achieves the rank of Captain. Sylvia is puzzled and even frightened by her husband's rejection of his heritage which she senses is also a rejection of her. When she begins reading about the Nazi atrocities in Germany she develops an almost pathological identification with the victims, and shortly after succumbs to a mysterious paralysis which confines her to a wheelchair. The couple turn for help to a friend of Sylvia's family, Dr Harry Hyman.

When it becomes evident there is no physical cause of the paralysis, Dr Hyman (an amateur Freudian) immediately suspects that the ailment has a sexual basis. By a combination of charm and compassion he gradually worms out details of their marriage. He learns of Phillip's impotence, and of the fact that Sylvia had embarrassed and infuriated him by revealing his infirmity to her father who passed the information along to the rabbi. Over a few days, Hyman comes to what he considers to be the root of the problem. In his view, Sylvia's resentment at being forced to remain at home has been combined with a growing sense of insecurity caused by her husband's fear and suspicions of others. Phillip's own self-loathing and attempts to deny his Jewish identity have led her to associate him with other anti-Semites. This anxiety develops into an irrational fear and finally hysterical paralysis.

For his part, Phillip has felt effectively castrated by his wife's resentment and lack of forgiveness so that the couple have not had sexual relations for twenty years. Unable to discuss the matter, they share a guarded relationship in which Phillip, as a result of his own feelings of inadequacy, alternately worships and abuses his wife. When he loses the confidence of his employer, and feels unjustly suspected of aiding a competitor, he suffers a heart attack and is bedridden. Able at last to speak openly of their feelings, each admits contributing to the failure of the relationship. Sylvia recognizes that she had chosen to remain in the marriage and was therefore responsible for her own unhappiness. Phillip realizes that his own fears had been communicated to his wife and been one of the causes of her paralysis. He asks for her forgiveness and his emotional turmoil leads to a second heart attack which renders him unconscious. In her concern for her husband, Sylvia struggles out of her wheelchair to go to him and finds that she can stand. The curtain falls before it is clear whether Phillip is alive or dead.

The play is a kind of psychological detective story - an investigation into the causes of Sylvia's collapse and the marital breakdown. The trail leads to the couple's response to anti-Semitism. Each tries to deal with minority anxiety in a different way. Phillip would like to settle his Jewish identity once and for all and sees two paths open to him. He could accept his difference, go to *shul* with the old men and become a full-time Jew; or he could overcome his sense of difference and inferiority by trying to disappear into the gentile community. He chooses the latter with disastrous results. Sylvia had not considered her religion a problem until her marriage to Phillip with his obsessive preoccupation with the subject. When she does develop a sense of her Jewishness, however, it is as a potential victim. Instead of establishing her own identity (perhaps through work), she becomes increasingly fearful until, with the news of the Nazi persecution in Germany, she comes to believe irrationally that all the Jews everywhere will be exterminated. In spite of the sexual ramifications, the root of the Gellburgs' problem seems to be their failure to deal with the question of their Jewish identity. It is Phillip who feels the problem most acutely. 'Why is it so hard to be a Jew', he asks. 'Why must we be different? Why is it? What is it for?' Hyman's answer is that Jews are no different from other people, that everybody is persecuted by someone, and that Jews and gentiles alike must take responsibility for their own lives and forgive others rather than blaming them.

Broken Glass is an interesting example of how Miller's thematic and technical preoccupations become modified in his late plays. Characteristically the work is an optimistic tragedy in which the death of a deluded protagonist provides illumination for surviving characters and for the audience. It is an exploration of hidden forces, both external and internal, that affect the principal characters in their search for self-fulfilment. But it is somewhat more narrowly focused than earlier plays, and considerably more explicit in its analysis of Miller's perennial obsessions – politics and sex. On one level it is the last, and most mordant, of a long line of marriage plays. These begin in the mid-forties with the loving relationship between David and Hester Beeves in *The Man Who Had All the Luck* and continue through the increasingly bitter marital experiences of the Kellers, Lomans, Proctors and Carbones until the final catastrophe of Quentin and Maggie in *After the Fall*. Surprisingly, the post-Marilyn marriage plays are scarcely more harmonious although the causes of dissension are more varied. These range from differing material expectations (*Price, Clock, Last Yankee*) to outright deception and betrayal (*Ride Down Mount Morgan*). Furthermore, while the earlier unhappy unions invariably end in suicide (in one form or another), the later partnerships tend to limp along with the disappointed spouses learning to accept or transcend their discontent.

In *Broken Glass* the situation of the Gellburgs is quite different. To begin with, their marriage is more calamitous than the others in that both partners are seriously damaged. Their illnesses, however, are only indirectly a product of their relationship – Sylvia's paralysis being an hysterical reaction to her fear, and Phillip's heart attack a consequence of his anxiety about his job. Furthermore, the ending is ambiguous since we don't know if Phillip is dead. David Thacker, who directed the play in England, was convinced that Sylvia could only stand *because* her husband had died.[1] But such an interpretation puts an excessive weight on the sexual nature of her illness and discounts the importance of the sympathy and forgiveness she feels in the final scene. Phillip's death (if it is a death) also breaks the pattern in that he is much more a victim than a prompter of fate.

It is in its exploration of the social and psychological forces at work in the marriage, however, that the play is most surprising. While Miller had long been concerned with Jewish identity, he had for some time avoided dealing with it directly in his plays. Consequently families such as the Kellers or the Lomans, although exhibiting many Jewish characteristics, are ethnically neutral. The novel *Focus* confronts the problem head on, but from the point of view of the Gentile rather than the Jew. Even *Incident at Vichy* tends to show Jews as types or as broadly representative of certain characteristics rather than as individuals. Only in the 1990s with *Plain Girl* and *Broken Glass* does Miller examine what it feels like to be a Jew from the inside. Phillip's denial of his true nature and calamitous pursuit of the wrong dream is a familiar Miller narrative. But, interestingly, this play appears to be a repudiation of his earlier Marxist internationalism. By showing the folly of Phillip's attempt to assimilate into gentile society, the playwright seems to be acknowledging the limits of universal love, and approving a separate tribalism within the larger human community.

But the torment brought on by living in a world of anti-Jewish prejudice is only part of the Gellburgs' difficulty. Like so many of Miller's characters, they also have problems with sex. And as usual, the relationship between the sex and the politics is not clear. Certainly the analysis of sexual dysfunction in this play is much more probing and clinical than in any of Miller's other works. It is also more explicitly Freudian. The aptly named Dr Hyman (Hymen the god of marriage), protests that he is only an amateur psychoanalyst and, indeed, his efforts seem both blunt and highly unprofessional. Nevertheless, the pattern of hysteria, repression, impotence and sexual fantasy the doctor uncovers is presented as a serious representation of the couple's problems. Sylvia's halting steps at the end of *Broken Glass* suggest that she has overcome her sexually-induced hysterical paralysis and with it her irrational fears. But the prognosis is not altogether hopeful. The dream of a wholly innocent, guilt-free sexuality seems as remote and inaccessible as the vision of a society of universal love. If Phillip survives, however, they may be able to rebuild their lives on a better understanding of themselves and others.

22
Mr Peters' Connections (1998)

At a dinner party at Sardi's following a PEN celebration of his birthday in October 1995, Miller was approached by a gossip columnist from the *New York Daily News*. After a few routine questions, the reporter asked, 'Do you ever dream about Marilyn Monroe? What kind of dreams are they?' Rising in a fury, the eighty-year old playwright pursued the younger man, knocking him into the buffet table, and thereby attracting the attention of a reporter from the *New York Post* and a headline in the next day's edition of that tabloid.[1] Whether or not that incident was the catalyst, by the end of the year Miller had written some sixty-five pages of a play that deals at length with dreaming about Marilyn Monroe.

Mr Peters' Connections is the playwright's most experimental work to that date, incorporating elements from Beckett and perhaps Pinter, but essentially elaborating his own form of psychodrama, a form he had been developing since *Death of a Salesman*. Carrying the subjectivity of *Ride Down Mount Morgan* still further, he creates a kind of stream of semi-consciousness, presenting the memories, regrets, dreams, and occasionally the real experiences of an elderly man nearing death. Miller described it as 'a play in which the narrative is simply the fluctuating moods and emotions of this old guy who has a nap in the afternoon'.[2] The action takes place on the threshold of the protagonist's mind, that region between waking and sleeping from which the restless sleeper can look backward into daylight or forward into the 'misty depths' of memories and conjectures.[3] The purpose of this reverie (if it can be said to be purposeful) is to try to make some sense of a life that has come to seem meaningless - to discover the connections or unifying subject that will give coherence to his disparate experiences.

The result is a text closer to music than traditional drama. Speech, sound effects, setting and action are combined according to the laws of free association rather than logic to produce the kind of psychic portrait that might emerge from a session of psychoanalysis. On the 'realistic' level, the play takes place in an abandoned night club in New York City where the elderly Mr Harry Peters has come after purchasing a pair of shoes, to rest and wait for his wife who apparently wants to look over the property with a view to buying it. While waiting, Peters meets a young couple who have come to the night club to allow the young woman to rest. When Peters' wife, Charlotte, finally arrives, she expresses enthusiastic interest in the club, and begins to calculate the costs of purchasing and redecorating it.

In Mr Peters' imagination, however, these material surroundings and living people have no more reality than the ghosts of his imagination. So his thoughts move back and forth from past to present as he connects his dead brother, Calvin, and lover, Cathy-May, with his living wife, Charlotte, and his daughter, Rose, and her friend, Leonard. He also introduces into his day-dream wholly imaginary persons such as Adele, a black bag lady who acts as observer and commentator, and Larry, the conjectural later husband of Cathy-May.

The dramatic representation of this reverie is a kind of verbal theme and variations on the subject of love. The atmosphere (or key) of the composition is established by the setting – an abandoned night club with a piano, some chairs and an old cabaret stand. Off stage (never seen but frequently mentioned) is the ladies' powder room. The environment is extremely ambiguous. The foreground is redolent of departed glamour, drunken confessions and the sentimental nostalgia induced by piano renditions of popular American show tunes. The powder room, off-limits to men, a refuge for ladies, speaks of the eternal mystery of Woman. For Mr Peters, it is a source of anxiety; talking about it is obscene, a reminder of the lust he can no longer satisfy and a reminder of his failure to act his age. In this evocative setting, the protagonist explores the full range of love from the explosive power of sexual passion to the tranquility of parental affection.

The dominant and recurring motif in this confessional narrative is Peters' dead lover, Cathy-May, who appears on four separate occasions. His first memory of her comes unexpectedly, stirring old passions and awakening forgotten happiness. He participates in a rather formal dance with her before she disappears and Peters' mood sours. His second recollection is of his trying to teach Cathy-May to walk by his side. When he fails, he becomes angry, jumps up and down, and finally gets Calvin to applaud her. But to no avail. 'She loves me but she's forgotten', he says, but admits that two people cannot occupy the same space. A third dream is sparked by the recollection of her death. Peters wonders whether, if she had lived, their love could have matured into a less tempestuous relationship. He imagines them dancing to the music of a big band. The tune is *Just One of Those Things* about a love 'too hot not to cool down'. But the vision fades as Cathy-May disappears into darkness. The final memory is the most elegiac. Peters first envisions a sort of spiritual reunion in which the two breathe in total synchronization and Cathy-May assures him, 'You were loved, Harry!' This union is shattered by the appearance of Cathy-May's husband, Larry, who abuses and humiliates her until she becomes inert. Peters is distraught at the idea of her dying alone, and as she seems to expire, he kisses his finger and touches it to her lips.

It is impossible not to see in these scenes allusions to Miller's life with Marilyn Monroe – from his dancing with her at a Hollywood party in 1951, to his futile efforts to help her in the days when her career made it impossible for him to pursue his own, to his horror and outrage at how she was treated by Hollywood and the media (and possibly by her husband, Joe DiMaggio), to his pity for her lonely death and regret that they could not have made a life together.

In a kind of counterpoint to the story of Peters' reminiscences of his dead lover are a number of other relationships. The most puzzling is that with his wife, Charlotte. Afraid that she might have got lost on her way to the night club, Peters asks Leonard to look out for her but discovers that he has forgotten her name. 'We are sick of each other', he says. 'Her imagination is destroying me. We're happy.' When Charlotte does arrive, it turns out that she is temperamentally very different from her husband. While he suffers from melancholia, she has been happy since she was a baby and has never changed. She is energetic, hopeful, enthusiastic and imaginative. She is also slightly contemptuous of Peters' philosophy. Where she is full of longings and plans for the improvement of her environment, her husband loses himself in Utopian dreams which he cannot reconcile with his own experience. Peters is more comfortable with Calvin who seems at first to be the proprietor of the night club. Of roughly the same age, the two men share many memories of growing up in the 1920s, and Calvin explains the history of the club which had originally been a bank, then a library, and finally a cafeteria before it became a night club. Later (inexplicably) it turns out that Calvin is Peters' brother and many years dead. Peters is less at ease with the young people who arrive at the night club. Not only do Rose and Leonard not share his memories, but their mode of thought seems alien to him. He feels that they are incapable of carrying out a logically coherent argument, refusing (or being unable) to discriminate between what is and is not relevant. He finds their endless digressions mentally exhausting, and deplores their indecisiveness.

What is revealed by this kaleidoscope of experiences and opinions is a personality very different from the kind of protagonist we have come to associate with Miller's plays. Harry Peters has led a comparatively disengaged life. After the heroic certainties of the War, he has failed to find a sense of purpose in civilian life. As an airline pilot, he has observed the world from the sidelines, deploring the decline in dignity and morals that characterized the second half of twentieth-century America, but he has contributed little to its improvement. When we meet him he has lost whatever energy and interests he once had, and feels more at home with the dead than the living. He mourns his lost convictions but, while not described, these do not appear to have been political or social creeds. Instead his 'philosophy' is a kind of futile utopianism. He dreams of escaping from his wife and cluttered domesticity into a perfect room where nothing is painful to him or out of place. Or he imagines that the human race has descended from the avaricious outcasts of some distant Edenic planet. Despairing that nothing he believed has turned out to be true, he nevertheless still believes in God while admitting that He is never there when you need Him.

Harry Peters, therefore, is a surprisingly ineffectual individual whose quest is the reverse of heroic. Indeed his journey to the underworld in search of his Eurydice is an attempt to join her, not to bring her back with him. When he understands the danger of looking backward, and is forced to return empty-handed, he faces a choice between suicide and a meaningless life. He is saved for life by two women. Adele, the black bag lady acting as a kind of chorus, explains the secret of her stoicism. 'I am a brokenhearted person,' she says, but 'at the same time I am often full of hope.' And periodically, for no apparent reason, her sorrow leaves her so that she lives in hope of those temporary respites. Grasping for a cogent reason for such hope, Peters searches for something to give his life meaning and enable him to face life. As he begins to fall asleep, all the figures but his daughter fade from his consciousness. Rose begs her father to 'stay' and tells him she loves him. She puts her head on his knee and hums a lullaby, serenading both her father and her unborn child. Peters seems at last to find the 'connections' he has been seeking in his love for his daughter and for the ongoing flow of life.

There is no doubt that the play presents real difficulties for a theatre audience, and it is not surprising that many of them have found the style murky and the ideas opaque. The text is somewhat more accessible to a reader than to a spectator and is very much in the modernist tradition of James Joyce and Samuel Beckett, something of a novelty for Miller and surprising to his fans. Nevertheless, it represents the playwright's ongoing determination to find the proper form for his artistic vision (and perhaps a slight contempt for the audience). If this is an experiment in absurdist aesthetics, however, it is by no means an endorsement of its nihilism. For, in the teeth of fashion, Miller subscribes to a kind of hopeful existentialism founded on his irrepressible optimism and astonishment at the wonder of life.

23
Resurrection Blues (2002)

For a Jewish agnostic, Arthur Miller has long shown a surprising interest in theology. In *The Creation of the World and Other Business* he explored man's fall and attendant alienation from God as depicted in the Old Testament. For his first play of the new millennium he turned his attention to the Christian New Testament and the story of the crucifixion with its promise of reconciliation and forgiveness. *Resurrection Blues*, for all its affinities with earlier works, was startlingly novel in its mixture of scriptural allusions, scathing political satire, philosophical speculation and almost scatological humour. Critics and audiences found it hilarious, shocking and confusing in about equal measure.

The story is set in an unnamed 'far away' country which has been enduring a thirty-eight year, narcotic-fueled civil war similar to the one in Colombia where Miller had travelled. Some years before the story begins, the rebels had been inspired by a mysterious, rarely-seen leader not unlike the Commandante Marcos who led the revolt in the Mexican region of Chiapas. What sets the imaginary country apart, however, and places it firmly in the realm of fantasy, is its continued use of crucifixion as a method of execution. The central situation of the story is the capture and threatened execution of a rebel leader widely believed by his followers to be the son of God.

In this mythic context, the story deals with the history of a single family that can trace its ancestry back to the conquistadores under Cortes. The dual drives of the original invaders - conquest and religion - have become separated in succeeding generations into ruthless militarism and intellectual inquiry. Two cousins in this family, Felix and Henri, embody this division. After a relatively innocent childhood, Felix joins the army and rises to become the military dictator of the country. His cousin, Henri, becomes a successful businessman, owning several pharmaceutical companies and raising fighting bulls on his estate. He marries, but spends little time with his family and neglects his business interests, losing himself in a search for truth. When he discovers Marxism, he decides he must resist the policies of the regime, and joins the rebels to fight the military dictatorship of his cousin, Felix. Inspired by his example, his daughter, Jeanine, follows him to the mountains. There, however, Henri quickly grows disillusioned with the struggle and leaves to continue his studies, finally becoming a professor of philosophy in Munich. Jeanine, meanwhile, leads a small brigade of teenaged freedom fighters who are captured and shot. Because of her relationship to Felix, Jeanine is spared, returns to civilian life and marries. Haunted by guilt, however, she takes to drugs, becomes an addict, loses her husband, and finally attempts suicide by jumping out of a third story window. Miraculously, she survives and, thanks to the love and encouragement of a new friend, she feels that she has died and come back to life.

The action of the play begins with Henri returning home to attend to his convalescing daughter, recognizing the harm he has done her, and resolving to nurse her back to health. In the process he begins to understand that he has been blind to those closest to him - his daughter and his wife - and that he has lived without love. Meanwhile, it turns out that Jeanine's new friend is the mysterious rebel leader, and that he has been captured by Felix's security forces and now faces execution. Henri tries to persuade Felix to abandon his grotesque plans, and meets a series of obstacles. To begin with, a New York advertising agency has agreed to pay $75 million for the exclusive rights to televise the crucifixion. When Henri tries to convince the American TV crew of the impropriety of their project, he is met by incomprehension. As a second strategy, he asks Emily, the young director who has attracted the attention of the dictator, to use her wiles to change Felix's mind. Finally, in a private meeting with the film company's account executive, Henri argues that the mysterious 'Messiah' is probably an illusion and, when that fails, appeals unsuccessfully to the man's conscience.

A resolution to these problems appears within reach when Felix returns from his rendezvous with Emily, apparently willing to bring the rebel leader into his government and to establish a democratic society. Hope is quickly dashed, however, as the various parties begin quarreling, and a disciple of the 'Messiah' arrives to report that his leader is starting to think that he has a duty to sacrifice himself for the common good. When it becomes apparent that a crucifixion would likely provoke envy among different villages all vying for the Right to host the event and take the attendant profits, there is general agreement that the 'Messiah' must be persuaded to leave. As Jeanine observes, they do not yet have the 'greatness to deserve his death'.

The world premiere of *Resurrection Blues* took place in Minneapolis at the Guthrie Theatre on 3 August 2002. It was greeted with a kind of respectful bewilderment. Bruce Weber of the *New York Times* called it a 'disappointingly unpersuasive work', and (rather surprisingly for a metropolitan critic) objected to 'the general's persistent sex jokes' which he found 'juvenile and truly beneath a playwright of Mr. Miller's stature'.[1] The play was subsequently produced at the Old Globe Theatre in San Diego in 2004, and two years later at the Old Vic in London where it fared little better. Critics acknowledged Miller's seemingly new-found talent in comedy and trenchant political satire, but the feeling remained that America's greatest living playwright has added little lustre to his reputation with this peculiar work.

A major obstacle to easy comprehension of the play is the puzzling juxtaposition of scenes of low, even crude comedy with political satire and serious philosophical speculation. It is a form of drama closer, perhaps, to the Old Comedy of Aristophanes than to anything more recent in the history of Western theatre. To the Greeks, collocations of satirical attacks on contemporary politicians, fantastical situations, encounters between mortals and gods, and commentary on the foibles of Athens and its citizens were regular fare. Phallic humour, rather than being a source of distraction or embarrassment was a reminder of the origins of dramatic art in ancient fertility rites. In employing such a capacious and discordant comic form, Miller may have been trying to reconcile the apparent contradictions of Apollo and Dionysus, head and heart, philosophy and sex. Or he may (as he suggested to Michael Billington), simply have wanted the audience to experience the frustration of looking for meaning and not finding it.[2] Any attempt at analysis, therefore, runs the serious risk of falling into a skilfully prepared trap.

The play is about resurrection to the extent that it deals with the revival of suppressed or transmuted feelings. Felix has had to repress his emotions in order to rule and it has led to his sexual impotence. In trying to kill her feelings of guilt and disappointment with drugs, Jeanine has found only isolation and despair. Henri has escaped from reality into ideology and imagination, sacrificing his real emotions for the pseudo feelings of politics and art. All three are brought back to life through the agency, or the influence, of the supposed Messiah. But the work is a 'blues' because the 'rebirth' these characters experience is short-lived. The longed-for paradise they hope to share is beyond their capacity to build. Change can no longer be effected by heroes or by grand political gestures. Politics no longer exists, and it would seem that nothing remains in which to believe.

That this is not the final message of the play is suggested by the presentation of the multi-named 'Messiah'. Since the figure never appears to the audience except as a burst of light, he remains an enigma – something different for each character. For Jeanine and the peasants he represents hope and love; for Felix he is a threat to his authority; for Henri he is possibly nothing more than the product of over-active imaginations. The 'Messiah', of course, is not God, but the son of God, an intermediary through whom we communicate with the Divine, and, as such, himself fallible. He is also dangerous in that he seems helpless to prevent the violence perpetrated in his name. Would it not be better, therefore, as the disciple, Stanley, suggests that, instead of taking on the attributes of God, the 'Messiah' settled for being merely 'god-like ... in a more general, inspirational way', and left the actual improvements up to individual human beings? Having had something of a Messiah complex himself as a boy, Miller knew all too well the dangers of trying to interpret the Divine. *Resurrection Blues* implies that, if God is not dead, He is certainly incommunicado and we must learn to live 'in the garden of one's self'.[3]

24
Non-Theatrical Writing

Arthur Miller made his name as a playwright, and it is as a playwright that he will chiefly be remembered. But it was not his plays that first brought him attention; nor has he ever confined his interest to the stage. Indeed, not since George Bernard Shaw has a practicing playwright turned his hand to such a variety of literary, critical and journalistic enterprises. Initially these sorties into other genres were the attempts of a young writer to find his own voice. *Situation Normal* (1944) was a volume of reportage salvaged from research for an unrealized film project; *Focus* (1945), a novel written out of despair stemming from the failure of his first Broadway play. As his career prospered and his fame grew, however, Miller turned more deliberately to non-dramatic forms as a means of expanding and clarifying his ideas or as an alternative to writing plays. The series of short stories written between 1955–62 and collected under the title *I Don't Need You Any More* (1967) reflects the author's years with Marilyn Monroe when his involvement with her film career curtailed his own dramatic output. The travel books describing Russia and China are a product of his collaboration with his photographer wife, Inge Morath. In addition to these major publications, Miller has over the years engaged in an ongoing public *apologia* in speeches, interviews, articles in the New York newspapers, and in his sweeping autobiography, *Timebends* (1987). Then in his final years he returned to the short story form, publishing six poignant tales of loss and disappointed hope. If his plays remain his most deeply considered explorations of the human dilemma, Miller's non-theatrical writings provide the context in which those plays can best be understood.

(i) Reportage

Two assumptions underlie all of Miller's work – that man is a social being and that it is the writer's function to explore the implications of that fact. These beliefs are given their most explicit expression in several volumes of reportage, the first of which was his earliest publishing success. *Situation Normal* (1944) is an account of Miller's investigation of American training bases undertaken as background for the screenplay of *The Story of G.I. Joe.* The series of vivid sketches of officers and enlisted men, interspersed with reflections by the author, reveals less about the American fighting man, perhaps, than about the hopes of the young reporter. At the time Miller was anything but objective. Because he himself saw the war so clearly as a crusade against fascism in defence of democracy and the principle of equality, he wanted the American soldiers to see it in the same light. But he had to admit they did not. 'It is terrible to me that everything is so personal.... I can't seem to find men who betray a social responsibility as a reason for doing or not doing anything.'[1] Because of his own convictions, however, Miller could not accept the evidence of his senses. So he attributed to the men a kind of subconscious understanding of the war. 'I can't give up the idea that political and economic beliefs have something to do with how these men react ... I am beginning to think that perhaps those beliefs are there in a totally unsuspected guise.'[2] He also attributed to the fighting men an almost mystic solidarity. No man', he claimed with no personal experience, 'has ever felt identity with a group more deeply and intimately than a soldier in battle'.

A second deeply held conviction expressed in the book is his sense that, without a clear idea of why he had fought and what he had accomplished, the returning veteran would become a prey to the destructive tendencies in American life. Opposed to the ideal of community experienced in the foxholes is the evil of a civilian society of selfish competition in which each person tries to outdo his neighbours. Unless the returning soldier's attachment to his home is overwhelming, he is going to feel the loss of a social unit, a social goal worth his sacrifice. The only thing that could rejoin such a soldier with America is a belief in the rightness, the justness, the necessity of his fight. The writer must help by finding a meaning in the war, by showing something sane coming out of the horror. Merely to report what the soldier feels or does at a particular time is only part of the truth. It is the writer's responsibility to capture the 'idea' behind surface appearances and, by articulating it, help to instil the necessary understanding.[3]

After his success on Broadway in 1947 Miller abandoned journalism to concentrate on the dramatic representation of human experience, and it was more than twenty years before he returned to a reportorial study of society. Then, following his marriage to Inge Morath in 1962, Miller began to develop a broader international outlook. During the late 1960s he made two trips to Russia – the first to Moscow in 1965 where, as the newly-elected President of PEN, he tried (unsuccessfully) to persuade the

Soviet Writers' Union to join the Association of Poets, Essayists and Novelists, and a second in 1969 following the Soviet invasion of Czechoslovakia. The two visits made a profound impression on him, allowing him to judge at first hand the success of the world's first socialist state. On his return he incorporated his conclusions in a volume of photographs and commentary which he published with his wife under the title, *In Russia* (1969).

In the book he claims that his account of his experiences is 'bereft of political nationalism or cultural partisanship'.[4] But every encounter he describes is coloured by the dreams of his own youth, by what he calls 'the old illusion which the great October Revolution raised before the world – that a government of and by the insulted and injured had finally risen on the earth, a society which had somehow abolished the motivations for immorality, the incarnation at long last of the human community'.[5] Since his most recent visit to the country post-dated both the 20th Congress of the Communist Party at which the excesses of Stalinism had been exposed, and the crushing of the 'Prague Spring' of Communism with a human face, he could have been under no misapprehension as to the monstrous tyranny of Soviet rule during the previous fifty years. But he was deeply impressed by the people he met, especially the older writers who had suffered under Stalin but had nevertheless retained hope for their country. Miller found that he could identify with their suffering and even understand their reluctant faith. The source of this empathy is perhaps implicit in the simile he used to express their disillusion. It was, he says, 'a little like a man trying to explain how he fell in love with a perfect woman who turned out to be murderous, vain, even insane, and cared nothing for him, a woman to whom he had dedicated his works, his life, and his highest idealistic feelings'.[6] Miller well knew how impossible it is to part from a beloved without leaving something behind. He also sensed that the power of the Communist ideal was like that of a religious belief – seductive because it called for sacrifice to a worthier ideal than one's own selfish interests. In 1969 Miller was writing for an audience still hostile to the Soviet Union and reluctant to hear good news of the enemy. He seems to have been anxious to avoid the anti-Communist stereotypes and, like many of the writers he met, undoubtedly put the best possible face on what he saw. Nevertheless his comments now seem surprisingly optimistic about the possibilities of Communism and unduly sanguine about its past atrocities.

He got a second chance to observe the Communist system at first hand in 1978 when he and Inge travelled to China. There, although technically tourists, they were able to meet with a number of prominent

Chinese artists and intellectuals as well as several American expatriates and obtain a glimpse into a country in transition (a glimpse made considerably more vivid by Inge's ability to speak Chinese). Their arrival in China coincided with a new openness to the west after the introverted decade of the Cultural Revolution. The people they met were willing to discuss the past, but for the most part remained at a loss to explain their painful experiences. During the decade from 1965–75, Mao and/or the advisors around him had attempted to revive the revolutionary fervour of earlier years by applying Marxist egalitarian ideals with unprecedented rigour. The intention, widely supported throughout the country, was to eradicate the last vestiges of feudal inequality, but the effect had been catastrophic. What began as a reform movement degenerated into civil war and eventually into total anarchy in the course of which hundreds of thousands of individuals deemed to be 'elitist' were imprisoned, tortured, or sent to be reeducated through manual labour. The result was the silencing or immobilization of the entire intellectual and artistic classes. Since few were willing to believe that Mao himself had intended so effectively to destroy the educated infrastructure of the state, the excesses of the period were blamed on Mao's wife, Jiang Qing, and her three associates known collectively as 'the Gang of Four'.

Miller's account of the anguish caused by these events is a moving picture of the unsettling effects of a shattering loss of belief. For none of the individuals he interviewed, not the Chinese artists who had suffered humiliation and loss, not the American and British expatriates who had watched from the sidelines, could bring themselves to condemn the Cultural Revolution altogether. Compared with the incalculable benefit of the Liberation in destroying Chinese feudalism, recent excesses seemed to them like minor abuses. Feelings toward the Party, however, were profoundly ambivalent. While regretting the lack of safeguards against the abuse of power, few of the individuals Miller spoke to would agree with him about the importance of an independent press and judiciary. Nor was there much enthusiasm, or even interest, in civil rights. Miller took this to be a consequence of the Chinese (and Russian) Revolutions preaching the pre-eminence of the State whereas the American Revolution had promoted the rights of the individual. Miller's American prejudices and inherent optimism are amply reflected in the volume he published when he returned to the United States. Modestly titled *Chinese Encounters* (1979), it concludes, rather too sanguinely as it turned out, that post-Mao China was searching for democratic institutions that might prevent a recurrence of the fascist tendencies possible in a one party state and exemplified by the tyranny of the 'Gang of Four'.

Two of the individuals Miller met on his first visit to China were Cao Yu, playwright and head of the Beijing People's Art Theatre, and Ying Ruocheng, a leading actor and director with the same company. Both of these men had spent time in the United States and, when China began to open to the west under the new policies of Deng Xiaoping, they were determined to include more modern western plays in their repertoire. In 1982, they approached Miller and persuaded him to return to China to direct a production of *Death of a Salesman* in a translation by Ying who would play the leading role. *Salesman in Beijing* (1984) is Miller's account of that experience based on a log he kept between morning and evening rehearsals in the spring of 1983.

The journal is a vivid picture of the surprising mingling of two seemingly incompatible cultures. In the face of skeptics, Miller maintained that, beneath their ethnic and cultural differences, Chinese and Americans share a common humanity which it is the function of art to reveal. In order to focus on what unites rather than what divides them, he insisted that attempts to imitate the outward appearance of Americans by using wigs and makeup should be abandoned. Working with actors trained in a much more formal, even ritualistic, tradition, Miller struggled to get his cast to understand the emotional truth of their characters. To help them ground their performances in genuine, rather than imagined, feeling he encouraged them to draw on their own experiences of frustration, self-delusion, yearning and disappointment during the years of the Cultural Revolution. Since actors had been particularly targeted by the Red Guards, most of the cast members had suffered badly during the decade before 1975. Miller's description of his attempts to understand and shape a company whose language he could not speak is a vivid illustration of the way theatre can provide a meeting ground for cultural strangers, and a vindication of his conviction that below superficial differences lies a common human nature.

(ii) Novels

The claims of such a common humanity constitute an ongoing preoccupation of the playwright throughout his career. Under what conditions do such claims take precedence over those of individual survival or self-realization? He explored this question in two novels written nearly fifty years apart. *Focus* (1945) was prompted by the author's alarm over the strength of fascist sentiment in the United States and deals with the awakening of social conscience in a Gentile who suddenly himself experiences the effects of anti-Semitism. Lawrence Newman is a personnel officer in a large New York firm who is responsible for enforcing the company's policy against hiring Jews. When he buys himself a badly needed pair of glasses he begins to be taken for a Jew himself, and when the supervisor tries to move him to a less conspicuous office he resigns in indignation. He is finally taken on by a Jewish firm where he encounters a woman he had previously refused to hire on the mistaken assumption that she was Jewish. Seeing her now in an entirely different light, he falls in love with her and marries her.

Following his purchase of glasses, and increasingly after his marriage, Newman is subjected to pressures to join a movement to drive a Jewish merchant out of the Brooklyn neighbourhood in which they both live. Prompted by his wife, who realizes that they must either join with the Christian Front or be attacked by it, Newman attends a Front rally. There he is mistaken for a Jew and thrown out. A couple of nights later, in the company of his wife, he is assaulted by a group of young toughs who also attack the Jewish merchant. In the mêlée Newman and Finklestein find themselves fighting side by side until they finally drive off their assailants. Newman reports the incident to the police only to be mistaken for a Jew himself. Understanding at last the true brotherhood of man, he allows the mistake to go uncorrected.

Focus is about anti-Semitism, of course, but it is also about masks - the kinds we don ourselves (however unwittingly) and those that are forced upon us by the prejudice or ignorance of others. The discrepancy between perceived and real identity is a theme running through all of Miller's work, but it appears most arrestingly in his only other novel written near the end of his career. *Plain Girl* (1992) also deals with anti-Semitism and physical appearance, but in a much more complex fashion. Janice Sessions, the homely heroine, is the daughter of middle class New York parents whose immigrant roots were obliterated in the nineteenth century when their father's Russian name was changed to one the United States immigration officer could pronounce. She comes to think of herself as unattractive, sensing her mother's disappointment in her as well as the indifference of the boys she meets at parties. Feeling unwanted, she settles for a loveless marriage with a young Jewish Communist whose passionate idealism she admires and tries to imitate.

Janice's relationship with her first husband, Sam, is one based on shared ideals. She looks up to him and is inspired by his fierce commitment. But she is disappointed that he can see nothing in paintings but the political ideology of the artist, and eventually explodes in frustration at his inability to take pleasure in the moment because of his obsession with a Utopian future. When war breaks out, Sam enlists and, while he is in Europe, Janice is awakened physically during a brief sexual encounter.

A little later she meets a Polish professor of art history who seduces her with snippets of existential philosophy. He persuades her that she has been a slave to the war which has made it impossible for her to express anything but her goodness. She needs to free herself from the slavery to Communism and fascism, learn to take what is offered, regret nothing and accept that she has chosen to be what she is. When her husband returns from the war, therefore, she asks him for a divorce.

Once more on her own, she meets and marries a blind man, Charles, whose sightless attention makes her feel free, able finally to look outward without holding her breath and waiting for the world's disapproval. Charles proves to be not only an unjudgemental mirror, but also a guide into the world of the dark. Under his loving hands she learns to submerge her intellect in passion, discovering a truth beyond reason and speech. She also learns how to forgive herself for the naiveté of her youthful beliefs and to enjoy the pleasures of the moment. After Charles dies she feels the 'implosion of causes and purposes she had once known' and can no longer find the strength to call them back from the quickly disappearing past.[7] She gives thanks for fourteen years of married happiness and for her luck in being loved for her self rather than for her appearance.

Focus and *Plain Girl*, therefore, are complementary studies of anti-Semitism seen respectively from the point of view of the perpetrator and the victim. Newman in *Focus* overcomes his prejudice by figuratively seeing the world through the eyes of a Jew and learning the credo of the bullied: 'Don't allow yourself to be victimized'. It is the lesson that Janice too must learn. Her self-perceived plainness, a metaphor for her Jewishness, is as much in her mind as in her face. She finds release in the arms of her blind lover, partly because he is (figuratively) unprejudiced, but mainly because she has already inured herself against the hostile gaze of others. By choosing to accept who she is, Janice preempts criticism thus making her mask unnecessary. Whereas in *Focus* Miller emphasizes our obligation to others and the universality of human nature, in *Plain Girl* he celebrates the uniqueness of the individual and the importance of living an authentic life both intellectually and sexually.

(iii) Essays on Drama

After the modest success of *Focus* (90,000 copies sold), Miller might reasonably have considered pursuing a career as a novelist. After all, for a socially committed writer, the drama is perhaps the least likely form to choose as a vehicle of expression. Not only is it the medium in which the author's own personality and opinions are most obliquely set forth, but it is also the one over which he has least control. Even in those cases where the playwright is intimately involved in the process of production, the collaborative nature of the art precludes the possibility of a single, unchangeable effect. But after his study with Kenneth Rowe, Miller became convinced that drama was 'as close to being a total art as the race has invented. It can tell, like science, what is - but more, it can tell what ought to be ... there lies within the dramatic form the ultimate possibility of raising the truth-consciousness of mankind to a level of such intensity as to transform those who observe it'.[8] Hopelessly idealistic as such a belief may seem now, at the time the success of *All My Sons* and the triumph of *Death of a Salesman* appeared, to Miller at least, to vindicate it. But his embracing of the quintessentially impersonal genre of the drama did not prevent him from engaging with his public more directly. As a result, beginning with 'Tragedy and the Common Man' in the *New York Times* (27 February, 1949), and continuing throughout most of his career, Miller entered into an ongoing debate with the critics and the general public about the nature of drama and the condition of the American theatre. Collectively these articles constitute the most comprehensive discussion of the playwright's art by a practicing dramatist since the prefaces and criticism of George Bernard Shaw. Miller's reflections touch on three main subjects - the nature of tragedy, the function of drama, and the practice of playwriting.

Miller's initial defence of *Salesman* as a tragedy owed much to his view of life as expressed in *Focus*. The tragic feeling is invoked in an audience by the spectacle of a character willing to lay down his life to secure his sense of personal dignity. The catastrophe is a consequence of the hero's indignation at being displaced from his rightful place in society and his resulting compulsion to 'evaluate himself justly'. What distinguishes the tragic hero from the mass of ordinary men is his willingness to question and attack the system that degrades him. The spectacle of the hero's attack suggests an evil in his environment; his destruction hints at the existence of a moral law.[9] The conflict in tragedy as Miller understood it, therefore, was not between man and some irresistible fate (the traditional Greek view), nor was it inevitable; it showed the hero struggling against social forces that could be changed or overcome. For, as Miller says, tragedy must always show how the catastrophe might have been avoided, how good might have been allowed to express itself instead of succumbing to evil.[10] Over the years Miller modified his views slightly, moving closer to Bernard Shaw's conception of the morality-challenging 'superman' who must co-operate with a creative 'life force' to bring about a better world.[11]

Finally, in his autobiography in 1987, he proposed an entirely novel definition of the tragic according to which fate is a punishing, but benevolent 'power of the invisible world' which reflects 'Nature's endless self-correcting urge, her aversion to man-destroying waste'. [12] From being the common man indignant at his displacement in society, the tragic hero becomes a Promethean figure able to pass over the boundaries of the accepted mores of his people in order to move towards man's 'fated excellence'.

Miller's initial ideas about drama were formed in the 1930s when he came to believe that a play could change the world. It could do this by showing people the way to a better life, helping them to understand themselves, showing them a higher consciousness, making them more human.[13] But it should also bring news of the inner life, the hidden laws of reality, to make sense of the chaos of life.[14] Ultimately, however, Miller had to admit that the author's intention and the audience's response are not always the same thing and that the stage, far from serving as a pulpit, is more like an arena of suggestion for the onlooker.[15] While he had finally to concede that art could never pierce the human mystery, he continued to the end to maintain that those works that attempt to do so will be the ones that endure.[16]

Miller's notions of how the playwright might best communicate his insights also changed over the years. Misunderstood and criticized for presenting an unduly pessimistic picture of America in his plays, Miller had laid out his artistic *credo* in a letter to the chairman of HUAC following his refusal to name names in 1956. In it he explained:

> I was looking for the world that would be perfect .... For a time [I sought] in Marxism a fount of authority from which might flow a stream of values ... in which I could wholly have faith. ... What I sought to find from without I subsequently learned must be created within.[17]

The process of his search for inner truth is described in some detail in a series of interviews the playwright conducted with the psychologist Richard Evans in 1969. For Miller, a play doesn't begin with an idea or theme, but with an event or character. First comes the collection of evidence, notebook after notebook of ideas, images, scraps of dialogue, even suggested set designs, until gradually a pattern begins to emerge. Then follows the most difficult step - the writing of scenes that will illustrate that pattern. In this process the playwright portions himself out among the various characters, testing his own attitudes, exploring different aspects of his own personality, even (and perhaps especially) those aspects of which he is ashamed. In this way he 'puts himself on the line', usually secretly or symbolically, so that the characters are not real persons, but the playwright's hidden and veiled reactions to the world.[18] The truth that the finished work reveals, therefore, is not a Law handed down from a mountain, but a result of a search of the darkest parts of the self which the playwright believes is part of a universal human nature.

In the 1970s and 1980s Miller's views came to seem more and more old fashioned as stylistic experimentation and fashionable despair seized the attention of American theatre critics, and Miller found his new work unwelcome on the fiercely commercialized Broadway stages. He continued his own experiments with form, but he eschewed the more extreme gestures of the absurdists and the alternative companies. Instead he held stubbornly to his belief that the reports of God's death were exaggerated and that the responsibility of the artist was to celebrate life not death.

(iv) Short Stories

During the period of his greatest success as a playwright, Miller had little cause to resort to other forms of narrative art, but in the late 50's during a lull in his dramatic career, he produced a handful of exquisite short stories collected and published in 1967 under the title *I Don't Need You Anymore.* These works, quieter in tone, more intimate, less desperate in their striving after meaning, constitute a neglected aspect of his work. Many of them are thinly disguised portraits of individuals Miller has met or known. Some of the subjects are easily identifiable – Marilyn Monroe in 'Please Don't Kill Anything' or Isidore Miller in 'Search for a Future'; others remain nameless – the cowboys Miller met in Las Vegas ('The Misfits') or the jockey portrayed in 'Glimpse of a Jockey'. Of greatest interest, perhaps, are the two tales in which the subject is clearly the author himself – 'Fame' and 'I Don't Need You Anymore'. The first explores the awkward self-consciousness of a newly famous playwright. But it is the second, which shows the origins of an artistic vocation, that is the most absorbing.

The story is an account of a young Jewish boy's ambivalent feelings towards his family on the last day of a seaside holiday. The piece undoubtedly draws heavily on Miller's recollections of his own childhood and is one of the few extended accounts of his memories of that time before the 'fall' of 1929. The story, told from the point of view of its five year-old protagonist, Martin, takes place during Yom Kippur and recounts the contradictory emotions of a young boy as he stands between childhood and maturity. The central incident is Martin's retaliation against what he senses as his mother's withdrawal of love when, in a moment of anger, he strikes out at her, shouting, 'I don't need you any more'. This and subsequent outbursts of childish violence disturb the holiday atmosphere and provoke short-lived tensions in the relationships of his parents and brother.

A marked characteristic of the story, and an obstacle to simple interpretation, is the intense, almost hallucinatory nature of the boy's experience. A somewhat out-of-focus perspective is partly the result of Martin's youth and imperfect understanding. His father and older brother have gone to the synagogue, leaving him at home with his mother, where he feels a sense of frustration at this exclusion from the adult male world of sacrifice (it is a fast day), responsibility and understanding. His previously close relationship with his mother has also altered as a result of her pregnancy and his gradual exclusion from his parents' bedroom as he approaches an age of sexual awareness. Martin senses this alteration of his position in the family, but his understanding of what is happening is distorted by his hyperactive imagination. Once an infallible means of winning astonishment and approval, his storytelling ability has also begun to fail him as he detects clearer and clearer evidence of a lack of interest, or even belief, on the part of his listeners. Now he begins to see that his own experiences do not correspond with those of his parents and brother. There are certain things which cannot be told without unpredictable consequences.

The first information Martin acquires that he knows he must keep to himself is the fact that his mother almost married someone other than his father. The knowledge that his family is not eternal, that his mother and father do not have absolutely inseparable lives, seems to Martin a terrible burden which he must guard in order to protect them. Another secret he cannot impart to the others is his vision of God, whom he perceives to be in the ocean along with the bearded sins which have been shed on the day of atonement. That night he goes down to the beach where he experiences what is almost a religious call.

> He yearned to know what he should do for God .... He now vowed obedience to the sea, the moon, the starry beach and the sky, and the silence that stretched its emptiness all around him. What exactly its command was he did not know, but an order was coming to him from the night ... and it made him better and no longer quite alone.

> He felt ... he was the guardian of Ben's and his parents' innocence. Vaguely he felt that with some words which he knew were somewhere in his head he had almost sent them all screaming and roaring at one another and at him, so that - had he said what he could say, they would all be horrified at the mere sight of one another and there would be a terror of crashing. He must keep them from that knowledge .... In league with rule, in charge of the troubled peace, he slept in the strength of his ministry.[19]

After an interim of more than thirty years during which his attention was directed to other genres, Miller returned to the short story in his final years with the publication of six tales that appeared in various literary periodicals from 2001 to 2005.[20] Considerably more elegiac than his earlier fiction, these stories speak of loneliness, lost love, the cruelty of time and the relentless search for solutions to the unanswerable questions. Foremost among these latter are the mysteries of sex and political conviction. While these themes have been implicit in most of Miller's work from the beginning, they here become central and are treated much more frankly.

The title story of the published volume, *Presence* (2003), sets the tone of the collection in that it explores the borderline between illusion and truth, imagination and fact, reality and dream. During an early morning walk, the narrator encounters a young woman on an almost deserted beach. He follows her into the water where they swim together, sink beneath the waves, kiss and then part. Moments later the girl disappears and the man cannot be sure the experience actually took place. A more earthbound sexual adventure is recounted in 'Bulldog' (2001). In that story, a thirteen year-old boy is introduced to the mysteries of passion by the woman from whom he buys a bulldog puppy. Too embarrassed to look her in the face, the boy finds the experience disgusting and knows he must keep it secret. While this excludes him from totally honest intimacy with his family, he finds that the loss of his innocence stimulates his creative imagination and he is able to improvise melodies on the piano in a new and exciting way.

The links between sex, creativity and love are set forth in a much more complex manner in 'The Bare Manuscript' (2002). In that story, Clement, a once successful but now struggling author is suffering from writer's block. He attributes his artistic problems partly to his lost youth, and partly to the failure of his marriage to Lena which has dwindled from its early happiness into a loveless, embittered relationship. One day Clement sees a young girl walking in the sunlight on a beach and imagines writing on her naked body. The idea obsesses him to the point that he places an ad in the newspaper through which he locates Carol Mundt, a young woman willing to participate in his odd experiment. Aroused by the touch of Carol's body, Clement finds his creativity is released and that he is once more able to 'write with his groin' as he had when he was young. What he writes, however, is not about Carol, but about his early happiness with Lena. Indeed he hopes that perhaps the story may help to reconcile the two of them. When Lena returns home, however, he finds himself once again filling up with hate for her wilful self-destruction which has prematurely aged her. He realizes that he still has a remnant of love somewhere in his brain, but he cannot bring it out except as art paradoxically inspired by the younger woman.

Miller is a product of the 1930s and 40s and the world-wide struggle between communism and fascism. As a young man he wholeheartedly embraced the socialist dream of a world of social justice and racial harmony and firmly believed that through his art he was helping to bring it closer. During his maturity he was to lose that conviction and to begin to look for alternative certainties. It was a search that preoccupied him for the rest of his life. It forms the core of *Resurrection Blues* (2002) and informs two of his last short stories. In 'The Performance' (2002), the narrator tries to make sense of a story he first heard in 1947. It had been told to him by a thirty-five year-old Jewish tap dancer by the name of Harold May who, in 1936, had appeared in a single performance before Adolph Hitler. So impressed was the dictator that he asked May to form a dance school. The dancer turned down the offer, but before he did he spent several days in Berlin during which time he had been impressed by the cleanliness of the streets and the congeniality of the people. Sitting in a New York café after the war, therefore, he found it difficult to grasp how the Germans had been seduced by Nazism. He concludes that the entire nation must have been in some kind of dream. Looking out at the street, however, he wonders if other countries, perhaps even America, might not be similarly afflicted. The narrator is disturbed by the story and by the implication that American dreams might be unreal or dangerous. But he puts this frightening idea aside, preferring to think hopeful thoughts and to believe that good things can come out of dreaming.

What those good things might be like is suggested in 'The Turpentine Still' (2004), an allegory of the failure of the socialist vision. The story tells of the sentimental journey of the seventy-two year-old Mark Levin to Haiti in search of the meaning of an experience he had there 33 years before. On holiday with his wife, Adele, he had met an eccentric expatriate New Yorker by the name of Douglas who was trying to set up a distillery to produce turpentine from the mountain pines and provide some help for the impoverished islanders. Levin had left the island before the completion of the enterprise and in the intervening years had almost forgotten about it. After the death of his wife and most of his friends, however, he determines to return to ascertain whether or not the Quixotic undertaking had been a success. He finds the island devastated by crime and corruption, the forest illegally stripped, and the population hopeless and apathetic. Only an old peasant remembers the turpentine still which had been in operation for only a few months before the owner went bankrupt because of his feckless generosity.

Standing in front of the immense, improbable structure, Levin is awestruck by the impulse that had led Douglas to abandon a job on Madison Avenue and sacrifice his wife and children to this impractical vision that he thought would give meaning to his life. Douglas seems to Levin like an artist driven by some creative urge and a desire to be useful whose efforts have been completely defeated. It seems inevitable that all of Douglas's life will be forgotten and that no one will ever feel the quality of his crazy hope again. In spite of the seeming futility of the project, Levin admires the man's aspiration and wishes that he could have been as careless with his own life. Afraid that the world has become too hostile to the generous impulses represented by the abandoned still, however, and feeling, perhaps, helpless to accomplish anything himself, he seeks consolation in music and remembered love.

(v) Interviews

Much less formal than his stories, but no less interesting for that, are the interviews Miller granted almost prodigally throughout his life.[21] Sometimes rambling, sometimes cantankerous, seldom apologetic, these interviews provide an invaluable insight into the author's preoccupations at particular moments in his career and occasionally an unguarded exposure of his inner life. But as Miller cheerfully admits, we all wear masks. Even in his seemingly confessional autobiography, *Timebends*, (1987) there are lacunae and silences – veils over a self which, unlike Eddie Carbone, Miller does not want wholly known.

25
Finishing the Picture (2004)

By the turn of the century, Miller's reputation was at its peak. In America, not only were there revivals of his early works including *A View From the Bridge* (1998), *Death of a Salesman* (1999), *The Price* (2000), but also successful productions of his more recent plays - *Broken Glass* (1994) and *The Ride Down Mount Morgan* (2000). Each year brought new awards and honours, not only American and British, but Spanish and Japanese. In England, a survey conducted by the National Theatre named Miller the greatest playwright of the twentieth century.[1] Worldwide there was probably not a week when one of his plays was not being performed.

In October 2000, the University of Michigan held a major three-day symposium to celebrate the eighty-fifth birthday of its famous alumnus, but without the guest of honour. Two weeks prior to the event, Miller had tripped over a curb, breaking several ribs and making it impossible for him to travel to Ann Arbor. Instead he was forced to carry on an interview with the Conference Chairman, Enoch Brater, by satellite link from his Roxbury home. It began with the familiar questions about his early years at the University, the sources of his plays, his attitude to film adaptations. But then came an unexpected enquiry: 'Why have so many writers of your generation with a Jewish background had such a major impact on theatre and literature?' Miller's answer is revealing. Jews write about America, he said, because for the first time in two thousand years they felt that they would be judged by their character and their work rather than by their race. For Jews, America is a 'blazing society that has all kinds of endless hope ... full of incredible failings which they want to understand and eliminate'.[2] Miller's response encapsulates his own ambivalent attitude to the country of his birth - an uncomfortable mixture of fierce patriotism and bitter disappointment.

In many ways, the University of Michigan Conference of 2000 was emblematic of Miller's situation at eighty-five. The huge TV image of the playwright in the University auditorium was a considerable distortion of the truth. Miller, sitting at home in his Roxbury home, was less self-assured than his impressive public persona. Not only was he no longer confident that he had found the truth, but he sensed his powers waning. His memory was fading[3] and he found he could no longer focus. 'I don't have any big answers', he told a reporter. 'I struggle with everything, just like everyone else.'[4]

A search for big answers has always been implicit in Miller's work, but he has only occasionally (as in *The Creation of the World*) approached the subject head-on. Then, early in 2001, he set out to examine the dilemma of belief - political and religious - in a radically new satirical fashion. During most of 2001 he laboured on a play which he called *Resurrection Blues*. While he was at work on the piece, however, Inge developed a slight pain in her back which, alarmingly, was diagnosed as lymphatic cancer. After undergoing a regime of chemotherapy, however, the doctors assured her the disease had been arrested and she resolved to pursue a photo project she had been planning with an Austrian friend - a journey back to the area where she grew up, near the Austrian-Slovenian border. It would give her an opportunity to reconnect with friends she had not seen for many years and also to recapture something of her youth.

During the assignment, however, the pain returned, making the work more and more difficult. She doggedly completed the assignment, but back in Roxbury she learned that the cancer had returned and was far advanced. Recognizing the inevitable, she nevertheless refused to go to New York, entering a hospital only the day before she died on 31 January 2002. To her family, her death was doubly poignant - in part because they had believed the cancer had been beaten, and partly because Inge had not lived to see her second grandson, born just four months later. Miller was particularly devastated and wrote to Inge's brother: 'I am still astonished by the happiness that was ours for forty years ... She was a courageous fine woman. We were all blessed in being so close to her.'[5]

The months following were an emotional roller-coaster ride for the playwright. The birth of Rebecca's son in May was closely followed by the death of Robert Whitehead in June; the opening of his new play, *Resurrection Blues*, at the Guthrie Theatre in Minneapolis in August, and the Broadway revival of *The Crucible* in September were triumphs clouded by the death of his brother Kermit on 17 October 2003, ironically his own eighty-eighth birthday. Never had he been so conscious of his own mortality. And yet, not long after Inge's death, Miller told a reporter that he was 'getting better ... coming up from underneath'.[6] Sometime during this period at a dinner party given by friends he met an intensely lively thirty-two year-old painter by the name of Agnes Barley. Attracted by her youth and vitality, Miller began to court her, seeing her for dinner four or five times a week. Within months she had moved in with him.[7] Agnes gave Miller a new lease on life, allowing him to resume his writing routine of spending every morning in his studio. Soon he was working on a new play.

Paradoxically, the new project involved a return to the period of his greatest unhappiness - the making of *The Misfits* in Nevada in the summer of 1960. The subject (abandoned twenty-five years earlier when he was unable to complete it) was the crisis during the shooting of the film when Marilyn Monroe had to be flown to a Hollywood hospital for a week's convalescence. But the theme, according to Miller, was the perversion of the American Dream.[8] As he worked on the play, Miller poured into it not only his anguish over the failure of his relationship with Monroe and his bitter disenchantment with the 'blazing society', but also his perennially optimistic faith in the possibility of rebirth and renewal. He called it *Finishing the Picture.*

The action of the play[9] takes place in the Nevada hotel where the film's New York producer, Phillip Oschner, has come in an attempt to save the project (already several million dollars over budget) which is threatened by the physical and psychological collapse of its star, Kitty. Oschner, a Brooklyn-born former militant Marxist now millionaire businessman, has already managed to have a one-night fling with the star's forty year-old assistant, Edna. He is stunned by the encounter, having 'cemented' himself in a wall of loneliness after his wife's recent death. It seems to both, however, that something genuine has happened between them, although Edna wants to keep the affair secret.

Oschner summons the various participants in the catastrophe to his hotel suite where director, Derek Clemson, cameraman, Terry Case, and the writer and husband of the star, Paul, consider their options. These would seem to include: shutting down the film at great financial loss (and the likely termination of Kitty's career); suspending shooting for a week to allow the star to get medical treatment; or somehow coaxing or compelling Kitty to return to the set to finish the picture. The next day the situation is further complicated by the arrival of Jerome Fassinger, Kitty's drama teacher who, in response to a frantic appeal from the star, has flown in from New York to join his wife, Flora, already in Nevada as Kitty's acting coach. One by one the concerned parties visit the star's bedside in an effort to cajole or threaten her back to work. As each confronts the drugged and immobile actress, they reveal their differing assessments of her personality, as well as their own involvement in the exploitation of her fragile beauty. If these interviews tell us little about Kitty, they expose many of the corrupting forces at work in the entertainment industry with its relentless pursuit of celebrity. In spite of the poisonous influences revealed, the play ends hopefully. The distant forest fire that has threatened the project has been contained; Kitty is to be sent to a hospital; and Edna prepares for a dinner with Phillip Oschner.

The problem with the work (which it shares with several of Miller's late plays) is that there is too much talk, too little action, and a puzzling tone that alternates between grotesque satire and pathos. The central situation provides a convenient metaphor for several of Miller's perennial concerns – the relationship between power and art, the destructive effects of celebrity, and the limits of love. Once again, however, because the central relationship of Kitty and Paul so closely mirrors that of Miller and Monroe, it is difficult to think beyond the particular to the wider social implications that Miller wants us to see in the story. The question of our responsibility for each other is overshadowed by the wickedly funny caricature of Jerome and Flora Fassinger (Lee and Paula Strasberg); the overarching theme of destruction and regeneration (implied by the forest fire's power to generate new growth) is obscured by the pathos of the failure of Kitty and Paul's relationship. 'I didn't save her, I didn't bring the miracle ... and she didn't save me.' The complex web of ideas is bogged down in a rather static and repetitious plot.

Looking about for a sponsor for his new play, Miller was drawn to the Goodman Theatre in Chicago which had staged the triumphant fiftieth anniversary production of *Death of a Salesman* in 1999. That production had gone on to great success on Broadway winning critical acclaim and four Tony Awards. Hoping to duplicate this earlier triumph, Artistic Director, Robert Falls, and producer, David Richenthal, hired a cast of prominent New York and Californian actors. The 5 October 2004, world premiere of *Finishing the Picture* attracted international interest, but the reviews were distressingly mixed. A number of Chicago critics were enthusiastic, one even calling the work among Miller's best. There was general respect for the playwright, and a kind of voyeuristic curiosity about the originals of the thinly veiled characters, but few of the notices were without qualifications. Some, no doubt hoping for some new insight into the personality of Marilyn Monroe, regretted Miller's decision to leave the character of Kitty undefined, a shadowy figure without dialogue, the object of others' speculation. Some regretted a certain coldness or detachment in the character of Paul which rendered the character opaque. Few responded to the larger social issues discussed. The one point of agreement was that the lampoon of the Strasbergs, while quite possibly spiteful and cruel, was nevertheless wickedly funny and the best thing in the play.

For a transfer to Broadway to be feasible, however, there needed to be encouragement from the New York press. *The New York Times'* Ben Brantley was rather casually dismissive, but the critic from the *Wall Street Journal* was positively scathing. In such a case it would have been foolhardy to attempt a move to New York without revisions. By the time the Chicago production ended on 7 November, however, Miller was ill. Suffering from cancer and heart problems, he could no longer work and turned his attention to ordering his personal affairs. In December, in defiance of the menacing future, he announced his intention to marry Agnes Barley. But it may have been the past that haunted him more compellingly. For after nearly forty years of neglect, he finally offered a gesture of reconciliation to his so-long-unacknowledged son, Daniel. In separate trust documents drawn up with his last will and signed on 30 December, 2004, he named Daniel as an equal heir with his three other children.[10] Shortly thereafter, however, his condition worsened and he was forced to enter the Sloan-Kettering Memorial Cancer Hospital in New York. He was discharged at the end of the year, but only to move into his sister's apartment near Central Park where he required twenty-four hour nursing care. Feeling the end to be near, he asked to go home and was taken by ambulance to Roxbury where a bed was set up for him in the downstairs study. From it he could look out at the rolling hills of Connecticut, the pine forest he had planted, and the garden to which he liked to retreat when life seemed pointless or too difficult to grasp. And there, on 10 February 2005, his long search ended.

26
Conclusion

Arthur Miller spent most of his adult life trying to make sense of the events through which he and his contemporaries had passed. His entire career as a writer can be seen as an attempt to find justification for his own hope. In his youth he believed that socialism was inevitable and that society could be changed through art; then he sought salvation in personal relationships; in his later work, he seemed to have formulated for himself a kind of existential optimism. Miller's disillusion with an early faith and determined effort to find an acceptable substitute are, in many ways, the quintessential modern experience. Where Miller differs from many of his contemporaries, however, is in his guarded optimism in the face of the great mass of evidence that had accumulated in the twentieth century to undermine it.

Miller came to prominence as a realistic dramatist strongly influenced by the Greek tragedians and Ibsen. In their shadow he wrote tightly plotted social tragedies like *All My Sons* and *A View From the Bridge* in which a protagonist is driven by selfishness or passion to commit an anti-social act and then led to confront his own involvement in the evil plaguing his society. During the McCarthy era, when problems of ethical choice became complicated by social and political coercion, he modified the form into what could be called the drama of self-definition. Plays such as *The Crucible*, *Incident at Vichy*, *The Archbishop's Ceiling* and *Playing for Time* explore how a protagonist is faced with competing moral claims or social pressures which he must decide between. Whether he chooses to preserve his life (through collaboration or betrayal) or lose it (through defiance or sacrifice) depends on how he defines himself in relation to others. The most probing of these is also the one most ingeniously devolved from its Greek source. *The Price* presents a situation in which the competing claims of selfishness and altruism remain unresolved, Victor and Walter defining their actions according to their own criteria rather than by the demands or expectations of others. While all these plays are fascinating studies of agonizing moral choice, there is a mystery at the heart of each one since (as Miller admitted in the case of Von Berg) the deepest well-springs of a decision to sacrifice oneself for another are unfathomable.

Recognizing the inadequacies of strict stage realism to probe the inner life, Miller made several efforts to extend its reach. The first and most successful of these was *Death of a Salesman* in which he used a mixture of dramatized memories and imaginary conversations to explore the doubts, self-justifications and dreams that Willy cannot express openly. In its mixture of external actions and inner thoughts, *Salesman* was revolutionary and led Miller to push his experiments in this mode still further in *After the Fall*, *The Ride Down Mount Morgan* and *Mr Peters' Connections*. The problem in all four of these 'stream of consciousness' plays is the relationship between subjective and objective truth. Whereas the aim is to show more vividly the connection between past and present, emotional trauma and intellectual consequence, that aim is defeated if the audience is given no means of establishing 'objective' reality. In *Salesman* and *Ride Down Mount Morgan*, characters existing in the 'real' world provide a standard against which we can judge the protagonist's more extravagant statements. In *Fall* and *Mr Peters*, however, such checks are largely missing.

Miller's one attempt at 'epic theatre', *The American Clock*, is a blend of his own memories and those of anonymous survivors of the Depression as recorded by the oral historian, Studs Terkel. In it Miller returned to that time of his life he came to regard as pivotal, the period before and after the 'fall' of 1929 when the world seemed to be turned upside down. That and many succeeding disillusionments had led the playwright to search for some kind of certainty that would give coherence to his memories and meaning to his life. In his youth he expected the explanation to be rational. As he matured, however, he came to feel the need of something more intangible - a ground for conscience and imagination. Miller's search for the roots of belief is evident in many of his realistic plays, but it is most explicit in his fantasies such as *The Creation of the World and Other Business* and *Resurrection Blues*. The first he called the most complete exposition of his religious beliefs that he had come to. In it he portrayed a loving, but long-since-departed God who can be reached only through conscience. *Resurrection Blues* presents a similar picture of the alienation of God, and man's need to work out his own salvation.

Each of Miller's plays has been a fresh attempt to find a suitable form for his dramatic vision. In his search for new techniques, however, he has for the most part avoided the more extreme innovations of the surrealists, expressionists, absurdists and other twentieth-century theatrical iconoclasts. His experimentation has always been directed towards making his characters more psychologically real, not rendering them mechanical, faceless or depersonalized; making the causal connections between things more understandable, not suggesting a world without meaning. To Miller, whatever their limitations, reason and language remained our most reliable tools for understanding the world. Attempts to discredit them or to substitute a 'poetry of the theatre' for poetry *in* the theatre struck him as misguided. His own contribution in this respect has been his creation of an effective stage speech that combines the power of formal rhetoric with an impression of colloquial conversation. His most extreme experiment with deliberately heightened dialogue is *The Crucible* where the historical setting gives a certain licence for highly figurative diction. Miller's evocation of seventeenth-century language in this play has been much admired, but it is no more successful than his metamorphosis of contemporary American speech in several of his other works. Willy Loman's indignant or despairing outcries ('a man is not a piece of fruit' or 'the woods are burning') or Gregory Solomon's expostulations ('five hundred dollars they'll pay a lawyer to fight over a bookcase it's worth fifty cents') are random examples of the way in which Miller transmutes the idiom of the New York streets into something powerfully moving. Miller's best dialogue is that based on the slangy, wisecracking speech of ill-educated or bilingual New York immigrants, mainly Jewish and Italian. Within this seemingly narrow compass of regional idiom the playwright expresses a remarkable range of feeling.

During his lifetime Arthur Miller acquired an international eminence as playwright, celebrity, social activist and political gadfly that is almost without precedent. Not surprisingly, his often trenchant criticisms of American life were not always enthusiastically received in his own country where his popularity has fluctuated wildly. There is no question that Miller's greatest triumph is *Death of a Salesman*. A brilliant mixture of the particular and the symbolic, it lays bare the contradictions at the heart of the American Dream - the seductive attraction of its promise as well as the corrosive effects of its single-minded pursuit. Equally highly regarded is *The Crucible*, a chilling dissection of ideological tyranny which has been instantly recognized as relevant wherever such tyranny is practiced.

Also likely to endure are Miller's plays dealing with family life - *All My Sons, The Price, Broken Glass.* Few playwrights have better understood the conflicts at the heart of the family or represented them more honestly. This is largely a product of his own continual introspection. Indeed, in this respect, Miller seems less like a dramatist than a lyric poet 'dazzled', as Milan Kundera put it in another context, 'by his own soul and by desire to make it heard'.[1] Like the analyst looking for general psychological laws in the freely associated memories of a patient, Miller hopes that by trying to make sense of his own deeply personal experiences he will reveal universal human truths. While this self-analysis has contributed substantially to the lifelikeness of his portraiture, it has also resulted in a fairly narrow canvas. The typical Miller family consists of an ill-educated father, a mother with some cultural aspirations, and two sons. Sisters, grandparents and very young children hardly ever appear; nor are their problems discussed. Furthermore, the families are almost invariably lower-middle-class. There are no 'movers and shakers' in the plays and little concern with the problems of the 'rulers', whether these are considered to be politicians, scientists, engineers, financiers, or even writers and artists. The professional class is represented almost exclusively by lawyers, and the intellectual questions raised in the plays are discussed, for the most part, by non-intellectuals. Furthermore, he focuses fairly narrowly on the Judeo-Christian tradition. Problems of the blacks during the civil rights struggle, the agonies of the Vietnamese, as well as the concerns of feminists and gays find only the faintest echo in his plays.

Even within this limited family unit it is only the men who are convincingly portrayed. It is one of the weaknesses of the plays as a whole that Miller fails to create believable women. The female characters in the plays are rarely shown except in their relationship to some man. They are not presented as individuals in their own right, but rather as mothers, wives or mistresses. The moral dilemma in a Miller play is almost invariably seen from a man's point of view, and to a large extent women exist outside the arena of real moral choice. They seldom experience the career or identity crises that affect men; nor are they shown having trouble relating to their parents or lovers. It is significant, too, that the obvious exceptions to this generalization, Maggie, Fania Fenelon and Sylvia Gellburg, are closely patterned on specific individuals.

Arthur Miller is usually thought of as a social critic or political commentator, a railer against perversions of the American Dream. But like earlier social prophets, he is less concerned with establishing utopias than with saving souls. Systems – whether they be capitalism, socialism, McCarthyism or even Nazism – are not Miller's prime concern. They provide the fire in which the individual is tested, but it is the way in which the protagonist responds that is of interest to the playwright. It is in this context that one can speak of 'sins' and indeed Miller sometimes seems almost medieval in his concern with such topics as conscience, presumption, despair and faith. Miller is quintessentially an explorer of the shadowy region between pride and guilt, selfishness and sacrifice. His characters are a peculiar combination of insight and blindness, doubt and assertiveness, which makes them alternately confront and avoid their innermost selves. To the tangled pathways between self-criticism and self-justification there is probably no better guide.

Miller is the spokesman for those who yearn for the comfortable certainty of a belief, but whose critical intelligence will not allow them to accept the consolations of traditional religions. What seems certain to ensure his continued popularity in a world grown weary of the defeatism of so much modern literature is his hopefulness. Like the Puritan theologians of old, Miller has come to realize that the greatest enemy to life is not doubt, but despair. And against despair, the individual has only faith and hope. In *Playing for Time* Miller presents the artist as the individual who refuses to avert his eyes from the horrors of the concentration camp in order that he may bear witness before heaven and mankind. It is Miller's chief merit as an artist that the evidence he presents in his plays seems, on the whole, more balanced than that of some of his contemporaries. For if he has not hesitated to look on the evil in himself and others, neither has he been willing to shut his eyes to the good.

Notes

1 Beginnings

1. Unless otherwise noted, details of Miller's life have been gleaned from Arthur Miller's autobiography, *Timebends* (London: Methuen, 1987) and Martin Gottfried, *Arthur Miller: A Life* (London: Faber and Faber, 2003).
2. Kenneth Rowe, *Write That Play* (New York: Funk and Wagnalls, 1939), pp. 45–52.

2 Golden Years

1. *The Golden Years*, in Arthur Miller *Plays: Four* (London: Methuen, 1994), p. 96.
2. Edwin Seaver, (ed.), *Cross-Section; A Collection of New American Writing* (New York: Fischer, 1944), p. 550.
3. 'Introduction', Arthur Miller, *Plays: One* (London: Methuen, 1988), pp. 14–15.
4. *Plays: Four*, p. 185.
5. 'Introduction', *Plays: One*, p. 15 .
6. *Plays: Four*, p. ix.

3 All My Sons

1. 'Introduction', *Plays: One*, p. 19.

4 Salesman

1. 'The *Salesman* has a Birthday', *New York Times* (5 Feb., 1950), reprinted in Robert A. Martin, (ed.), *The Theatre Essays of Arthur Miller*, 2nd edn (London: Methuen, 1994), p. 13.
2. Richard Evans, *Psychology and Arthur Miller* (London: Methuen, 1981), p. 23.
3. *Plays: One*, p. 180.
4. *Ibid.*, p. 222.

5 Betrayals

1. Gottfried, *op. cit.*, p. 145.
2. *Ibid.*, p. 145.
3. Elia Kazan, *A Life* (New York: Alfred Knopf, 1988), p. 365.
4. Arthur Miller, *Timebends*, p. 194.

5. 'The Crucible in History', reprinted in Steven Centola, (ed.), *Arthur Miller, Echoes Down the Corridor: Collected Essays 1944–2000* (London: Methuen, 2000), p. 285.
6. Miller archives at the Harry Ransom Library at the University of Texas, quoted by Gottfried, p. 189.
7. Elia Kazan, *A Life*, p. 461.
8. 'Journey to *The Crucible*', *The New York Times* (8 Feb., 1953).
9. Evans, *op. cit.*, p. 72.
10. Letter to James Stern (4 Nov. 1954) in the British Library (ADD 80869 3007B).
11. *Congressional Record*, Vol. CII, Part II, 14530.

6 The Crucible

1. Marion Starkey, *The Devil in Massachusetts* (Garden City, N.Y.: Doubleday, 1949).
2. *Plays: One*, p. 331.

7 Memory and View

1. 'Introduction', *Plays: One*, p. 46.
2. Stern-Miller correspondence in the British Library (4 Nov. 1954).
3. 'A View from the Bridge', *Theatre Arts*, XL (Sept., 1956), p. 62.
4. *Ibid.*, p. 62.
5. *Ibid.*, p. 62.
6. *Ibid.*, p. 63.
7. 'A View from the Bridge', *Plays: One*, p. 437.
8. *Ibid.* p. 439.
9. Sheila Huftel, *Arthur Miller: The Burning Glass* (New York: Citadel, 1965), p. 161.
10. 'Introduction', *Plays: One*, pp. 52-3.

8 Celebrity

1. Quoted by Gottfried, p. 321.
2. A.J. Weatherby, Jr, *Conversations with Marilyn* (London: Robson Books, 1976), quoted in Gottfried, p. 338.

9 Misfits

1. 'Author's Note', *The Misfits* (London: Methuen, 2002).
2. James Goode, *The Story of 'The Misfits'* (Indianapolis: Bobbs-Merrill, 1963), p. 75.
3. 'The Misfits' in *I Don't Need You Anymore* (New York: Bantam, 1968), p. 93.
4. *Ibid.*, p. 89.

5. *Timebends*, p. 458.
6. *Ibid.*, p. 473.
7. *Ibid.*, p. 472.
8. *The Misfits* (2002).
9. *Timebends*, p. 465.
10. Goode, *op. cit.*, p. 300.

10 Refuge

1. *New York Times* (25 Jan., 1961).
2. *Timebends*, p. 594.
3. Stern-Miller correspondence in the British Library (6 April, 1961).
4. Inge Morath and Regina Strassegger, *Last Journey* (Munich: Prestel Verlag, 2002), p. 176.
5. *Ibid.*, p. 147.
6. *The Observer* (13 Feb., 2005).
7. *Timebends*, p. 531.
8. *New York Times* (29 Sept., 1962).
9. The birth was not reported in the press and only a few close friends seem to have known about it. Some of those friends set Daniel's birth in November, 1966. See Suzanna Andrews, 'Arthur Miller's Missing Act', *Vanity Fair* (September, 2007), p. 254.
10. Gottfried, *op.cit.,* p. 347.
11. *New York Times* (29 Dec., 2002).
12. Introduction, *Psychology and Arthur Miller.*

11 After the Fall

1. *After the Fall* (New York: Bantam, 1974), p. 123.

12 The Price

1. *The Price* in *Plays: Two* (London: Methuen, 1981), p. 361.
2. *Ibid.*, p. 366.
3. *Ibid.*, p. 369.
4. *Ibid.*, p. 370.
5. *Ibid.*, p. 372.
6. *Ibid.*, p. 373.

13 Alienation

1. Stern-Miller correspondence in the British Library (15 Feb., 1968).
2. Miller quoted by Benedict Nightingale, *The Times* (3 July, 2000).
3. Peter Applebaum, *New York Times* (29 Jan., 1999).

4. Suzanna Andrews, *Vanity Fair* (September, 2007) 260.
5. Reuters (17 Oct., 1995).

14 Creation of the World

1. 'The Story of Adam and Eve' in David Rosenberg, (ed.), *Genesis: As It Is Written* (San Francisco: Harper San Francisco, 1996), p. 39.
2. 'Guilt and *Incident at Vichy*', *New York Times Magazine* (3 Jan., 1965), reprinted in *Echoes Down the Corridor*, p. 74.
3. Tom Buckley, *New York Times* (29 Aug., 1972).
4. Clive Barnes, *New York Times* (1 Dec., 1972).
5. *The Creation of the World* in *Plays: Two*, p. 385.

15 The Archbishop's Ceiling

1. *Timebends*, p. 570.
2. Inge Morath and Arthur Miller, *In Russia* (New York: Viking, 1969), pp. 18, 22.
3. Arthur Miller, 'The Prague Winter', *New York Times* (16 July, 1975).
4. *The Archbishop's Ceiling* in *Plays: Two*, p. 95.
5. Arthur Miller, 'Introduction', *The Archbishop's Ceiling* (New York: Grove Press, 1989), p. x.

16 The American Clock

1. *Timebends*, p. 588.
2. 'Introduction', *The American Clock* (New York: Grove Press, 1989), p. xiv.
3. Frank Rich, *The New York Times* (21 Nov., 1980).
4. Miller was so pleased with the London production that he authorized its publication - *The Archbishop's Ceiling, The American Clock* (New York: Grove Press, 1989) in spite of the fact that an earlier version had appeared in 1982.
5. Irving Wardle, *The Times* (London, 19 Dec., 1986).
6. Miller interviewed by Christopher Bigsby in *Arthur Miller: A Critical Study* (Cambridge: Cambridge University Press, 2005), pp. 341, 343.

17 Incident and Playing

1. *Plays: Two*, p. 110.
2. 'Guilt and *Incident at Vichy*', *New York Times Magazine* (3 Jan., 1965), reprinted in *Echoes Down the Corridor*, pp. 70, 72.
3. *Playing for Time* (Woodstock: The Dramatic Publishing Company, 1985).
4. *Playing for Time: A Screenplay* (New York: Bantam, 1981), p. 46.
5. Interview with Ralph Tyler, *New York Times* (17 June, 1979).

18 One-Act Plays

1. Bob Peck in Christopher Bigsby, (ed.), *Arthur Miller and Company* (London: Methuen, 1990), p. 173.
2. 'Introduction', *Two-Way Mirror* (London: Methuen, 1984), p. 1.
3. *Timebends*, p. 590.
4. *Theatre Essays*, p. 427.
5. *Timebends*, p. 590.
6. *Timebends*, p. 503.

19 The Ride Down Mount Morgan

1. Quoted in Christopher Bigsby, (ed.), *The Cambridge Companion to Arthur Miller* (Cambridge: Cambridge University Press, 1997), p. 172.
2. Mel Gussow, *Conversations with Miller* (New York: Applause Theatre and Cinema Books, 2002), p. 150.
3. *Ibid.*, p. 150.
4. *The Ride Down Mount Morgan* (London: Methuen, 1991), p. 34.
5. Bruce Weber, *New York Times* (10 April, 2000).
6. Arthur Miller quoted by Christopher Bigsby, *Companion to Arthur Miller*, p. 171.

20 The Last Yankee

1. *Time* (8 Feb., 1993).
2. Frank Sheck, *Christian Science Monitor* (28 Jan., 1993).
3. David Richards, *New York Times* (31 Jan., 1993).
4. Melanie Kirkpatrick, *Wall Street Journal* (27 Jan., 1993).
5. 'About Theatre Language' in *The Last Yankee* (London: Methuen, 1994).
6. *Ibid.*, pp. 92–4.
7. *Time* (8 Feb., 1993).

21 Broken Glass

1. Gottfried, *op. cit.*, p. 441.

22 Mr Peters' Connections

1. Gottfried, *op. cit.*, pp. 442–3.
2. *Ibid.*, p. 444.
3. 'Preface', *Mr. Peters' Connections* (London: Methuen, 2000).

23 Resurrection Blues

1. *New York Times* (15 Oct., 2002).
2. *Times* (London, 3 July, 2000).
3. *Resurrection Blues* (London: Methuen, 2006), p. 65.

24 Non-Theatrical Writing

1. *Situation Normal* (New York: Reynal & Hitchcock, 1944), p. 44.
2. *Ibid.*, p. 44.
3. *Ibid.*, p. 167.
4. Inge Morath and Arthur Miller, *In Russia* (New York: Viking, 1969), p. 8.
5. *Ibid.*, p. 23.
6. *Ibid.*, p. 19.
7. *Plain Girl* (London: Methuen, 1995), p. 76. The novel first appeared in the United States in 1992 as *Homely Girl: A Life.*
8. 'The Family in Modern Drama', *Atlantic Monthly* CXCVII (April, 1956), pp. 35-41; reprinted in *Theatre Essays*, (TE), p. 84.
9. 'Tragedy and the Common Man', *The New York Times* (27 Feb., 1949), in TE, p. 4.
10. 'Arthur Miller on The Nature of Tragedy', *New York Herald Tribune* (27 Mar., 1949), in TE, p. 11.
11. 'On Social Plays', preface to *A View from the Bridge* (New York, 1955), in TE, pp. 51-68.
12. *Timebends*, p. 233.
13. 'Introduction', *Collected Plays, Volume One* (New York: Viking, 1957) in TE, p. 123.
14. 'The Shadows of the Gods', *Harpers*, CCXX (Nov. 1960), in TE, p. 177.
15. Miller quoted in *Psychology and Arthur Miller*, p. 26.
16. 'About Theatre Language', p. 98.
17. Congressional Record Vol. 102, Part II, 14532.
18. *Psychology and Arthur Miller.*
19. *I Don't Need You Anymore*, pp. 39-40.
20. *Presence* (New York: Viking, 2007).
21. These are less easily accessible, but several are recorded in Mel Gussow, *Conversations With Miller*, and Matthew Roudane, *Conversations With Arthur Miller* (Jackson: University Press of Mississippi, 1987).

25 Finishing the Picture

1. Annette Witheridge, *Mail on Sunday* (13 Feb., 2005).
2. Interview in Enoch Brater, (ed.), *Arthur Miller's America* (Ann Arbor: University of Michigan Press, 2005), p. 251.
3. Gussow, *Conversations*, p. 202.
4. *USA Today* (14 Sept. 2001).

5. Letter reproduced in Inge Morath, *Last Journey*, p. 176.
6. John Peter, *Sunday Times* (13 Feb., 2005).
7. David Usborne, *The Independent on Sunday* (1 Feb., 2004).
8. Miller quoted by Stephen Kinger, *New York Times* (4 Mar., 2004).
9. Details of the play are from Christopher Bigsby's account of the unpublished typescript in *Arthur Miller: A Critical Study*, pp. 437–43.
10. Suzanna Andrews, *Vanity Fair* (Sept., 2007) 265.

26 Conclusion

1. *The Guardian* (3 Mar., 2007).

Bibliography

Works by Arthur Miller

(i) Collections

Plays: One (London: Methuen, 1988). [*All My Sons, Death of a Salesman, The Crucible, A Memory of Two Mondays, A View from the Bridge* (two-act version)].

Plays: Two (London: Methuen, 1988). [*The Misfits, After the Fall, Incident at Vichy, The Price, The Creation of the World and Other Business, Playing for Time*].

Plays: Three (London: Methuen, 1990). [*The American Clock, The Archbishop's Ceiling, Two-Way Mirror*].

Plays: Four (London: Methuen, 1994). [*The Golden Years, The Man Who Had All the Luck, Danger Memory*].

Plays: Five (London: Methuen, 1995). [*The Last Yankee, The Ride Down Mount Morgan, Almost Everybody Wins*].

The Portable Arthur Miller (New York: Viking, 1971) [*Death of a Salesman, The Crucible, Incident at Vichy, The Price, The Misfits*].

Echoes Down the Corridor: Collected Essays 1944–2000, Steven Centola, (ed.) (London: Methuen, 2000).

The Theatre Essays of Arthur Miller, 2nd edn, Robert A. Martin, (ed.) (London: Methuen, 1994).

(ii) Individual Works

The Man Who Had All the Luck, in Edwin Seaver, (ed.), *Cross-Section: A Collection of New American Writing* (New York: Fischer, 1944).

Situation Normal (New York: Reynal & Hitchcock, 1944).

Focus (New York: Reynal & Hitchcock, 1945; London: Victor Gollancz, 1949; London: Secker and Warburg, 1974; Harmondsworth: Penguin, 1978).

All My Sons (New York: Reynal & Hitchcock, 1947, and Viking: 1957; Harmondsworth: Penguin, 1961 [with *A View from the Bridge*]).

Death of a Salesman (New York: Viking, 1949, and Bantam, 1951; Harmondsworth: Penguin, 1961) and in Gerald Weales (ed.), Viking Critical Library Edition (New York: Viking, 1967; Harmondsworth: Penguin, 1977).

An Enemy of the People (adaptation) (New York: Viking, 1951; Harmondsworth: Penguin, 1977).

The Crucible (New York: Viking, 1953; Harmondsworth: Penguin, 1968) and in Gerald Weales (ed.), Viking Critical Library Edition (New York: Viking, 1971; Harmondsworth: Penguin, 1977).

A View from the Bridge (one-act version) (New York: Viking, 1955), and in *Theatre Arts*, xi, (Sep. 1956); (two-act version) (London: Cresset, 1957; New York:

Compass, 1960, and Bantam, 1961; Harmondsworth: Penguin, 1961 [with *All My Sons*]).
Memory of Two Mondays (New York: Viking, 1955 [with *A View from the Bridge*]).
The Misfits (New York: Viking, 1961; Harmondsworth: Penguin, 1961; London: Methuen, 2002).
Jane's Blanket (New York: Collier-Macmillan, 1963).
After the Fall (New York: Viking, 1964, and Bantam, 1965; Harmondsworth: Penguin, 1968; New York: Bantam, 1974) (Television adaptation).
Incident at Vichy (New York: Viking, 1965, and Bantam, 1967).
I Don't Need You Anymore (New York: Viking; London: Secker & Warburg; Harmondsworth: Penguin, 1967; New York: Bantam, 1968).
The Price (New York: Viking, 1968; Harmondsworth: Penguin, 1970).
In Russia (with Inge Morath) (New York: Viking, 1969).
The Portable Arthur Miller, Harold Clurman (ed.) (New York: Viking, 1971).
The Creation of the World and Other Business (New York: Viking, 1973).
In the Country (with Inge Morath) (New York: Viking, 1977).
Chinese Encounters (with Inge Morath) (New York: Farrar, Straus, Giroux, 1979).
Playing for Time (New York: Bantam, 1981 (Television version); Chicago: Dramatic Publishing Company, 1985) (Stage version).
The American Clock (New York: Dramatists Play Service, 1982; London: Methuen, 1983; New York: Grove Press, 1989 [with *The Archbishop's Ceiling*]).
Salesman in Beijing (New York: Viking, 1984).
The Archbishop's Ceiling (London: Methuen, 1984).
Two-Way Mirror (London: Methuen, 1984). [*Elegy for a Lady, Some Kind of Love Story*].
Danger: Memory! (London: Methuen, 1986; New York: Grove Press, 1987) [*I Can't Remember Anything, Clara*].
Timebends (New York: Viking, 1987; London: Methuen, 1987).
The Golden Years and *The Man Who Had All the Luck* (London: Methuen, 1989.)
Everybody Wins (London: Methuen, 1990).
The Ride Down Mount Morgan (London: Methuen, 1991; London: Penguin, 1999) (Revised version).
Homely Girl; A Life (New York: Peter Blum Books, 1992) (Subsequently published as *Plain Girl* (London: Methuen, 1995 and Minerva, 1996).
The Last Yankee (London: Methuen, 1993; London: Penguin, 1994) (with 'About Theatre Language').
Broken Glass (New York: Penguin, 1994).
Mr. Peters' Connections (New York: Penguin, 1999; London: Methuen, 2000).
'The Crucible' in History and Other Essays (London: Methuen, 2000).
Resurrection Blues (London: Methuen, 2006).
Presence (New York: Viking, 2007).
Stern, James, Arthur Miller correspondence. British Library ADD80869 3007B.

(iii) Conversations and Interviews

Bigsby, C.W.E. (ed.), *Arthur Miller and Company* (London: Methuen, 1990).
Bigsby, C.W.E. (ed.), *Remembering Arthur Miller* (London: Methuen, 2005).

Centola, Steven, *Arthur Miller in Conversation* (Dallas, Texas: Northouse, 1993).
Evans, Richard I., *Psychology and Arthur Miller* (New York: Dutton, 1969; London: Methuen, 1981).
Gussow, Mel, *Conversations With Miller* (New York: Applause Theatre and Cinema Books, 2002).
Roudane, Matthew C., *Conversations With Arthur Miller* (Jackson: University of Mississippi Press, 1987).

Works by Other Authors

(iv) Full Length Studies

Brater, Enoch, *Arthur Miller: A Playwright's Life and Works* (London: Thames and Hudson, 2005).
Bigsby, C.W.E, *Arthur Miller: A Critical Study* (Cambridge: Cambridge University Press, 2005).
Gottfried, Martin, *Arthur Miller: A Life* (London: Faber and Faber, 2003).
Huftel, Sheila, *Arthur Miller: The Burning Glass* (New York: Citadel, 1965).
Nelson, Benjamin, *Arthur Miller: Portrait of a Playwright* (London: Peter Owen, 1970).
Schlueter, Jane and James K. Flanagan, *Arthur Miller* (New York: Unger, 1987).
Welland, Dennis, *Miller: A Study of His Plays* (London: Eyre Methuen, 1979); *Miller the Playwright*, 3rd edn (London: Methuen, 1985).

(v) Background

Bentley, Eric (ed.), *Thirty Years of Treason; Excerpts from Hearings Before the House Committee on Un-American Activities* (New York: Viking, c. 1971).
Clurman, Harold, *The Fervent Years* (London: Dennis Dobson, 1946) A history of the Group Theatre.
Fenelon, Fania with Marcel Routier (trans. Judith Landry), *The Musicians of Auschwitz* (London: Sphere Books, 1979).
Goode, James, *The Story of the Misfits* (Indianapolis: Bobbs-Merrill, 1963).
Guiles, Fred L, *Norma Jean* (New York: McGraw-Hill, 1969).
Kazan, Elia, *A Life* (New York: Alfred A Knopf, 1988).
Loewenstein, Rudoph M., *Christians and Jews* (New York: Dell, 1963).
Matthews, Jane, *The Federal Theatre 1935–39* (Princeton University Press, 1967).
Rowe, Kenneth, *Write That Play* (New York: Funk and Wagnalls, 1939).
Starkey, Marion, *The Devil in Massachusetts* (Garden City, NY: Doubleday, 1949).
Strassegger, Regina and Inge Morath, *Last Journey* (Munich: Prestel Verlag, 2002).
Weatherby, A.J. Jr, *Conversations With Marilyn* (London: Robson Books, 1976).

(vi) Criticism

Bigsby, C.W.E., *The Cambridge Companion to Arthur Miller* (Cambridge: Cambridge University Press, 1997).

Brater, Enoch, *Arthur Miller's America* (Ann Arbor: University of Michigan Press, 2005).
Centola, Steven, *The Achievement of Arthur Miller* (Dallas, Texas: Contemporary Research Press, 1995).
Centola, Steven and Michelle Cirulli, *The Critical Response to Arthur Miller* (London: Praeger Publishers, 2006).
Corrigan, Robert W. (ed.), *Arthur Miller: A Collection of Critical Essays* (Englewood Cliffs, N.J.: Prentice-Hall, 1969).
Griggin, Alice, *Understanding Arthur Miller* (Columbia S.C.: University of South Carolina Press, c. 1996).
Marino, Stephen A., *A Language Study of Arthur Miller's Plays: The Poetic in the Colloquial* (Lewiston, N.Y.: E Mellon Press, c. 2002).
Martin, Robert A. (ed.), *Arthur Miller: New Perspectives* (Englewood Cliffs, N.J.: Prentice-Hall, 1982).
Martine, James J., *Critical Essays on Arthur Miller* (Boston: G.K. Hall, 1979).
Weales, Gerald (ed.), '*The Crucible*': *Text and Criticism* (New York: Viking, 1971).
Weales, Gerald (ed.), '*Death of a Salesman*': *Text and Criticism* (New York: Viking, 1967).

(vii) Study Aids

Bigsby, C.W.E., *File on Miller* (London: Methuen, 1987).
Koorey, Stefani, *Arthur Miller's Life and Literature: An Annotated and Comprehensive Guide* (London: Scarecrow Press, 2000).

(viii) Internet Sites

The Arthur Miller Society, www.ibiblio.org/miller.
University of Michigan, www.umich.edu/~amfiles.

Index

Actors' Studio, 35
Amagansett, 56
American Legion, 34
ANTA (American National Theatre and Academy) Washington Square Theatre, 70, 73
Anti-Semitism, 7, 14, 32, 110
Arthur Miller Centre for American Studies, 93
Auschwitz, 110

Barley, Agnes, 158-9, 161
Beijing People's Art Theatre, 147
Biltmore Theatre, 92, 107
Bloomgarden, Kermit, 20, 31, 49, 57
Bolton Theatre, 92
Booth Theatre, 92
Broadway, 1, 2, 14, 34, 91
Brook, Peter, 56
Brown, Kay, 49
Burns, David, 72

Calder, Alexander, 119
China, 145-7
Clurman, Harold, 19, 91
Clift, Mongomery, 63
Columbia Pictures, 32
Comedy Theatre, 56
Communism, 30, 31, 32, 37
Congress, 36, 56
Coronet Theatre, 19, 52
Cottesloe Theatre, 107
Czechoslovakia, 100, 101

Depression, 4, 105, 106-8
DiMaggio, Joe, 34

Eisenhower Theatre, 92
Ensemble Studio Theatre, 126
Eyre, Richard, 92

Falls, Robert, 160
Fascism, 5, 8, 110
Federal Theatre Project, 7
Fenelon, Fania, 110, 112, 113
Flanagan, Hallie, 7
Fried, Walter, 20
Freud, 32

Gable, Clark, 63, 65
Goodman Theatre, 160
Greene, Milton, 35, 56
Grosbard, Ulu, 71, 72
Group Theatre, 6, 18
Guthrie Theatre, 140

Harold Clurman Theatre, 92
Harris, Barbara, 91
Hingle, Pat, 72, 91
Hiss, Alger, 31
Hollywood, 11, 31, 32, 33
Holocaust, 110
Hopwood literary prizes, 5, 6
House Committee on Un-American Activities, 7, 30, 31, 32, 33, 34, 35, 36, 37, 52, 55
HUAC, *see* House Committee on Un-American Activities
Huston, John, 58, 63-4

Ibsen, Henrik, 5, 16, 30

Joseph Papp Public Theatre, 125

Kazan, Elia, 19, 20, 28, 29, 31, 32, 33, 52, 69, 71, 73, 74
Kennedy Center, 92

Lincoln Center, 69, 70, 92
Loden, Barbara, 74
Loewenstein, Rudolph, 111
Long Wharf Theatre, 92

Manhattan Theatre Club, 92, 127
Martin Beck Theatre, 33
Mielziner, Jo, 20, 73, 74
Miller, Arthur,
awards, 28, 33, 93, 107, 157, 160
critical reception, 1, 2, 27, 28, 33, 47, 70-1, 79, 92, 93, 157, 164
divorces, 35, 58, 65
dramatic influences, 5, 134
dramatic technique, 6, 12, 13, 14, 16, 17, 21, 27, 28, 40, 47, 48, 49, 52, 54, 57, 60, 62, 70, 73, 75, 88, 97, 106, 111, 120, 123, 132, 134, 141, 163-4
dramatic theory, 53, 150-2
education, 4, 5
fame, 29-30, 36, 55
family, 2, 3, 4, 10, 20, 29, 30, 65
film writing, 11, 34, 62-4
ideas, 13, 26, 40, 44, 69, 165-6
income, 5, 10, 91
Jewishness, 2
marriages:
Mary Slattery, 10, 11, 20, 29, 30, 32, 35
Marilyn Monroe, 52, 55-9, 63, 67, 70, 74
Ingeborg Morath, 66-7, 68-9, 93, 94, 158
method of composition, 32, 124, 151-2, 164-5
political activity, 35, 36, 69
private life, 29, 34, 35, 56, 58, 67-8, 93
psychoanalysis, 32
reputation, 33, 34
socialism 30, 31
temperament, 29-30, 66
theatrical experience, 72, 91
travels, 33, 66, 69, 93, 100, 144-7
youth, 2, 3, 4
works, dramatic:
After the Fall, 70, **73-80**
All My Sons, ***14–19***
American Clock, The, ***92, 105–9***
Archbishop's Ceiling, The, ***92, 100–4***
Bridge to a Savage World, *34*
Broken Glass, *92*, ***130–3***
Children of the Sun (The Golden Years), **7-9**
Clara, ***118–19***
Creation of the World and Other Business, The, *91*, ***95–9***
Crucible, The, *33*, ***33–46***, *58, 67, 71*
Danger: Memory!, 92
Death of a Salesman, ***20–8***, *91, 147, 160*
Elegy for a Lady, ***116–17***
Enemy of the People, An, *30*
Finishing the Picture, **159-61**
Golden Years, The, *7–9*
Grass Still Grows, The, 6
Great Disobedience, The, *6*
Half Bridge, The, 10
Honors at Dawn, 6
I Can't Remember Anything, **119-20**
Incident at Vichy, 70, 71, **110-12**
Inside of His Head, The, *20*
Last Yankee, The, *92*, ***126–9***
Man Who Had All the Luck, The, 10, 11, 12
Memory of Two Mondays, A, 34, **47-8**
Mr. Peters' Connections, 92, **134-8**
No Villain, 5, 6
Playing for Time, 92, **112-15**
Plenty Good Times, 20, 34, 57
Price, The, 71, **81-90**
Resurrection Blues, **139-42**
Ride Down Mount Morgan, The, 92, 93, **121-5**
Some Kind of Love Story, **117-18**
They Too Arise, 6
Two Way Mirror, 92
View from the Bridge, A, 20, 34, 35, **49-54**, 56, 66, 67, 71

Miller, Arthur - *continued*
works, non-theatrical:
'Bare Manuscript, The', 154
'Bulldog', 154
Chinese Encounters (travel), **145-6**
Focus (novel), 14, **147-8**
I Don't Need You Anymore (short stories), **152-4**
In Russia (travel), 145
In the Country, 93
'Misfits, The', 56, **60-2**
'Performance, The', 155
Plain Girl, 148-9
Presence (short stories), 154
Salesman in Beijing, 147
Situation Normal (reportage), 11, 144
'Turpentime Still, The', 155
works, film:
Bridge to a Savage World, 34
Crucible, The, 94
Hook, The, 31
Misfits, The, 57, 58, **62-4**
Miller, Augusta (mother), 3, 65
Miller, Daniel (son), 68, 94, 161
Miller, Isidore (father), 3, 65
Miller, Jane (daughter), 11, 94
Miller, Joan (sister), 2, 94, 161
Miller, Kermit (brother), 2, 6, 10, 14, 158
Miller, Mary (wife) *see* Mary Slattery
Miller, Rebecca (daughter), 68, 94, 158
Miller, Robert (son), 20, 94
Monroe, Marilyn, 24, 25, 32, 34, 35, 52, 55-9, 63, 67, 70, 74
films:
As Young as You Feel, 32
Bus Stop, 35
Let's Make Love, 58
Misfits, The, **57-8**, 62
Prince and the Showgirl, The, 35
Some Like it Hot, 57
Montand, Yves, 58
Morath, Ingeborg, 66, 67, 68, 69, 93, 94, 158

National Theatre of Great Britain, 71, 92, 93, 107
New York Ensemble Studio Theatre, 92

Odets, Clifford, 6
The Flowering Peach, 34, 47
Old Globe Theatre, 141
Old Vic Theatre, 141
Olivier, Sir Laurence, 35, 55, 56, 71

Peck, Gregory, 58
PEN (Poets, Essayists and Novelists), 69, 100
Pulitzer Prize, 28
Pyle, Ernie, 11

Redgrave, Vanessa, 113
Repertory Theatre of Lincoln Center, 69, 71, 73
Richenthall, David, 160
Ritt, Martin, 47, 49, 52
Robards, Jason Jr., 74
Roosevelt, President F.D., 105, 109
Rosenberg, Julius and Ethel, 32, 45
Rowe, Kenneth, 5, 6, 57
Roxbury, 20, 29, 30, 55, 57, 65-6, 67-9, 93, 161

Salem witch trials, 33, 38-9
Second World War, 10
Shaw, George Bernard, 143, 150
Signature Theatre, 92
Slattery, Mary, 5, 6, 10, 11, 20, 29, 30, 32, 35
Spanish Civil War, 5
Spoleto Festival, 92, 106
Starkey, Marion (*The Devil in Massachusetts*), 39
Stern, James, 47
Stewart, Patrick, 125
Story of G.I. Joe, The, 11
Strasberg, Lee, 35, 160
Strasberg, Paula, 35, 56, 160
Studio Theatre, 92

Taylor, Frank, 57
Terkel, Studs (*Hard Times*), 105
Thacker, David, 92
Theatre Guild, 6, 7, 92
Twentieth Century Fox, 33

University of Michigan, 4, 5, 157
University of East Anglia, 93

Vivian Beaumont Theatre, 70, 92

Walter, Francis E., 35
Warden, Jack, 71
Whitehead, Robert, 47, 68, 69, 70, 71, 91, 92, 158
Williamstown Theatre Festival, 125
Williams, Tennessee:
  The Glass Menagerie, 14
  Streetcar Named Desire, 31
Wood, Peter, 107
WPA (Works Progress Administration), 7
Wright, Frank Lloyd, 57

Young Vic, 92, 127
Youth Board of NYC, 34